WITHDRAWN

TWENTIETH CENTURY VIEWS

The aim of this series is to present the best in contemporary critical opinion on major authors, providing a twentieth century perspective on their changing status in an era of profound revaluation.

Maynard Mack, *Series Editor*
Yale University

JANE AUSTEN

A COLLECTION OF CRITICAL ESSAYS

Edited by

Ian Watt

A SPECTRUM BOOK

Prentice-Hall, Inc., *Englewood Cliffs, N. J.*

Current printing (last digit):

13 12 11 10 9 8 7 6 5

© 1963 BY PRENTICE-HALL, INC.

ENGLEWOOD CLIFFS, N.J.

LIBRARY OF CONGRESS CATALOG CARD NO.: 63-9516

Printed in the United States of America-C

Table of Contents

SPECIAL TOPICS

Introduction

by Ian Watt

Literary, unlike divine, masterpieces do not need prophets or scientists to reveal their essences; so there is much to be said against literary criticism, and even more against anthologies of it. The reader's direct relation to the novel or poem is what really matters, and anything that intrudes upon this relation, or, worse, becomes a substitute for it, has much to answer for. So, no doubt, would Jane Austen, the most lucid and the least recondite of authors, have thought after she had recovered from the shock of discovering that writings about her, by people she didn't even know, and who sometimes got quite personal, were being read by students in universities. To Jane Austen such guided entrance into her life and writings would certainly have seemed an eccentric betrayal of the proper purposes of a university, as well as an unwarranted invasion of her cherished privacy. In Jane Austen's day, of course, women didn't go to college and the men studied classics, mathematics, and theology, not English literature, and certainly not novels; while on the one occasion when she might have met a literary lion (admittedly a French one, Madame de Staël), she declined.

And yet, apart from the vanity of authors, which is probably quite as reliable a constant as their professed alarm at finding themselves in an academic context, Jane Austen might well have been interested and amused by the present collection. For, among other things, it would at least have afforded her an opportunity of verifying one of the cardinal postulates of her novels: that our conversations to and about other people are actually unveilings of a more consequential reality, the self; that the ultimate purport of all our pronouncements is unwitting self-definition, an unconscious revelation of our manners, our passions, our intellectual capacities, and our operative moral values. Both Jane Austen's novels and the present anthology testify to the truth that although talk may not always illuminate its ostensible subject, it can at least be depended on to enlighten us about the talker.

Jane Austen's works have certainly provoked those who have written about them to reveal as much about themselves as about the novels; but besides the satisfaction of our insatiable appetites for ironic contemplation, there are other reasons for reading the critics. Once we are interested in anything, we want to talk about it and compare our private sense of it with other people's. If we find ourselves agreeing, the discovery that others see the object as we do is fortifying; our faith in our personal vision needs continual strengthening; we're never quite certain we've actually seen something until we know that someone else has seen it too. If, on the other hand, we find ourselves disagreeing, forced reconsideration of our notions may be salutary; and there is always the possibility of learning something new. If we're genuinely interested in a book we can even bring ourselves to be grateful when others draw our attention to things in it we've missed or misunderstood.

For most readers these various ways of sharing a vision of the literary object are probably the main value of literary criticism; but it has another one, to which this introduction is more particularly addressed. The development of a writer's reputation is itself of considerable intrinsic interest; and the literary vision of the past can also clarify our own critical perspective, if only by reminding us that for the most part we look at literature, as at life, through spectacles that have already been used by others.

I

If the current view of Jane Austen is that she is first and foremost a critical observer of humanity who uses irony as a means of moral and social judgment, who enlarges the reader's understanding of experience through making him realize how limited is that of her fictional characters, then we may say that such an attitude is peculiar to the present century. Jane Austen had many admiring readers in the nineteenth century, but they stopped short of seeing the tiny stage of Jane Austen's novels as a microcosm of some larger moral universe; their approbation, rather, came from their enthusiasm for Jane Austen's scrupulous and initiated fidelity to ordinary social experience.

The first and most enduring of the critical problems that Jane Austen's works raise is one of scale: does the patent restriction of her subject matter of itself exclude her from the ranks of the great novelists? That the restriction was deliberate there is no doubt. In a letter to her young niece Anna, who was beginning to experiment in writing fiction, Jane Austen commended her for "collecting your People delightfully, getting them exactly into such a spot as is the delight of my life:—3 or 4 Families in a Country Village is the very thing to work on." So limited a choice of character and environment was necessarily accompanied by a narrative technique analogous to the miniaturist's. In a letter to her literary brother Edward about his "strong, manly, spirited Sketches," Jane Austen jokingly excused herself from the possible intention of plagiarizing from them for her own novels: "How could I possibly join them on to the little bit (two Inches wide) of Ivory on which I work with so fine a Brush, as produces little effect after much labour?"

That Jane Austen chose limited subjects does not, of course, mean that she did not take her art very seriously; and a good many of her contemporary readers were well aware of how fully she had mastered it. An anonymous reviewer in the *Edinburgh Magazine* (1818), for instance, foresaw that there might eventually be found "more permanent delight in those familiar cabinet pictures, than even in the great historical pieces of our more eminent modern masters." The main allusion was no doubt to Sir Walter Scott, the most famous poet and novelist of the day; and no less a contemporary than Robert Southey found it very difficult to decide whether he "had rather be the Author of Miss Austen's novels or Walter Scott's." Scott himself, whose anonymous praise in a review of *Emma* in the *Quarterly Review* (1816) had delighted Jane Austen, wrote later in his private journals:

> Also read again, and for the third time at least, Miss Austen's very finely written novel of *Pride and Prejudice*. That young lady had a talent for describing the involvements and feelings and characters of ordinary life, which is to me the most wonderful I ever met with. The Big Bow-wow strain I can do myself like any now going; but the exquisite touch, which renders ordinary commonplace things and characters interesting, from the truth of the description and the sentiment, is denied to me.

Despite such public and private homage Jane Austen's position in the world of early nineteenth century letters was relatively obscure. The Romantic movement and its Victorian aftermath was in general unlikely to be favorable to Jane Austen's classical sense of order and control. All the Romantics were seeking in some way to transcend the limitations of actuality, to go beyond the bounds of society, reason, and individual experience, whether through political reform, through the imagination, or through spiritual self-exploration; and so it is not surprising that we find Keats, Shelley, and Byron silent about Jane Austen. Unlike these, Wordsworth read and commented upon Jane Austen's novels; but Sara Coleridge reports that, rather too predictably, "Mr. Wordsworth used to say that though he admitted that her novels were an admirable copy of life, he could not be interested in productions of that kind; unless the truth of nature were presented to him clarified, as it were, by the pervading light of the imagination, it had scarce any attractions in his eyes." Wordsworth's characteristic gravity also played a part in his lack of enthusiasm: as Sara Coleridge remarked, Wordsworth "never in his life appreciated any genius in which [humour] is a large element. Hence his disregard for Jane Austen's novels."

Jane Austen has always offended both the imaginative sensibility which yearns to transcend common experience, and the passionate temperament impatient of restraint, with which it is often combined. Among the Victorians, Carlyle's summary dismissal of Jane Austen's novels as mere "dish-washings!," for instance, can be attributed to his desire for an ampler and more heroic way of life that would transcend the everyday realities of Jane Austen's world; and Charlotte Brontë's impatience had a similar origin. Writing in 1848 to an Austen enthusiast, George Henry Lewes, she described *Pride and Prejudice* as "An accurate, daguerreotyped portrait of a commonplace face; a carefully fenced, high-cultivated garden, with neat borders and delicate flowers"; comparing Jane Austen to George Sand, she found the latter "sagacious and profound," while Miss Austen was "only shrewd and observant"; and she concluded by telling Lewes that "Miss Austen being, as you say, without 'sentiment,' without *poetry,* maybe *is* sensible, real (more *real* than *true*), but she cannot be great."

Reaction to Jane Austen's novels can be roughly classed according to the general antithesis between the "heart" and the "head." Such admirers as Scott, Whately, Macaulay, themselves mainly dominated by the head, are content to see the exquisite operation of reason and intelligence and judgment in Jane Austen's novels, even though they operate on limited subjects; while advocates of the reasons of the "heart," such as Charlotte Brontë, interpret limitation as synonymous with an unimaginative and complacent acceptance of the intolerable confinements of mundane reality. Between them, these two schools of thought divide most of the Romantic and early Victorian response to Jane Austen. Both schools agreed that Jane Austen presented rather limited areas of experience; they disagreed in their estimate of her only because they made different demands upon life. The literary implications of these different demands can be briefly suggested by Horace Walpole's famous dictum: "This world is a comedy to those that think, a tragedy to those that feel." Jane Austen's novels are comedies, and can have little appeal to those who, consciously or unconsciously, believe thought inferior to feeling.

Jane Austen's admirers are confronted with a different critical problem. They may in general accept the view that comedy can present as profound a picture of human life as tragedy, and yet find that in the case of Jane Austen it is still difficult to reconcile the apparently superficial nature of her subject matter with the absolute command of experience implied by the way it is presented.

George Henry Lewes seems to have been the first to begin to resolve the critical dilemma created by this recurrent antithesis between the maturity of the form and the social and spiritual narrowness of the content. Several earlier critics had likened Jane Austen's powers of dialogue and characterization to Shakespeare's. As early as 1821, Archbishop Richard

Whately wrote that Jane Austen conducted her dialogue "with a regard to character hardly exceeded even by Shakespeare himself"; and it was Jane Austen's power of characterization which had inspired Macaulay's famous encomium: "among the writers who . . . have approached near-est to the manner of [Shakespeare's characterization] we have no hesita-tion in placing Jane Austen." In 1847, however, in the course of a com-parison between Shakespeare and Walter Scott, Lewes went a good deal further than earlier critics in giving a reason for his conviction that Jane Austen was in some way closer to Shakespeare: "The two minds [of Scott and Shakespeare]," he wrote, "have certainly some peculiarities in com-mon, but they belong altogether to a different species. Now Miss Austen has been called a prose Shakespeare; and, among others, by Macaulay. In spite of the sense of incongruity which besets us in the words *prose* Shakespeare, we confess the greatness of Miss Austen, her marvelous dramatic power, seems more than any thing in Scott akin to the greatest quality in Shakespeare."

By drawing attention to Jane Austen's dramatic power, to the great objectivity with which she presented her characters and their relation-ships, Lewes went some way toward explaining how, although the stage and the cast of Jane Austen's novels may be small, the play is not. Yet even in Lewes's later tribute that Jane Austen was "the greatest artist that has ever written, using the term to signify the most perfect mastery over the means to her end," we can see that Lewes still conceded the small scale of Jane Austen's fictional world. For him the best that could be said was "Her circle may be restricted, but it is complete. Her world is a perfect orb, and vital."

The way out of the dichotomy of form and content was more thor-oughly explored in 1870, when there appeared an essay by Richard Simp-son, a Roman Catholic friend of Newman's, and a Shakespearean scholar of some note. He viewed Jane Austen primarily as a critic of her society whose works were an expression of her ironic sense. In developing the implications of the distance between Jane Austen and her fictional sub-ject matter Simpson introduced for the first time what were to become two of the most frequently noted themes of modern Jane Austen criticism: humor as a way of criticizing characters and their society; and irony as a means of moral evaluation, a means of transcending the limitations of the novel's characters and their concerns. Using the Shake-spearean parallel, Simpson pointed out that Jane Austen's humor was far from complacent:

> It is clear she began, as Shakespeare began, with being an ironical censurer of her contemporaries. . . . She began by being an ironical critic; she manifested her judgment of them [Romances] not by direct censure, but by the indirect method of imitating and exaggerating the faults of her

models, thus clearing the fountain by first stirring up the mud. This critical spirit lies at the foundation of her artistic faculty. Criticism, humour, irony, the judgment not of one that gives sentence but of the mimic who quizzes while he mocks, are her characteristics.

Simpson then proceeded to articulate a distinction between Jane Austen, the judging mind, and what she portrays in her fiction; many readers had mistaken the novels for a complacent mirror of that limited world, but they were really Jane Austen's mode of mastering it:

> She was conscious that, as a novelist, she was speaking somewhat in Cambyses' vein, and that the earnestness of her language was a little outdoing the truth of things. This consciousness gave her a superiority to her subject, which is one element in solving the secret of her wonderful power over it. . . .

II

Simpson's essay was in part the result of the increased interest in Jane Austen created by the publication of her first biography, which he was reviewing. In the Sixties, we are told, Tennyson "spoke of Jane Austen . . . as next to Shakespeare!" and went on to thank "God Almighty that he knew nothing of Jane Austen, and that there were no letters preserved either of Shakespeare's or of Jane Austen's, that they had not been ripped open like pigs." Tennyson was soon deprived of this particular satisfaction as regards Jane Austen, although the biographical operation was performed somewhat more delicately at the discreet hands of Jane Austen's nephew, James Edward Austen-Leigh, who published *A Memoir of Jane Austen* in 1870. After the Austen-Leigh *Memoir* there was much more information available about Jane Austen, even though the loyalty of successive generations of the Austen clan was to withhold for many years such minor skeletons in the family cupboard as the existence of Jane Austen's brother, George, who, in the laconic formula of R. W. Chapman, "was never able to take his place in the family." Despite these reticences, Jane Austen became much more widely discussed, and her reputation even crossed the Atlantic to the United States, where, for most of the nineteenth century, Jane Austen had been little known.

One may surmise that Jane Austen's view of life contains many elements of a peculiarly English nature which do not travel well: the class system, the insistence on manners and decorum, the reverence for whatever is established. These social elements combined with Jane Austen's growing reputation to provoke the violent antipathy of Mark Twain, the greatest of nineteenth century America's spokesmen for the liberated vernacular consciousness. In *Following the Equator,* speaking of the ship's library, Twain echoed the distaste of generations of schoolboys who have been forcibly exposed to *Pride and Prejudice* in the lower grades: "Jane Austen's books . . . are absent from this library. Just that one omission alone would make a fairly good library out of a library that hadn't a book in it." This contemptuously circuitous disparagement is Twain's most extensive published reference to Jane Austen, but he expressed his disgust at greater length, although hardly less flatly, in an unpublished manuscript entitled "Jane Austen." [1] The opening sentence of the essay sets the tone of Twain's general attitude: "Whenever I take up *Pride and Prejudice* or *Sense and Sensibility,* I feel like a barkeeper entering the Kingdom of Heaven." Twain's argument against Jane Austen is based primarily on the stiffness and propriety of her characters (he calls them "manufactures" which are unable to "warm up and feel a passion"), and on her exclusive concentration upon the genteel (he says that the whole thing is a matter of "taste," of artificial social values). Twain even calls Jane Austen's characters "Presbyterians"; and from his choice of that rather unhistorical, though expressive, designation, we may infer that his animus led him to align Jane Austen with the Calvinist-Puritan tradition in America which gave him so continual a sense of outrage.

But, above and beyond these elements in Twain's dislike of Jane Austen which were, in the nineteenth century, peculiarly American, it is clear that Twain stands with those other adversaries of Jane Austen whose instinctive revulsion springs from their hatred of everything in society, in religion, or in the literary tradition, which inhibits the spontaneous, the natural, and the physical forces in the individual life. The attitude of Henry James toward Jane Austen is somewhat more unexpected. Though hardly an Anglophobe, and at least as much an advocate of the claims of the head as of the heart, James was not, on the whole, an admirer. He made, it is true, several laudatory references to Jane Austen, and on one occasion even ranked her with Shakespeare, Cervantes, and Fielding among "the fine painters of life." But in his most extended discussion of Jane Austen, a 1905 lecture entitled "The Lesson of Balzac," James was curiously condescending. Jane Austen's great popularity drives him to the hypothesis that commercial pressures must be largely responsible:

This tide has risen high on the opposite shore, the shore of appreciation— risen rather higher, I think, than the high-water mark, the highest, of her intrinsic merit and interest; though I grant indeed—as a point to be made—

[1] MS. DV 201 (De Voto numbering), written about 1900-1905, now in the Mark Twain Papers at the University of California Library, Berkeley, © 1963, Mark Twain Co. I am indebted to the Mark Twain Company and the University of California Press for permission to quote from this manuscript.

that we are dealing here in some degree with the tides so freely driven up, beyond their mere logical reach, by the stiff breeze of the commercial, in other words of the special bookselling spirits; an eager, active, interfering force which has a great many confusions of apparent value, a great many wild and wandering estimates, to answer for. For these distinctively mechanical and overdone reactions, of course, the critical spirit, even in its most relaxed mood, is not responsible. Responsible, rather, is the body of publishers, editors, illustrators, producers of the pleasant twaddle of magazines; who have found their "dear," our dear, everybody's dear, Jane so infinitely to their material purpose, so amenable to pretty reproduction in every variety of what is called tasteful, and in what seemingly proves to be saleable, form.

Although such diverse admirers as Kipling, R. W. Chapman, and F. R. Leavis have seen Jane Austen as James's precursor in literary technique (especially in *Emma* where, in Leavis' words, "everything is presented through Emma's dramatized consciousness"), James's summary judgment on Jane Austen's art seems to exclude any possibility of indebtedness: "For signal examples of what composition, distribution, arrangement can do, of how they intensify the life of a work of art, we have to go elsewhere." The reason for this rather sweeping condemnation is no doubt that in the last analysis, James, like the Romantics, had his transcendental ambitions, though they were less a matter of seeking to escape from the confines of ordinary experience, than of transcending them through art, through a loftier conception of the scope and function of the novel. That it was this larger ambition for his art which lay behind James's derogation of Jane Austen is suggested when James makes an explicit contrast between the "great novelists" on the one hand, whose "immediate presence causes our ideas, whether about life in general or about the art they have exemplified in particular, to revive and breathe again, to multiply, more or less to swarm," and Jane Austen on the other, who, "with all her light felicity, leaves us hardly more curious of her process, or the experience in her that fed it, than the brown thrush who tells his story from the garden bough."

III

In the twentieth century, the literary and critical climate became more favorable to Jane Austen, especially in England, where the Victorians soon went out of fashion. The writers of the so-called Bloomsbury Group, in particular, were warm advocates of the eighteenth century view of life, of the values of wit, style, restraint, reason, skepticism; and this, combined with their emphasis on personal relationships as of ultimate importance, provided a congenial basis for a fuller appreciation of Jane Austen. Katherine Mansfield and Virginia Woolf were both devotees; but it is in E. M. Forster that Jane Austen found one of her most unqualified admirers, and certainly her greatest literary disciple.

In three short reviews of editions of Jane Austen, collected in *Abinger Harvest,* Forster was tempted by his subject to adopt the archest and coziest of his literary roles: he confessed to being "a Jane Austen-ite and therefore slightly imbecile about Jane Austen. . . . She is my favorite author! I read and re-read, the mouth open and the mind closed." His discussions of Jane Austen in *Aspects of the Novel* are of great critical interest. Forster singles out for especial praise the way that the characters in Jane Austen's novels are organically related to their environment and to each other; and he uses Jane Austen as a signal example of how to create what he calls "round" as opposed to "flat" characters, that is, characters who are three dimensional enough to develop, or to surprise us convincingly: "All her characters," Forster declares, "are round, or capable of rotundity."

Forster's admiration for Jane Austen is based partly on compatibility of temperament (just as Mark Twain's detestation is based partly on the reverse); but this affinity, of course, has larger moral and literary implications: both Jane Austen and E. M. Forster attempt to reconcile the claims of the head and the heart, and indeed make that conflict a central issue in their novels. But a rather specific and peculiarly English tradition in the novel is also involved, as a 1953 interview with Forster printed in the *Paris Review* showed. In answer to a question, Forster stated that Jane Austen and Proust were the authors from whom he had learned the most; and when asked "What did you learn from Jane Austen technically?" he answered: "I learned the possibilities of domestic humor." Forster is, then, and rather consciously, Jane Austen's successor in the tradition of the outwardly unambitious novel which deals humorously with ordinary middle-class domestic life in a relatively leisured society. There are, of course, important differences, as Forster indicated in the additional comment: "I was more ambitious. . . . I tried to hitch it [domestic humor] on to other things." Forster did not explain just how he was more ambitious; but it is clear that in his earlier novels, such as *A Room with a View,* he used domestic comedy as a means of exploring social and psychological conflicts of a much more problematic kind than those Jane Austen treats in her novels; while in his last novel, *A Passage to India,* what begins as a somewhat conventional story about a trip to India to arrange a marriage erupts into a matter of more universal import; the domestic comedy of Part I, "Mosque," turns into the metaphysical chaos of Part II, "Caves."

Jane Austen's popularity with the middle-brow reading public also reached new heights in the twentieth century; and, though less severely than Henry James, Katherine Mansfield, Virginia Woolf, and E. M. Forster all made the new cult a target for their irony. Obviously, many of Jane Austen's admirers have been mainly interested in her for non-literary reasons; suburban housewives are refreshed by a return to the days of poke-bonnets; snobs and Tories rejoice in whatever appears to reinforce their cherished conviction that the possibilities of life are extremely limited, particularly for other people. Just as the dislike of Jane Austen's detractors springs from their sense that she is coolly indifferent to the forward or the upward or the inward look which they favor, so her most uncritical devotees, the "Janeites," find in her a fortifying occasion for looking backward, or down their noses. The apogee of such tendencies is probably to be found in Rudyard Kipling's story "The Janeites," published in 1924. It is an embarrassingly smug tale whose message seems to be that an admiration for Jane Austen is the secret password among the elite, in this case composed of gallant artillery officers who are also successful professional men; as an unlettered cockney taxi-driver (who, of course, is ignorant of the fact that the lady so often discussed by his betters is a long-dead writer) reports with respectful awe: "this Secret Society woman I was tellin' you of—this Jane. She was the only woman I ever 'heard 'em say a good word for. 'Cordin' to them Jane was a none-such."

But the twentieth century was to see the reputation of Jane Austen grow as rapidly among professional scholars and critics as among novelists and Janeites. The essay on Jane Austen by the great Shakespearean critic A. C. Bradley, which appeared in 1911, is the first large-scale critical work on Jane Austen. Bradley was especially perceptive on the relationship between Jane Austen's irony and her narrative point of view: "In all her novels, though in varying degrees, Jane Austen regards the characters, good and bad alike, with ironical amusement, because they never see the situation as it really is and as she sees it. . . . We constantly share her point of view, and are aware of the amusing difference between the fact and its appearance to the actors." By distinguishing between Jane Austen's own values and those of the characters she portrays, Bradley developed the critical tradition begun by Richard Simpson forty years before; and so too did the excellent centenary essay by Reginald Farrer in the July 1917 *Quarterly Review,* an essay which enlisted him among the many critics who regard *Emma* as Jane Austen's supreme achievement.

In the Twenties, the indispensable scholarly basis for a fuller understanding of Jane Austen began to be supplied by the devoted labors of R. W. Chapman, who was something of a Janeite himself. Chapman's edition of the six novels appeared in 1923, of the letters in 1932, and of the juvenilia and the unfinished works in 1932 and 1951. Besides carefully editing and annotating Jane Austen's writings, Chapman also spoke up when her character or art was impugned; and one of his controversies, with an Oxford colleague, the scholar H. W. Garrod, is of some interest as an example of the total impasse between different personalities which the subject of Jane Austen so perennially provokes.[2]

In the years which followed Chapman's definitive edition of Jane Austen's novels, critical discussion increased. Edwin Muir's valuable book, *The Structure of the Novel* (1928), deserves particular mention because, although Muir conceived his book as in part an answer to Forster's *Aspects of the Novel,* he completely agreed with Forster's high estimate of Jane Austen's importance in the tradition of the novel, seeing her as "the first novelist who practised [the dramatic novel] with consummate success in England." There were many other equally admiring studies, too numerous to detail here; but it was not until 1939 that there appeared the first book-length critical study of Jane Austen to do justice to its subject—Mary Lascelles' *Jane Austen and her Art.*

During the thirties and forties the widespread influence of Freud and Marx led critics to set Jane Austen in new perspectives. There is, for example, something of Freud in the psychologist D. W. Harding's "Regulated Hatred: An Aspect of the Work of Jane Austen" (1940). This important study focuses on some elements in the novels which, consciously or unconsciously, are usually overlooked by the Janeites. The anthropologist Geoffrey Gorer's essay, "The Myth in Jane Austen," [3] was also concerned with the Janeites, trying to uncover the mystery of their cult in their unconscious identification with the Freudian pattern he attributed to the four central novels, *Sense and Sensibility, Pride and Prejudice, Mansfield Park, Emma*; in all of them there is a reversal of the usual Oedipal situation: the heroine hates her mother, loves her father, rejects a worthless suitor who stands for reprehensible sexual prowess, and eventually accepts a dependable lover who is really a father-substitute.

Studies of Jane Austen's representation of economic and class issues also flourished under the influence of Marxist thought. David Daiches' "Jane Austen, Karl Marx, and the Aristocratic Dance" (1948) saw Jane Austen as "in a sense a Marxist before Marx" who "exposes the economic basis of social behaviour with an ironic smile." This whole subject of Jane Austen's attitude to economic matters was most wittily expressed in W. H. Auden's 1937 "Letter to Lord Byron, Part I":

> You could not shock her more than she shocks me;
> Beside her Joyce seems innocent as grass.

[2] H. W. Garrod, "Jane Austen: A Depreciation," *Essays by Divers Hands: Transactions of the Royal Society of Literature,* Oxford, 1928; and R. W. Chapman, "Jane Austen: A Reply to Mr. Garrod," *Essays by Divers Hands: Transactions of the Royal Society of Literature,* Oxford, 1931.

[3] Mr. Gorer did not wish to have this essay given further circulation, though he writes that "there may be something to the point that charming deceivers [in Jane Austen's novels] tend to have names beginning with 'W.' "

It makes me feel uncomfortable to see
   An English spinster of the middle-class
   Describe the amorous effects of 'brass,'
Reveal so frankly and with such sobriety
The economic basis of society.

In 1949 the economic approach to Jane Austen was translated into the terms of literary criticism by Mark Schorer in his important essay "Fiction and the 'Matrix of Analogy' " (1949). Here the values of "commerce and property, the counting house and the inherited estate" are traced in Jane Austen's characteristic diction and metaphor. The date, the American provenance, and the combination of the sociological with the "New Critical" interest, of Schorer's essay herald the advent of the Fifties, the first decade in which there has been more critical and scholarly work on Jane Austen done in America than in England, and in which the main literary problems raised by the novels have at last been systematically investigated.

IV

Perhaps the firmest foundations for our understanding of Jane Austen during the past fifteen years have been contributed by historical scholarship. We have been given a much fuller sense of Jane Austen's position in her immediate social, political, and literary worlds by such articles as those of D. J. Greene, who explores Jane Austen's class affiliations, and of Alan D. McKillop, who has placed Jane Austen in the context of her immediate literary traditions. The work of such scholars could only have been done after the editorial work of R. W. Chapman had made the juvenilia and letters available for analysis. These sources were also the basis for an important critical study by Marvin Mudrick, *Jane Austen: Irony as Defense and Discovery* (1952), which works out in detail the relationship, first noted by Richard Simpson, between Jane Austen's attitude toward the literature of her time and her development of the use of irony for contrasting what is with what should be.

At the same time the way of considering literary works primarily as autonomous verbal structures, which is characteristic of the New Criticism, began to be applied to the novel in general and to Jane Austen in particular. The approach has done much to give more precise definition to the enduring problem of Jane Austen criticism: scale versus stature; the slightness of the matter and the authority of the manner. This school of criticism is represented here by Reuben Brower's demonstration of the complexity of verbal structure and psychological implication in *Pride and Prejudice*; written in 1945, the essay is one of the most illuminating, as well as one of the earliest, contributions to the modern analytical study of Jane Austen.

The new literary and political conservatism of the postwar world has also favored the present reputation of Jane Austen by relieving the critics from their earlier tacit obligation to dismiss anything which was not experimental in literary method and revolutionary in social attitude. This revived respect for the traditional can be seen, for example, in several essays by Lionel Trilling, essays which relate Jane Austen's novels to some of the profoundest conflicts in the values of Western civilization and the individual moral life. Trilling's views on *Mansfield Park* are of especial interest, because the straightforward didacticism of that work makes it the most awkward item in the Jane Austen canon; the unambiguous moralism of its plot and characterization could hardly be further removed from the wide-eyed and ironic complexity of attitude and effect found in *Pride and Prejudice* and, above all, in *Emma*; and these, of course, are the sides of Jane Austen which contemporary literary fashion prefers to emphasize.

In general, the criticism of Jane Austen in the last two decades is incomparably the richest and most illuminating that has appeared; but in demonstrating how the restrictions of her subject matter are the basis for a major literary achievement, recent criticism has perhaps failed to give the nature of Jane Austen's social and moral assumptions an equally exacting analysis. It is surely mistaken to assume that the affirmative elements in her morality and her humor are not as real as the subversive ironies which occasionally accompany them; or even to assume that awareness and insight, so often, and rightly, ascribed either to Jane Austen as narrator or to her major characters, are self-sufficient virtues: for how one sees is surely not more important than what one makes a point of seeing, or not seeing.

Since the publication of *Sense and Sensibility* in 1813, individual reaction to Jane Austen's novels has oscillated between the extremes of approbation and disdain, of adoration and condescension; but in general the history of her reputation shows an impressive pattern of consolidation and advance to a level of esteem much higher than the one to which she was assigned by most of her contemporaries. The ultimately indefinable powers which can transform a writer's image from that of a charming but inconsequential entertainer to that of mature but morally imperative artist, are surely deserving of our attention. We should, of course, approach the altar without genuflection; and, in this again taking our cue from Jane Austen herself, temper enthusiasm for the mode of delivery with a cool appraisal of what is delivered. With the aid of the pages that lie before him the reader may perhaps be able to create yet another image of Jane Austen, which may in turn be held up for public view. The present writer does not, certainly, agree with Philip Toynbee's recent admonition that "no novel of Jane Austen should be read more than once, and then only as a recognized indulgence," if only because such an attitude exhibits a puritan suspicion of entertainment more crass than anything in *Mansfield Park*. Yet even if we reject Toynbee's implied antithesis between entertainment and art, or between humor and moral commitment, we need not blind ourselves to the various consequences of the fact that Janes Austen was, in literature as in life, intensely aware of the limits of human possibility. She, certainly, would not have expected more justice than is contained in André Gide's finely balanced judgment that Jane Austen exhibits "an exquisite mastery of whatever can be mastered." [4]

NOTE: For this introduction I am much indebted to the works of Chapman, Duffy, Keynes, Link, which are listed in the bibliography; to W. H. Auden and Harcourt, Brace & World for permission to publish the stanza in *Letters from Iceland* (London, 1937); and to Walter Houghton and the Wellesley Index to Victorian Periodicals for identifying Richard Simpson as the author of the article in the *North British Review*. I wish to record my regret that the work of several excellent writers on Jane Austen could not be represented here; either, as in the case of Mary Lascelles, because their work did not seem to lend itself to abridgment, or, as in the case of Dr. Q. D. Leavis, because they were unwilling to accord their permission. I gladly acknowledge the help given me in the preparation of this volume by Joseph Fontenrose, Rena Fraboni, Patricia Runk, Marian Robinson, and Norair Taschian; lastly, I am deeply grateful to Joseph Cady who is mainly responsible for whatever may be new in this introduction.

Unless otherwise specified, all volume, chapter, and page references in this collection are to the third edition of *The Novels of Jane Austen*, ed. R. W. Chapman, Oxford, 1933.

[4] "Une exquise maîtrise de ce qui peut être maîtrisée" (*Journal*, 24 January, 1929).

Jane Austen

by Virginia Woolf

It is probable that if Miss Cassandra Austen had had her way we should have had nothing of Jane Austen's except her novels. To her elder sister alone did she write freely; to her alone she confided her hopes and, if rumour is true, the one great disappointment of her life; but when Miss Cassandra Austen grew old, and the growth of her sister's fame made her suspect that a time might come when strangers would pry and scholars speculate, she burnt, at great cost to herself, every letter that

This essay was based on "Jane Austen at Sixty," a review of R. W. Chapman's edition of *The Novels of Jane Austen*, in the *Nation*, December 15, 1923, p. 433. The review began:

Anybody who has had the temerity to write about Jane Austen is aware of two facts: first, that of all great writers she is the most difficult to catch in the act of greatness; second, that there are twenty-five elderly gentlemen living in the neighbourhood of London who resent any slight upon her genius as if it were an insult offered to the chastity of their Aunts. It would be interesting, indeed, to inquire how much of her present celebrity Jane Austen owes to masculine sensibility; to the fact that her dress was becoming, her eyes bright, and her age the antithesis in all matters of female charm to our own. A companion inquiry might investigate the problem of George Eliot's nose; and decide how long it will be before the equine profile is once again in favour, and the Clarendon Press celebrates the genius of the author of *Middlemarch* in an edition as splendid, as authoritative, and as exquisitely illustrated as this.

But it is not mere cowardice that prompts us to say nothing of the six famous novels, which in their new edition will shortly be celebrated in these columns by another hand. It is impossible to say too much about the novels that Jane Austen did write; but enough attention perhaps has never yet been paid to the novels that Jane Austen did not write. Owing to the peculiar finish and perfection of her art, we tend to forget that she died at forty-two, at the height of her powers, still subject to all those changes which often make the final period of a writer's career the most interesting of all. Let us take *Persuasion*, ...

From this point on, *The Common Reader* essay and the *Nation* review are similar except for three deletions from and three additions to the review text. The omitted passages are here given as notes; passages which do not occur in the review are enclosed in square brackets in the text.—*Ed.*

could gratify their curiosity, and spared only what she judged too trivial to be of interest.

Hence our knowledge of Jane Austen is derived from a little gossip, a few letters, and her books. As for the gossip, gossip which has survived its day is never despicable; with a little rearrangement it suits our purpose admirably. For example, Jane "is not at all pretty and very prim, unlike a girl of twelve. . . . Jane is whimsical and affected," says little Philadelphia Austen of her cousin. Then we have Mrs. Mitford, who knew the Austens as girls and thought Jane "the prettiest, silliest, most affected husband-hunting butterfly she ever remembers." Next, there is Miss Mitford's anonymous friend "who visits her now [and] says that she has stiffened into the most perpendicular, precise, taciturn piece of 'single blessedness' that ever existed, and that, until *Pride and Prejudice* showed what a precious gem was hidden in that unbending case, she was no more regarded in society than a poker or firescreen. . . . The case is very different now," the good lady goes on; "she is still a poker—but a poker of whom everybody is afraid. . . . A wit, a delineator of character, who does not talk is terrific indeed!" On the other side, of course, there are the Austens, a race little given to panegyric of themselves, but nevertheless, they say, her brothers "were very fond and very proud of her. They were attached to her by her talents, her virtues, and her engaging manners, and each loved afterwards to fancy a resemblance in some niece or daughter of his own to the dear sister Jane, whose perfect equal they yet never expected to see." Charming but perpendicular, loved at home but feared by strangers, biting of tongue but tender of heart—these contrasts are by no means incompatible, and when we turn to the novels we shall find ourselves stumbling there too over the same complexities in the writer.

To begin with, that prim little girl whom Philadelphia found so unlike a child of twelve, whimsical and affected, was soon to be the authoress of an astonishing and unchildish story, *Love and Freindship* [sic], which, incredible though it appears, was written at the age of fifteen. It was written, apparently, to amuse the schoolroom; one of the stories in the same book is dedicated with mock solemnity to her brother; another is neatly illustrated with water-colour heads by her sister. These are jokes which, one feels, were family property; thrusts of satire, which went home because all little Austens made mock in common of fine ladies who "sighed and fainted on the sofa."

Brothers and sisters must have laughed when Jane read out loud her last hit at the vices which they all abhorred. "I die a martyr to my grief for the loss of Augustus. One fatal swoon has cost me my life. Beware of Swoons, Dear Laura. . . . Run mad as often as you chuse, but do not faint. . . ." And on she rushed, as fast as she could write and quicker than she could spell, to tell the incredible adventures of Laura and

Sophia, of Philander and Gustavus, of the gentleman who drove a coach between Edinburgh and Stirling every other day, of the theft of the fortune that was kept in the table drawer, of the starving mothers and the sons who acted *Macbeth*. Undoubtedly, the story must have roused the schoolroom to uproarious laughter. And yet, nothing is more obvious than that this girl of fifteen, sitting in her private corner of the common parlour, was writing not to draw a laugh from brother and sisters, and not for home consumption. She was writing for everybody, for nobody, for our age, for her own; in other words, even at that early age Jane Austen was writing. One hears it in the rhythm and shapeliness and severity of the sentences. "She was nothing more than a mere good-tempered, civil, and obliging young woman; as such we could scarcely dislike her—she was only an object of contempt." Such a sentence is meant to outlast the Christmas holidays. Spirited, easy, full of fun verging with freedom upon sheer nonsense—*Love and Freindship* is all that; but what is this note which never merges in the rest, which sounds distinctly and penetratingly all through the volume? It is the sound of laughter. The girl of fifteen is laughing, in her corner at the world.

Girls of fifteen are always laughing. They laugh when Mr. Binney helps himself to salt instead of sugar. They almost die of laughing when old Mrs. Tomkins sits down upon the cat. But they are crying the moment after. They have no fixed abode from which they see that there is something eternally laughable in human nature, some quality in men and women that for ever excites our satire. They do not know that Lady Greville who snubs, and poor Maria who is snubbed, are permanent features of every ball-room. But Jane Austen knew it from her birth upwards. One of those fairies who perch upon cradles must have taken her a flight through the world directly she was born. When she was laid in the cradle again she knew not only what the world looked like, but had already chosen her kingdom. She had agreed that if she might rule over that territory, she would covet no other. Thus at fifteen she had few illusions about other people and none about herself. Whatever she writes is finished and turned and set in its relation, not to the parsonage, but to the universe. She is impersonal; she is inscrutable. When the writer, Jane Austen, wrote down in the most remarkable sketch in the book a little of Lady Greville's conversation, there is no trace of anger at the snub which the clergyman's daughter, Jane Austen, once received. Her gaze passes straight to the mark, and we know precisely where, upon the map of human nature, that mark is. We know because Jane Austen kept to her compact; she never trespassed beyond her boundaries. Never, even at the emotional age of fifteen, did she round upon herself in shame, obliterate a sarcasm in a spasm of compassion, or blur an outline in a mist of rhapsody. Spasms and rhapsodies, she seems to

have said, pointing with her stick, end *there;* and the boundary line
is perfectly distinct. But she does not deny that moons and mountains
and castles exist—on the other side. She has even one romance of her
own. It is for the Queen of Scots. She really admired her very much.
"One of the first characters in the world," she called her, "a bewitching
Princess whose only friend was then the Duke of Norfolk, and whose
only ones now Mr. Whitaker, Mrs. Lefroy, Mrs. Knight and myself." With
these words her passion is neatly circumscribed, and rounded with a
laugh. It is amusing to remember in what terms the young Brontës wrote,
not very much later, in their northern parsonage, about the Duke of
Wellington.

The prim little girl grew up. She became "the prettiest, silliest, most
affected husband-hunting butterfly" Mrs. Mitford ever remembered, and,
incidentally, the authoress of a novel called *Pride and Prejudice,* which,
written stealthily under cover of a creaking door, lay for many years
unpublished. A little later, it is thought, she began another story, *The
Watsons,* and being for some reason dissatisfied with it, left it unfinished.
The second-rate works of a great writer are worth reading because they
offer the best criticism of his masterpieces. Here her difficulties are more
apparent, and the method she took to overcome them less artfully concealed. To begin with, the stiffness and the bareness of the first chapters
prove that she was one of those writers who lay their facts out rather
badly in the first version and then go back and back and back and cover
them with flesh and atmosphere. How it would have been done we cannot say—by what suppressions and insertions and artful devices. But
the miracle would have been accomplished; the dull history of fourteen
years of family life would have been converted into another of those
exquisite and apparently effortless introductions; and we should never
have guessed what pages of preliminary drudgery Jane Austen forced
her pen to go through. Here we perceive that she was no conjuror after
all. Like other writers, she had to create the atmosphere in which her
own peculiar genius could bear fruit. Here she fumbles; here she keeps
us waiting. Suddenly she has done it; now things can happen as she likes
things to happen. The Edwardses are going to the ball. The Tomlin-
sons' carriage is passing; she can tell us that Charles is "being provided
with his gloves and told to keep them on"; Tom Musgrave retreats to
a remote corner with a barrel of oysters and is famously snug. Her genius
is freed and active. At once our senses quicken; we are possessed with
the peculiar intensity which she alone can impart. But of what is it
all composed? Of a ball in a country town; a few couples meeting and
taking hands in an assembly room; a little eating and drinking; and for
catastrophe, a boy being snubbed by one young lady and kindly treated
by another. There is no tragedy and no heroism. Yet for some reason the

little scene is moving out of all proportion to its surface solemnity. We have been made to see that if Emma acted so in the ball-room, how considerate, how tender, inspired by what sincerity of feeling she would have shown herself in those graver crises of life which, as we watch her, come inevitably before our eyes. Jane Austen is thus a mistress of much deeper emotion than appears upon the surface. She stimulates us to supply what is not there. What she offers is, apparently, a trifle, yet is composed of something that expands in the reader's mind and endows with the most enduring form of life scenes which are outwardly trivial. Always the stress is laid upon character. How, we are made to wonder, will Emma behave when Lord Osborne and Tom Musgrave make their call at five minutes before three, just as Mary is bringing in the tray and the knife-case? It is an extremely awkward situation. The young men are accustomed to much greater refinement. Emma may prove herself ill-bred, vulgar, a nonenity. The turns and twists of the dialogue keep us on the tenterhooks of suspense. Our attention is half upon the present moment, half upon the future. And when, in the end, Emma behaves in such a way as to vindicate our highest hopes of her, we are moved as if we had been made witnesses of a matter of the highest importance. Here, indeed, in this unfinished and in the main inferior story, are all the elements of Jane Austen's greatness. It has the permanent quality of literature. Think away the surface animation, the likeness to life, and there remains, to provide a deeper pleasure, an exquisite discrimination of human values. Dismiss this too from the mind and one can dwell with extreme satisfaction upon the more abstract art which, in the ball-room scene, so varies the emotions and proportions the parts that it is possible to enjoy it, as one enjoys poetry, for itself, and not as a link which carries the story this way and that.

But the gossip says of Jane Austen that she was perpendicular, precise, and taciturn—"a poker of whom everybody is afraid." Of this too there are traces; she could be merciless enough; she is one of the most consistent satirists in the whole of literature. Those first angular chapters of *The Watsons* prove that hers was not a prolific genius; she had not, like Emily Brontë, merely to open the door to make herself felt. Humbly and gaily she collected the twigs and straws out of which the nest was to be made and placed them neatly together. The twigs and straws were a little dry and a little dusty in themselves. There was the big house and the little house; a tea party, a dinner party, and an occasional picnic; life was hedged in by valuable connections and adequate incomes; by muddy roads, wet feet, and a tendency on the part of the ladies to get tired; a little principle supported it, a little consequence, and the education commonly enjoyed by upper middle-class families living in the country. Vice, adventure, passion were left outside. But of all this prosiness, of all this littleness, she evades nothing, and nothing is slurred over. Patiently and precisely she tells us how they "made no stop anywhere till they reached Newbury, where a comfortable meal, uniting dinner and supper, wound up the enjoyments and fatigues of the day." Nor does she pay to conventions merely the tribute of lip homage; she believes in them besides accepting them. When she is describing a clergyman, like Edmund Bertram, or a sailor, in particular, she appears debarred by the sanctity of his office from the free use of her chief tool, the comic genius, and is apt therefore to lapse into decorous panegyric or matter-of-fact description. But these are exceptions; for the most part her attitude recalls the anonymous lady's ejaculation— "A wit, a delineator of character, who does not talk is terrific indeed!" She wishes neither to reform nor to annihilate; she is silent; and that is terrific indeed. One after another she creates her fools, her prigs, her worldings, her Mr. Collinses, her Sir Walter Elliotts, her Mrs. Bennets. She encircles them with the lash of a whip-like phrase which, as it runs round them, cuts out their silhouettes for ever. But there they remain; no excuse is found for them and no mercy shown them. Nothing remains of Julia and Maria Bertram when she has done with them; Lady Bertram is left "sitting and calling to Pug and trying to keep him from the flower-beds" eternally. A divine justice is meted out; Dr. Grant, who begins by liking his goose tender, ends by bringing on "apoplexy and death, by three great institutionary dinners in one week." Sometimes it seems as if her creatures were born merely to give Jane Austen the supreme delight of slicing their heads off. She is satisfied; she is content; she would not alter a hair on anybody's head, or move one brick or one blade of grass in a world which provides her with such exquisite delight.

Nor, indeed, would we. For even if the pangs of outraged vanity, or the heat of moral wrath, urged us to improve away a world so full of spite, pettiness, and folly, the task is beyond our powers. People are like that—the girl of fifteen knew it; the mature woman proves it. At this very moment some Lady Bertram is trying to keep Pug from the flower beds; she sends Chapman to help Miss Fanny a little late. The discrimination is so perfect, the satire so just, that, consistent though it is, it almost escapes our notice. No touch of pettiness, no hint of spite, rouse us from our contemplation. Delight strangely mingles with our amusement. Beauty illumines these fools.

That elusive quality is, indeed, often made up of very different parts, which it needs a peculiar genius to bring together. The wit of Jane Austen has for partner the perfection of her taste. Her fool is a fool, her snob is a snob, because he departs from the model of sanity and sense which she has in mind, and conveys to us unmistakably even while she makes us laugh. Never did any novelist make more use of an impeccable sense of human values. It is against the disc of an unerring heart, an unfailing good taste, an almost stern morality, that she shows up those deviations from kindness, truth, and sincerity which are among the most delightful things in English literature. She depicts a Mary Crawford in her mixture of good and bad entirely by this means. She lets her rattle on against the clergy, or in favour of a baronetage and ten thousand a year, with all the ease and spirit possible; but now and again she strikes one note of her own, very quietly, but in perfect tune, and at once all Mary Crawford's chatter, though it continues to amuse, rings flat. Hence the depth, the beauty, the complexity of her scenes. From such contrasts there comes a beauty, a solemnity even, which are not only as remarkable as her wit, but an inseparable part of it. In *The Watsons* she gives us a foretaste of this power; she makes us wonder why an ordinary act of kindness, as she describes it, becomes so full of meaning. In her masterpieces, the same gift is brought to perfection. Here is nothing out of the way; it is midday in Northamptonshire; a dull young man is talking to rather a weakly young woman on the stairs as they go up to dress for dinner, with housemaids passing. But, from triviality, from commonplace, their words become suddenly full of meaning, and the moment for both one of the most memorable in their lives. It fills itself; it shines; it glows; it hangs before us, deep, trembling, serene for a second; next, the housemaid passes, and this drop, in which all the happiness of life has collected, gently subsides again to become part of the ebb and flow of ordinary existence.

What more natural, then, with this insight into their profundity, than that Jane Austen should have chosen to write of the trivialities of day-to-day existence, of parties, picnics, and country dances? No "suggestions to alter her style of writing" from the Prince Regent or Mr. Clarke could tempt her; no romance, no adventure, no politics or intrigue could hold a candle to life on a country-house staircase as she saw it. Indeed, the Prince Regent and his librarian had run their heads against a very formidable obstacle; they were trying to tamper with an incorruptible conscience, to disturb an infallible discretion. The child who formed her sentences so finely when she was fifteen never ceased to form them, and never wrote for the Prince Regent or his librarian, but for the world at large. She knew exactly what her powers were, and what material they were fitted to deal with as material should be dealt with by a writer whose standard of finality was high. There were impressions that lay outside her province; emotions that by no stretch or artifice could be properly coated and covered by her own resources. For example she could not make a girl talk enthusiastically of banners and chapels. She could not throw herself whole-heartedly into a romantic moment. She had all sorts of devices for evading scenes of passion. Nature and its

beauties she approached in a sidelong way of her own. She describes a
beautiful night without once mentioning the moon. Nevertheless, as we
read the few formal phrases about "the brilliancy of an unclouded night
and the contrast of the deep shade of the woods," the night is at once
as "solemn, and soothing, and lovely" as she tells us, quite simply, that
it was.

The balance of her gifts was singularly perfect. Among her finished
novels there are no failures, and among her many chapters few that sink
markedly below the level of the others. But, after all, she died at the
age of forty-two. She died at the height of her powers. She was still subject to those changes which often make the final period of a writer's
career the most interesting of all. Vivacious, irrepressible, gifted with
an invention of great vitality, there can be no doubt that she would
have written more, had she lived, and it is tempting to consider whether
she would not have written differently. The boundaries were marked;
moons, mountains, and castles lay on the other side. But was she not
sometimes tempted to trespass for a minute? Was she not beginning, in
her own gay and brilliant manner, to contemplate a little voyage of discovery?

Let us take *Persuasion,* the last completed novel, and look by its light
at the books she might have written had she lived.* There is a peculiar
beauty and a peculiar dullness in *Persuasion.* The dullness is that which
so often marks the transition stage between two different periods. The
writer is a little bored. She has grown too familiar with the ways of
her world[; she no longer notes them freshly]. There is an asperity in
her comedy which suggests that she has almost ceased to be amused by
the vanities of a Sir Walter or the snobbery of a Miss Elliott. The satire
is harsh, and the comedy crude. She is no longer so freshly aware of the
amusements of daily life. Her mind is not altogether on her object.
But, while we feel that Jane Austen has done this before, and done it
better, we also feel that she is trying to do something which she has
never yet attempted. There is a new element in *Persuasion,* the quality,
perhaps, that made Dr. Whewell fire up and insist that it was "the most
beautiful of her works." She is beginning to discover that the world is
larger, more mysterious, and more romantic than she had supposed. We
feel it to be true of herself when she says of Anne: "She had been forced
into prudence in her youth, she learned romance as she grew older—
the natural sequel of an unnatural beginning." She dwells frequently
upon the beauty and the melancholy of nature[, upon the autumn where
she had been wont to dwell upon the spring]. She talks of the "influence

* The review read ". . . had she lived to be sixty. We do not grudge it him, but her
brother the Admiral lived to be ninety-one."—*Ed.*

so sweet and so sad of autumnal months in the country." She marks "the tawny leaves and withered hedges." "One does not love a place the less because one has suffered in it," she observes. But it is not only in a new sensibility to nature that we detect the change. Her attitude to life itself is altered. She is seeing it, for the greater part of the book, through the eyes of a woman who, unhappy herself, has a special sympathy for the happiness and unhappiness of others, which, until the very end, she is forced to comment upon in silence. Therefore the observation is less of facts and more of feelings than is usual. There is an expressed emotion in the scene at the concert and in the famous talk about woman's constancy which proves not merely the biographical fact that Jane Austen had loved, but the aesthetic fact that she was no longer afraid to say so. Experience, when it was of a serious kind, had to sink very deep, and to be thoroughly disinfected by the passage of time, before she allowed herself to deal with it in fiction. But now, in 1817, she was ready. Outwardly, too, in her circumstances, a change was imminent. Her fame had grown very slowly. "I doubt," wrote Mr. Austen Leigh, "whether it would be possible to mention any other author of note whose personal obscurity was so complete." Had she lived a few more years only, all that would have been altered. She would have stayed in London, dined out, lunched out, met famous people, made new friends, read, travelled, and carried back to the quiet country cottage a hoard of observations to feast upon at leisure.

And what effect would all this have had upon the six novels that Jane Austen did not write? She would not have written of crime, of passion, or of adventure. She would not have been rushed by the importunity of publishers or the flattery of friends into slovenliness or insincerity. But she would have known more. Her sense of security would have been shaken. Her comedy would have suffered. She would have trusted less (this is already perceptible in *Persuasion*) to dialogue and more to reflection to give us a knowledge of her characters. Those marvellous little speeches which sum up, in a few minutes' chatter, all that we need in order to know an Admiral Croft or a Mrs. Musgrove for ever, that shorthand, hit-or-miss method which contains chapters of analysis and psychology, would have become too crude to hold all that she now perceived of the complexity of human nature. She would have devised a method, clear and composed as ever, but deeper and more suggestive, for conveying, not only what people say, but what they leave unsaid; not only what they are, but what life is.* She would have stood farther away from her characters, and seen them more as a group, less as individuals. Her

* The review read ". . . but (if we may be pardoned the vagueness of the expression) what life is."—*Ed.*

satire, while it played less incessantly, would have been more stringent and severe. She would have been the forerunner of Henry James and of Proust—but enough. Vain are these speculations; [the most perfect artist among women, the writer whose books are immortal,] * died "just as she was beginning to feel confidence in her own success."

* In the review ". . . these speculations; she died just as . . ."—*Ed.*

A Note on Jane Austen

by C. S. Lewis

I begin by laying together four passages from the novels of Jane Austen.

(1) Catherine was completely awakened. . . . Most grievously was she humbled. Most bitterly did she cry. It was not only with herself that she was sunk, but with Henry. Her folly, which now seemed even criminal, was all exposed to him, and he must despise her for ever. The liberty which her imagination had dared to take with the character of his father, would he ever forgive it? The absurdity of her curiosity and her fears, could they ever be forgotten? She hated herself more than she could express . . . Nothing could be clearer than that it had been all a voluntary, self-created delusion, each trifle receiving importance from an imagination resolved on alarm, and everything forced to bend to one purpose by a mind which, before she entered the Abbey, had been craving to the frightened. . . . She saw that the infatuation had been created, the mischief settled, before her quitting Bath. . . . Her mind made up on these several points, and her resolution formed, of always judging and acting in future with the greatest good sense, she had nothing to do but forgive herself and be happier than ever.

(Northanger Abbey, Chapter 25)

(2) "Oh! Elinor, you have made me hate myself forever. How barbarous have I been to you!—you, who have been my only comfort, who have borne with me in all my misery, who have seemed to be suffering only for me!" . . . Marianne's courage soon failed her, in trying to converse upon a topic which always left her more dissatisfied with herself than ever, by the contrast it necessarily produced between Elinor's conduct and her own. She felt all the force of that comparison; but not as her sister had hoped, to urge her to exertion now; she felt it with all the pain of continual self-reproach, regretted most bitterly that she had never exerted herself before; but it brought only the torture of penitence, without the hope of amendment. . . . [Elinor later saw in Marianne] an apparent composure of mind which, in being the result, as she trusted, of serious reflection, must eventually lead

" A Note on Jane Austen" by C. S. Lewis. From *Essays in Criticism,* IV (October 1954), 359-371. Reprinted by permission of the author and the editor of *Essays in Criticism.*

her to contentment and cheerfulness. . . . "My illness has made me think. . . . I considered the past: I saw in my own behaviour nothing but a series of imprudence towards myself, and want of kindness to others. I saw that my own feelings had prepared my sufferings, and that my want of fortitude under them had almost led me to the grave. My illness, I well knew, had been entirely brought on by myself, by such negligence of my own health as I felt even at the time to be wrong. Had I died, it would have been self-destruction. I wonder . . . that the very eagerness of my desire to live, to have time for atonement to my God and to you all, did not kill me at once. . . . I cannot express my own abhorrence of myself."

(Sense and Sensibility, Chapters 37, 38, 46)

(3) As to his real character, had information been in her power, she had never felt a wish of inquiring. His countenance, voice, and manner had established him at once in the possession of every virtue. . . . She perfectly remembered everything that had passed in conversation between Wickham and herself, in their first evening at Mr. Philip's. . . . She was *now* struck with the impropriety of such communications to a stranger, and wondered that it had escaped her before. She saw the indelicacy of putting himself forward as he had done, and the inconsistency of his professions with his conduct. . . . She grew absolutely ashamed of herself. . . . "How despicably have I acted!" she cried; "I, who have prided myself on my discernment! . . . who have often disdained the generous candour of my sister, and gratified my vanity in useless or blamable distrust. How humiliating is this discovery! yet, how just a humiliation! Had I been in love, I could not have been more wretchedly blind. But vanity, not love, has been my folly. . . . I have courted prepossession and ignorance, and driven reason away. . . . Till this moment I never knew myself."

(Pride and Prejudice, Chapter 36)

(4) Her own conduct, as well as her own heart, was before her in the same few minutes. . . . How improperly had she been acting by Harriet! How inconsiderate, how indelicate, how irrational, how unfeeling, had been her conduct! What blindness, what madness, had led her on! It struck her with dreadful force, and she was ready to give it every bad name in the world. . . . Every moment had brought a fresh surprise, and every surprise must be matter of humiliation to her. How to understand it all? How to understand the deceptions she had been thus practising on herself, and living under! The blunders, the blindness, of her own head and heart! She perceived that she had acted most weakly; that she had been imposed on by others in a most mortifying degree.

(Emma, Chapter 47)

Between these four passages there are, no doubt, important distinctions. The first is on a level of comedy which approximates to burlesque. The delusion from which Catherine Morland has been awakened was an innocent one, which owed at least as much to girlish ignorance of the world as to folly. And, being imaginative, it was a delusion from which an entirely commonplace or self-centred mind would hardly have suffered. Accordingly, the expiation, though painful while it lasts, is brief, and Catherine's recovery and good resolutions are treated with affectionate irony. The awakening of Marianne Dashwood is at the opposite pole. The situation has come near to tragedy; moral, as well as, or more than, intellectual deficiency has been involved in Marianne's errors. Hence the very vocabulary of the passage strikes a note unfamiliar in Jane Austen's style. It makes explicit, for once, the religious background of the author's ethical position. Hence such theological or nearly theological words as *penitence,* even the *torture of penitence, amendment, self-destruction, my God.* And though not all younger readers may at once recognize it, the words *serious reflection* belong to the same region. In times which men now in their fifties can remember, the adjective *serious* ("serious reading," "Does he ever think about serious matters?") had indisputably religious overtones. The title of Law's *Serious Call* is characteristic. Between these two extracts, those from *Pride and Prejudice* and *Emma* occupy a middle position. Both occur in a context of high comedy, but neither is merely laughable.

Despite these important differences, however, no one will dispute that all four passages present the same kind of process. "Disillusionment," which might by etymology be the correct name for it, has acquired cynical overtones which put it out of court. We shall have to call it "undeception" or "awakening." All four heroines painfully, though with varying degrees of pain, discover that they have been making mistakes both about themselves and about the world in which they live. All their *data* have to be reinterpreted. Indeed, considering the differences of their situations and characters, the similarity of the process in all four is strongly marked. All realize that the cause of the deception lay within; Catherine, that she had brought to the Abbey a mind "craving to be frightened," Marianne, that "her own feelings had prepared her sufferings," Elizabeth, that she has "courted ignorance" and "driven reason away," Emma, that she has been practising deceptions on herself. Self-hatred or self-contempt, though (once more) in different degrees, are common to all. Catherine "hated herself"; Marianne abhors herself; Elizabeth finds her conduct "despicable"; Emma gives hers "every bad name in the world." Tardy and surprising self-knowledge is presented in all four, and mentioned by name in the last two. "I never knew myself," says Elizabeth; Emma's conduct and "her own heart" appear to her, unwelcome strangers both, "in the same few minutes."

If Jane Austen were an author as copious as Tolstoi, and if these passages played different parts in the novels from which they are taken, the common element would not, perhaps, be very important. After all, undeception is a common enough event in real life, and therefore, in a vast tract of fiction, might be expected to occur more than once. But

that is not the position. We are dealing with only four books, none of
them long; and in all four the undeception, structurally considered, is
the very pivot or watershed of the story. In *Northanger Abbey* and *Emma,*
it precipitates the happy ending. In *Sense and Sensibility* it renders it
possible. In *Pride and Prejudice* it initiates that revaluation of Darcy,
both in Elizabeth's mind and in our minds, which is completed by the
visit to Pemberley. We are thus entitled to speak of a common pattern
in Jane Austen's four most characteristic novels. They have "one plot"
in a more important sense than Professor Garrod suspected. This is not
so clearly true of *Sense and Sensibility,* but then it has really two plots
or two "actions" in the Aristotelian sense; it is true about one of them.

It is perhaps worth emphasizing what may be called the hardness—at
least the firmness—of Jane Austen's thought exhibited in all these un-
deceptions. The great abstract nouns of the classical English moralists
are unblushingly and uncompromisingly used; *good sense, courage, contentment, fortitude,* "some duty neglected, some failing indulged," *impropriety, indelicacy, generous candour, blamable distrust, just humiliation, vanity, folly, ignorance, reason.* These are the concepts by which
Jane Austen grasps the world. In her we still breathe the air of the *Ram-
bler* and *Idler.* All is hard, clear, definable; by some modern standards,
even naïvely so. The hardness is, of course, for oneself, not for one's
neighbours. It reveals to Marianne her "want of kindness" and shows
Emma that her behaviour has been "unfeeling." Contrasted with the
world of modern fiction, Jane Austen's is at once less soft and less cruel.

It may be added, though this is far less important, that in these four
novels, self-deception and awakening are not confined to the heroines.
General Tilney makes as big a mistake about Catherine as she has made
about him. Mrs. Ferrars misjudges her son. Mr. Bennet is forced at last
to see his errors as a father. But perhaps all this does not go beyond
what might be expected from the general nature of human life and the
general exigencies of a novelistic plot.

The central pattern of these four has much in common with that of
a comedy by Molière.

Two novels remain. In *Mansfield Park* and *Persuasion* the heroine falls
into no such self-deception and passes through no such awakening. We
are, it is true, given to understand that Anne Elliot regards the breaking
off of her early engagement to Wentworth as a mistake. If any young
person now applied to her for advice in such circumstances, "they would
never receive any of such certain immediate wretchedness and uncertain
future good." For Anne in her maturity did not hold the view which
Lord David Cecil attributes to Jane Austen,[1] that "it was wrong to marry
for money, but it was silly to marry without it." She was now fully "on

---

[1] *Jane Austen,* Cambridge, 1936, p. 33.

the side of early warm attachment, and a cheerful confidence in futurity, against that over-anxious caution which seems to insult exertion and distrust Providence." (Notice, in passing, the Johnsonian cadence of a sentence which expresses a view that Johnson in one of his countless moods might have supported.) But though Anne thinks a mistake has been made, she does not think it was she that made it. She declares that she was perfectly right in being guided by Lady Russell who was to her "in the place of a parent." It was Lady Russell who had erred. There is no true parallel here between Anne and the heroines we have been considering. Anne, like Fanny Price, commits no errors.

Having placed these two novels apart from the rest because they do not use the pattern of "undeception," we can hardly fail to notice that they share another common distinction. They are the novels of the solitary heroines.

Catherine Morland is hardly ever alone except on her journey from Northanger Abbey, and she is soon back among her affectionate, if placid, family. Elinor Dashwood bears her own painful secret without a confidant for a time; but her isolation, besides being temporary, is incomplete; she is surrounded by affection and respect. Elizabeth always has Jane, the Gardiners, or (to some extent) her father. Emma is positively spoiled; the acknowledged centre of her own social world. Of all these heroines we may say, as Jane Austen says of some other young women, "they were of consequence at home and favourites abroad."

But Fanny Price and Anne are of no "consequence." The consciousness of "mattering" which is so necessary even to the humblest women, is denied them. Anne has no place in the family councils at Kellynch Hall; "she was only Anne." She is exploited by her married sister, but not valued; just as Fanny is exploited, but not valued, by Mrs. Norris. Neither has a confidant; or if Edmund had once been a confidant as well as a hero to Fanny, he progressively ceases to be so. Some confidence, flawed by one vast forbidden topic, we may presume between Anne and Lady Russell; but this is almost entirely off stage and within the novel we rarely see them together. Both heroines come within easy reach of one of the great archetypes—Cinderella, Electra. Fanny, no doubt, more so. She is almost a Jane Austen heroine condemned to a Charlotte Brontë situation. We do not even believe in what Jane Austen tells us of her good looks; whenever we are looking at the action through Fanny's eyes, we feel ourselves sharing the consciousness of a plain woman.

Even physically, we see them alone; Fanny perpetually in the East Room with its fireless grate and its touching, ridiculous array of petty treasures (what Cinderella, what Electra, is without them?) or Anne, alone beside the hedge, an unwilling eavesdropper, Anne alone with her sick nephew, Anne alone in the empty house waiting for the sound of Lady Russell's carriage. And in their solitude both heroines suffer; far more deeply than Catherine, Elizabeth, and Emma, far more innocently than Marianne. Even Elinor suffers less. These two novels, we might almost say, stand to the others as Shakespeare's "dark" comedies to his comedies in general. The difference in the lot of the heroines goes with a difference in the "character parts." Mrs. Norris is almost alone among Jane Austen's vulgar old women in being genuinely evil, nor are her greed and cruelty painted with the high spirits which make us not so much hate as rejoice in Lady Catherine de Bourgh.

These solitary heroines who make no mistakes have, I believe—or had while she was writing—the author's complete approbation. This is connected with the unusual pattern of *Mansfield Park* and *Persuasion*. The heroines stand almost outside, certainly a little apart from, the world which the action of the novel depicts. It is in it, not in them, that self-deception occurs. They see it, but its victims do not. They do not of course stand voluntarily apart, nor do they willingly accept the role of observers and critics. They are shut out and are compelled to observe: for what they observe, they disapprove.

It is this disapproval which, though shared both by Fanny and Anne, has perhaps drawn on Fanny, from some readers, the charge of being a prig. I am far from suggesting that Fanny is a successful heroine, still less that she is the equal of Anne. But I hardly know the definition of *Prig* which would make her one. If it means a self-righteous person, a Pharisee, she is clearly no prig. If it means a "precisian," one who adopts or demands a moral standard more exacting than is current in his own time and place, then I can see no evidence that Fanny's standard differs at all from that by which Marianne condemns herself or Anne Elliot corrects Captain Benwick. Indeed, since Anne preaches while Fanny feels in silence, I am a little surprised that the charge is not levelled against Anne rather than Fanny. For Anne's *chastoiement* * of poor Benwick is pretty robust; "she ventured to recommend a larger allowance of prose in his daily study, and . . . mentioned such works of our best moralists, such collections of the finest letters, such memoirs of characters of worth and suffering, as occurred to her at the moment as calculated to rouse and fortify the mind by the highest precepts and the strongest examples of moral and religious endurances" (Chapter II). Notice, too, the standards which Anne was using when she first began to suspect her cousin, Mr. Elliot: "she saw that there had been bad habits; that Sunday travelling had been a common thing; that there had been a period of his life (and probably not a short one) when he had been, at least careless on all serious matters." Whatever we may think of these standards ourselves, I have not the least doubt that they are those of all the heroines, when they are most rational, and of Jane Austen herself. This is the hard core of her mind, the Johnsonian element, the iron in the tonic.

* Chastisement—*Ed.*

How, then, does Fanny Price fail? I suggest, by insipidity. *Pauper videri Cinna vult et est pauper.** One of the most dangerous of literary ventures is the little, shy, unimportant heroine whom none of the other characters value. The danger is that your readers may agree with the other characters. Something must be put into the heroine to make us feel that the other characters are wrong, that she contains depths they never dreamed of. That is why Charlotte Brontë would have succeeded better with Fanny Price. To be sure, she would have ruined everything else in the book; Sir Thomas and Lady Bertram and Mrs. Norris would have been distorted from credible types of pompous dullness, lazy vapidity, and vulgar egoism into fiends complete with horns, tails, and rhetoric. But through Fanny there would have blown a storm of passion which made sure that we at least would never think her insignificant. In Anne, Jane Austen did succeed. Her passion (for it is not less), her insight, her maturity, her prolonged fortitude, all attract us. But into Fanny, Jane Austen, to counterbalance her apparent insignificance, has put really nothing except rectitude of mind; neither passion, nor physical courage, nor wit, nor resource. Her very love is only calf love—a schoolgirl's hero-worship for a man who has been kind to her when they were both children, and who, incidentally, is the least attractive of all Jane Austen's heroes. Anne gains immensely by having for her lover almost the best. In real life, no doubt, we continue to respect interesting women despite the preposterous men they sometimes marry. But in fiction it is usually fatal. Who can forgive Dorothea for marrying such a sugarstick as Ladislaw, or Nellie Harding for becoming Mrs. Bold? Or, of course, David Copperfield for his first marriage.

Fanny also suffers from the general faults of *Mansfield Park,* which I take to be, if in places almost the best, yet as a whole the least satisfactory, of Jane Austen's works. I can accept Henry Crawford's elopement with Mrs. Rushworth: I cannot accept his intention of marrying Fanny. Such men never make such marriages.

But though Fanny is insipid (yet not a prig) she is always "right" in the sense that to her, and to her alone, the world of *Mansfield Park* always appears as, in Jane Austen's view, it really is. Undeceived, she is the spectator of deceptions. These are made very clear. In Chapter 2 we learn that the Bertram girls were "entirely deficient" in "self-knowledge." In Chapter 3 Sir Thomas departs for Antigua without much anxiety about his family because, though not perfectly confident of his daughters' discretion, he had ample trust "in Mrs. Norris's watchful attention and in Edmund's judgement." Both, of course, failed to justify it. In Chapter 12 when Crawford was absent for a fortnight it proved "a fortnight of such dullness to the Miss Bertram's as ought to have put them both on

* "Cinna wants to seem poor and he is" (i.e., not worth much). Martial *Epigrams* viii, No. 19.—*Ed.*

their guard." Of course it did not. In Chapter 16 when Edmund at last consents to act, Fanny is forced to raise the question, "was he not deceiving himself." In Chapter 34 when Crawford (whose manners are insufferable) by sheer persistence pesters Fanny into speech when she has made her desire for silence obvious, she says, "Perhaps, Sir, I thought it was a pity you did not always know yourself as you seemed to do at that moment." But deception is most fully studied in the person of Mary Crawford, "a mind led astray and bewildered, and without any suspicion of being so: darkened, yet fancying itself light." The New Testament echo in the language underlines the gravity of the theme. It may be that Jane Austen has not treated it successfully. Some think that she hated Mary and falsely darkened a character whom she had in places depicted as charming. It might be the other way round; that the author, designing to show deception at its height, was anxious to play fair, to show how the victim could be likeable at times, and to render her final state the more impressive by raising in us false hopes that she might have been cured. Either way, the gap between Mary at her best and Mary in her last interview with Edmund is probably too wide; too wide for fiction, I mean, not for possibility. (We may have met greater inconsistency in real life; but real life does not need to be probable.) That last interview, taken by itself, is an alarming study of human blindness. We may— most of us do—disagree with the standards by which Edmund condemns Mary. The dateless and universal possibility in the scene is Mary's invincible ignorance of what those standards are. All through their conversations she is cutting her own throat. Every word she speaks outrages Edmund's feelings "in total ignorance, unsuspiciousness of there being such feelings" (Chapter 47). At last, when we feel that her ghastly innocence (so to call it) could go no further, comes the master stroke. She tries to call him back by "a saucy, playful smile." She still thought that possible. The misunderstanding is incurable. She will never know Edmund.

In *Persuasion* the theme of deception is much less important. Sir Walter is, no doubt, deceived both in his nephew and in Mrs. Clay, but that is little more than the mechanism of the plot. What we get more of is the pains of the heroine in her role of compelled observer. Something of this had appeared in Elinor Dashwood, and more in Fanny Price, constantly forced to witness the courtship of Edmund and Mary Crawford. But Fanny had also, at times, derived amusement from her function of spectator. At the rehearsals of *Lovers' Vows* she was "not unamused to observe the selfishness which, more or less disguised, seemed to govern them all" (Chapter 14). It is a kind of pleasure which we feel sure that Jane Austen herself had often enjoyed. But whether it were that something in her own life now began to show her less of the spectator's joys and more of his pains, forcing her on from "as if we were God's spies" to "break my heart for I must hold my tongue," or that she is simply exploring a new literary vein, it certainly seems that Anne's unshared knowledge of the significance of things she hears and sees is nearly always in some degree painful. At Kellynch she has "a knowledge which she often wished less, her father's character." At the Musgroves', "One of the least agreeable circumstances of her residence . . . was her being treated with too much confidence by all parties, and being too much in the secret of the complaints of each house" (Chapter 6). One passage perhaps gives the real answer to any charge of priggery that might lie against her or Fanny for the judgments they pass as spectators. Speaking of Henrietta's behaviour to Charles Hayter, Jane Austen says that Anne "had delicacy which must be pained" by it (Chapter 9). This is not so much like the Pharisee's eagerness to condemn as the musician's involuntary shudder at a false note. Nor is it easily avoided by those who have standards of any sort. Do not our modern critics love to use the term "embarrassing" of literature which violently offends the standards of their own group? and does not this mean, pretty nearly, a "delicacy" on their part which "must be pained"? But of course all these spectator's pains sink into insignificance beside that very special, almost unendurable, pain which Anne derives from her understanding of Wentworth's every look and word. For *Persuasion,* from first to last, is, in a sense in which the other novels are not, a love story.

It remains to defend what I have been saying against a possible charge. Have I been treating the novels as though I had forgotten that they are, after all, comedies? I trust not. The hard core morality and even of religion seems to me to be just what makes good comedy possible. "Principles" or "seriousness" are essential to Jane Austen's art. Where there is no norm, nothing can be ridiculous, except for a brief moment of unbalanced provincialism in which we may laugh at the merely unfamiliar. Unless there is something about which the author is never ironical, there can be no true irony in the work. "Total irony"—irony about everything—frustrates itself and becomes insipid.

But though the world of the novels has this serious, unyielding core, it is not a tragic world. This, no doubt, is due to the author's choice; but there are also two characteristics of her mind which are, I think, essentially untragic. The first is the nature of the core itself. It is in one way exacting, in another not. It is unexacting in so far as the duties commanded are not quixotic or heroic, and obedience to them will not be very difficult to properly brought up people in ordinary circumstances. It is exacting in so far as such obedience is rigidly demanded; neither excuses nor experiments are allowed. If charity is the poetry of conduct and honour the rhetoric of conduct, Jane Austen's "principles" might be described as the grammar of conduct. Now grammar is something that anyone can learn; it is also something that everyone must learn. Compulsion waits.

I think Jane Austen does not envisage those standards which she so rigidly holds as often demanding human sacrifice. Elinor felt sure that if Marianne's new composure were based on "serious reflection" it "must eventually lead her to contentment and cheerfulness." That it might lead instead to a hair-shirt or a hermitage or a pillar in the Thebaïd is not in Jane Austen's mind. Or not there. There is just a hint in *Persuasion* that total sacrifice may be demanded of sailors on active service; as there is also a hint of women who must love when life or when hope is gone. But we are then at the frontier of Jane Austen's world.

The other untragic element in her mind is its cheerful moderation. She could almost have said with Johnson, "Nothing is too little for so little a creature as man." If she envisages few great sacrifices, she also envisages no grandiose schemes of joy. She has, or at least all her favourite characters have, a hearty relish for what would now be regarded as very modest pleasures. A ball, a dinner party, books, conversation, a drive to see a great house ten miles away, a holiday as far as Derbyshire—these, with affection (that is essential) and good manners, are happiness. She is no Utopian.

She is described by someone in Kipling's worst story as the mother of Henry James. I feel much more sure that she is the daughter of Dr. Johnson: she inherits his commonsense, his morality, even much of his style. I am not a good enough Jamesian to decide the other claim. But if she bequeathed anything to him it must be wholly on the structural side. Her style, her system of values, her temper, seem to me the very opposite of his. I feel sure that Isabel Archer, if she had met Elizabeth Bennet, would have pronounced her "not very cultivated," and Elizabeth, I fear, would have found Isabel deficient both in "seriousness" and in mirth.

A Long Talk About Jane Austen

by Edmund Wilson

There have been several revolutions of taste during the last century and a quarter of English literature, and through them all perhaps only two reputations have never been affected by the shifts of fashion: Shakespeare's and Jane Austen's. We still agree with Scott about Jane Austen, just as we agree with Ben Jonson about Shakespeare. From Scott, Southey, Coleridge, and Macaulay (to say nothing of the Prince Regent, who kept a set of her works "in every one of his residences") to Kipling and George Moore, Virginia Woolf and E. M. Forster, she has compelled the amazed admiration of writers of the most diverse kinds, and I should say that Jane Austen and Dickens rather queerly present themselves today as the only two English novelists (though not quite the only novelists in English) who belong in the very top rank with the great fiction-writers of Russia and France. Jane Austen, as Mr. Stark Young once said, is perhaps the only English example of that spirit of classical comedy that is more natural to the Latin people than to ours and that Molière represents for the French. That this spirit should have embodied itself in England in the mind of a well-bred spinster, the daughter of a country clergyman, who never saw any more of the world than was made possible by short visits to London and a residence of a few years in Bath and who found her subjects mainly in the problems of young provincial girls looking for husbands, seems one of the most freakish of the many anomalies of English literary history.

In *Speaking of Jane Austen,* by G. B. Stern and Sheila Kaye-Smith, two of Jane Austen's sister novelists have collaborated to pay her homage. Both Miss Stern and Miss Kaye-Smith have read the six novels again and again, and they have at their fingers' ends every trait, every speech, every gesture of every one of Jane Austen's people. Here they discuss, in alternate chapters, which give the effect of a conversation, a variety of aspects

"A Long Talk About Jane Austen." From *Classics and Commercials: A Literary Chronicle of the Forties* by Edmund Wilson (Farrar, Straus & Cudahy, Inc.). Copyright 1950 by Edmund Wilson. Published in Great Britain by W. H. Allen and Company, 1951. First appeared in *The New Yorker,* October 13, 1945. Reprinted by permission of the author.

of their subject. Miss Kaye-Smith is especially concerned with the historical background of the novels: she turns up a good deal that is interesting about the costume and food of the period and the social position of clergymen, and she traces the reflection, so meager and dim, of the cataclysmic political events that took place during Miss Austen's lifetime. Miss Stern is more preoccupied with the characters, whom she sometimes treats as actual people, classifying them on principles of her own and speculating about their lives beyond the story; sometimes criticizes from the point of view of a novelist who would see the situation in some cases a little differently, modifying or filling out a character or assigning a heroine to a different mate. The two ladies debate together the relative merits of the novels, agreeing that *Pride and Prejudice* belongs not at the top but toward the bottom of the list, and partly agreeing and partly not as to which of the characters are least successful. They have notes on Miss Austen's language and they underline some of her fine inconspicuous strokes. They make an effort to evoke the personalities of characters who are mentioned but never appear, and they have concocted a terrific quiz, which few readers, I imagine, could pass.

The book thus contains a good deal that will be interesting to those interested in Jane Austen, though neither Miss Stern nor Miss Kaye-Smith, it seems to me, really goes into the subject so deeply as might be done. My impression is that the long study of Jane Austen which has lately been published by Queenie Leavis in the English magazine called *Scrutiny* gets to grips with her artistic development in a way that the present authors, who do not mention Mrs. Leavis's essay, have scarcely even attempted to do. Yet *Speaking of Jane Austen,* an as informal symposium, revives the enthusiasm of the reader and stimulates him to think about the questions suggested by Miss Kaye-Smith and Miss Stern. Let me contribute a few comments of my own which will bring certain of these matters to attention:

(1) The half-dozen novels of Jane Austen were written in two sets of three each, with an interval of about ten years between the two: *Pride and Prejudice, Sense and Sensibility,* and *Northanger Abbey; Mansfield Park, Emma,* and *Persuasion.* The first of these lots, both in its satiric comedy and in the pathos of *Sense and Sensibility,* is quite close to the eighteenth century, whereas the second, with its psychological subtlety and such realism as the episode in *Mansfield Park* in which Fanny goes back to her vulgar home, is much closer to what we call "modern." In the second lot, the set comic character of the type of Lady Catherine de Bourgh, who at moments, as Miss Stern points out, falls in to the tone of an old-fashioned play, tends to give way to another kind of portraiture—as in the small country community of *Emma*—which is farther from cari-

cature and more recognizable as a picture of everyday life, and in *Persuasion,* a sensitivity to landscape and a tenderness of feeling appear that have definitely a tinge of the romantic. It is not true, as has been sometimes complained, that Miss Austen took no interest in nature, though this last novel is the only one of her books of which one clearly remembers the setting. Miss Kaye-Smith does note of *Persuasion* that "the weather and scenery have taken on some of the emotional force that permeates the whole book." But both authors seem to treat the novels as if they have always coexisted in time, instead of forming a sequence. What I miss in *Speaking of Jane Austen* is any account of the successive gradations, literary and psychological, which lead from *Pride and Prejudice* to *Persuasion.*

(2) The authors of this book both believe that there is something wrong with *Mansfield Park,* and they have a great deal to say about it. They feel that the chief figure, Fanny Price, a poor relation who immolates herself to the family of a great country house, is too meaching—too "creepmouse," Miss Kaye-Smith says—to be an altogether sympathetic heroine, and that in this case the author herself, in a way that is not characteristic, adopts a rather pharisaical attitude toward the more fun-loving and sophisticated characters. Miss Kaye-Smith tries to explain this attitude by suggesting that Jane Austen at this period may have come under the influence of the Evangelical Movement, to which two references are to be found in the book.

To the reviewer, this line of criticism in regard to *Mansfield Park* is already very familiar—it seems to represent a reaction which is invariable with feminine readers; yet I have never felt particularly the importance of the objections that are made on these grounds nor been shaken in my conviction that *Mansfield Park* is artistically the most nearly perfect of the novels. It is true that I have not read it for thirty years, so that I have had time to forget the moralizings that bother Miss Kaye-Smith and Miss Stern, but the sensations I remember to have had were purely aesthetic ones: a delight in the focusing of the complex group through the ingenuous eyes of Fanny, the balance and harmony of the handling of the contrasting timbres of the characters, which are now heard in combination, now set off against one another. I believe that, in respect to Jane Austen's heroines, the point of view of men readers is somewhat different from that of women ones. The woman reader wants to identify herself with the heroine, and she rebels at the idea of being Fanny. The male reader neither puts himself in Fanny's place nor imagines himself marrying Fanny any more that he does the nice little girl in Henry James's *What Maisie Knew,* a novel which *Mansfield Park* in some ways quite closely resembles. What interests him in Miss Austen's heroines is the marvellous portraiture of a gallery of different types of women, and Fanny, with her humility, her priggishness and her innocent and touching good faith, is a perfect picture of one kind of woman.

Whatever tone Jane Austen may sometimes take, what emerge and give the book its value are characters objectively seen, form and movement conceived aesthetically. It is this that sets Jane Austen apart from so many other women novelists—whether, like the author of *Wuthering Heights* or the author of *Gone With the Wind,* of the kind that make their power felt by a projection of their feminine day-dreams, or of the kind, from *Evelina* to *Gentlemen Prefer Blondes,* that amuse us by mimicking people. Miss Austen is almost unique among the novelists of her sex in being deeply and steadily concerned, not with the vicarious satisfaction of emotion (though the Cinderella theme, of course, does figure in several of her novels) nor with the skilful exploitation of gossip, but, as the great masculine novelists are, with the novel as a work of art.

(3) *Emma,* which both these critics adore, is with Jane Austen what *Hamlet* is with Shakespeare. It is the book of hers about which her readers are likely to disagree most; they tend either to praise it extravagantly or to find it dull, formless, and puzzling. The reason for this, I believe, is that, just as in the case of *Hamlet,* there is something outside the picture which is never made explicit in the story but which has to be recognized by the reader before it is possible for him to appreciate the book. Many women readers feel instinctively the psychological rightness of the behavior attributed to Emma, and they are the ones who admire the novel. Some male readers, like Justice Holmes, who was certainly a connoisseur of fiction yet who wrote to Sir Frederick Pollock that, "bar Miss Bates," he was "bored by *Emma,*" never succeed in getting into the story because they cannot see what it is all about. Why does Emma take up her two protégées? Why does she become so much obsessed by her plans for them? Why does she mistake the realities so and go so ludicrously wrong about them? Why does it take her so unconscionably long to reach the obvious rapproachment with Knightley?

The answer is that Emma is not interested in men except in the paternal relation. Her actual father is a silly old woman: in their household it is Emma herself who, motherless as she is, assumes the functions of head of the family; it is she who takes the place of the parent and Mr. Woodhouse who becomes the child. It is Knightley who has checked and rebuked her, who has presided over her social development, and she accepts him as a substitute father; she finally marries him and brings him into her own household, where his role is to reinforce Mr. Woodhouse. Miss Stern sees the difficulties of this odd situation. "Oh, Miss Austen," she cries, "it was *not* a good solution; it was a bad solution, an unhappy ending, could we see beyond the last pages of the book." But among the contretemps she foresees she does not mention what would surely have been the worst. Emma, who was relatively indifferent to men, was inclined to infatuations with women; and what reason is there to believe that her marriage with Knightley would prevent her from going on as she had done before: from discovering a new young lady as appealing as Harriet Smith, dominating her personality and situating her in a dreamworld of Emma's own in which Emma would be able to confer on her all kinds of imaginary benefits but which would have no connection whatever with her condition or her real possibilities? This would worry and exasperate Knightley and be hard for him to do anything about. He would be lucky if he did not presently find himself saddled, along with the other awkward features of the arrangement, with one of Emma's young protégées as an actual member of the household.

I do not mean to suggest for *Emma* any specific Freudian formula, but I feel sure that it is the one of her novels in which the author's own peculiar "conditioning" is most curiously and clearly seen. Jane Austen spent all her life with persons related to her by blood—her parents, her five brothers, her single unmarried sister—and the experience behind the relationships imagined by her in her novels is always an experience of relationships of blood, of which that between sisters is certainly the most deeply felt. Miss Stern and Miss Kaye-Smith are agreed with George Moore that Marianne's love for Willoughby in *Sense and Sensibility* is the most passionate thing in Jane Austen; but isn't it rather the emotion of Elinor as she witnesses her sister's disaster than Marianne's emotion over Willoughby of which the poignancy is communicated to the reader? The involvement with one another of the sisters is the real central theme of the book, just as the relation of Elizabeth to her sisters is so vital a part of *Pride and Prejudice*. For, though Miss Austen's intelligence was free to follow and understand other women when they were flirting or comfortably married, hunting husbands or breaking their hearts, she seems always to have been held suspended by the web of her original family ties. To some special equilibrium of the kind, which she never felt the necessity of upsetting, she must partly have owed the coolness, the patience, the poise, the leisure of mind to work at writing for its own sake, that made it possible for her to become a great artist. The solicitude of the sober Elinor Dashwood watching her giddy sister Marianne becomes in time the detached interest of the author looking on at the adventures of her heroines. In the last of her novels, *Persuasion,* one does find a different element and feel a personal emotion of the author's—a tinge of sadness at a woman's self-fulfilment missed—but the pattern is still much the same. Anne Elliot is herself a young sister: she, too, has a big sister, Lady Russell, who, like Emma, has misled her protégée—in this case, by discouraging her from marrying and nearly spoiling her life. Miss Stern and Miss Kaye-Smith do not care much for Lady Russell as a character; but she is worth thinking seriously about as a very important motif in Jane Austen. The comedy of the false sister-relationship of *Emma* has turned into something almost tragic.

On *Sense and Sensibility*

by *Ian Watt*

The basic conflict in *Sense and Sensibility* is by no means as remote from us as the society in which it is set. Many of Jane Austen's admirers, it is true, read her novels as a means of escape into a cosy sort of Old English nirvana, but they find this escape in her pages only because, as E. M. Forster has written, the devout "Janeites" "like all regular church-goers . . . scarcely notice what is being said."

An appreciation of what Jane Austen is really saying obviously involves, in the first place, some understanding of the very different social, literary, and linguistic conventions of her time.

We cannot, for example, see the characters clearly until we make allowances for the social order in which they are rooted. Even after their fall in the world the Dashwoods still keep two maids and a manservant; and when Jane Austen refers to the "work" of Elinor or Marianne, she only means elegant needlework. But we should not assume that the Dashwoods were self-pitying in thinking of themselves as poor; they really were, by the standards of their class; and what we would now be inclined to condemn as laziness or frivolity was then a universally accepted part of the leisure-class code. Similarly, it would be wrong to regard Edward Ferrars as an irresponsible sponger; in the reign of George the Third, young gentlemen with expectations of inherited wealth were not supposed to work. If they took up a profession, it was usually only as a matter of social convenience or prestige, and so Ferrars' concern about his vocation deserves much more credit than it would today. Nor is he hypocritical in deciding upon holy orders: his modest degree of religious commitment was certainly as great as, if not greater than, that normally found among the Anglican clergy of the period.

Even the code of Regency manners has some bearing on our interpretation of the characters and the plot. When Elinor is addressed as Miss Dashwood, for example, it is not because the speaker is being unduly formal in omitting her given name, but only because "Miss" and the

surname was the correct appellation for the eldest daughter. Nor is Elinor
herself to be regarded as a suspicious prude when she assumes, merely
from Willoughby's "addressing her sister by her christian name alone,"
that he and Marianne must be engaged. This was a fair deduction in the
more formal society of Jane Austen's England, and Mrs. Dashwood's
failure to clarify the position was, she later admits, a serious breach of
her duties as a mother.

The form of *Sense and Sensibility* is not in itself particularly remote
from us, since domestic comedy is a characteristically English literary
genre, although somewhat out of fashion today. The danger here is
rather that the novel's lightness of manner may lead us to underestimate
its real scope. Jane Austen restricted her means very consciously. She always "kept to her own style," a style which, as she described it, "dealt in
pictures of domestic life in country villages"; and each of these pictures
were painted "on to the little bit (two inches wide) of ivory on which I
work with so fine a brush, as produces little effect after much labour."
But the effect is not really so little, at least not for the kind of reader she
laughingly envisaged in a jingle (which is itself a parody of Sir Walter
Scott): "I do not write for such dull elves / As have not a great deal of ingenuity themselves." Nor do we need such a great deal of ingenuity to
see that all, or nearly all, the great issues in human life make their appearance on Jane Austen's narrow stage. True, it is only the stage of
petty domestic circumstance; but that, after all, is the only stage where
most of us are likely to meet them.

Jane Austen's stage, then, is narrow; it is also devoted to entertainment; and we may fail to recognize the great issues of life in their humor-
ous garb unless we are prepared to view the comic mode as an entertainment which can be both intellectually and morally serious. Jane Austen's
comedy belongs to the general category of what, in his essay "On the
Artificial Comedy of the Past Century" (1822), Charles Lamb was to call
"Comedy of Manners," referring to Restoration comedy and its successors.
Sense and Sensibility is certainly a narrative form of what Meredith
called "High Comedy"—the kind of comedy which arouses "thoughtful
laughter" at human weakness, folly, and affectation, usually presented in
their more sophisticated forms. Our attitude to such comedy must be ap-
propriately sophisticated and thoughtful; we must try to see all the
characters sufficiently objectively to be able to build up from their follies
and mistakes a coherent pattern of the positive norms from which the
characters have deviated.

Today we are less accustomed to look for universal norms in what we
read: partly because there is so much less common agreement about intellectual, moral, and social standards, and partly because we tend to see
life, and therefore literature, mainly in terms of individual experience.
Jane Austen's own standards—always present in her use of such abstract

terms as "reason," "civility," "respectability," and "taste"—were, like those of her age, much more absolute; and as a novelist she presented all her characters in terms of their relation to a fixed code of values. It follows that our attitude to her characters and their actions should be rather detached, both emotionally and intellectually; we must not be so bound up with the fate of Jane Austen's two heroines that we are blind to the emerging general pattern of values in the novel as a whole; if we confine all our attention to what is going to happen next to Elinor and Marianne, a great deal in the novel will seem redundant.

The most direct clue to the scheme of values which underlies *Sense and Sensibility* is its language. Jane Austen never bettered, and perhaps never equaled, the force and the brilliance of her verbal ironies in such scenes as those of John Dashwood and his wife discussing his father's dying wishes, or the grand dinner at which the Dashwoods entertain the Middletons, and where "no poverty of any kind, except of conversation, appeared." These ironies often depend on the power of abstract terms, as, for example, when Elinor smiles to see Mrs. Ferrars and her daughter being gracious to Lucy Steele "whom, of all others, had they known as much as she did, they would have been most anxious to mortify; while she herself, who had comparatively no power to wound them, sat pointedly slighted by both." Mark Schorer has finely observed that "there are none but verbal brutalities" in Jane Austen's novels. The brutalities are not gratuitous; they are the means whereby Jane Austen shocks us into seeing the disparity between proper norms of conduct and the actualities of human behavior, as in this case we are shocked into seeing the cruelty that underlies social pride.

The speech habits of the characters are also a means not only of psychological description but of placing each individual in Jane Austen's total scheme. The pretentious illiteracies of Lucy Steele, for instance, are less glaring than her sister's lamentably arch vulgarity; but they are nevertheless the means whereby the Dashwood sisters, and the reader, are enabled both to diagnose Lucy's sly and unscrupulous exploitation of the forms of intimacy, and to judge it in intellectual, social, and moral terms. Similarly, Marianne's proclaimed dislike of cliché is a sign of her genuine sense as well as of her verbal sensibility; and we must therefore balance her occasional lapses into the modish extravagancies of the sentimental novel against the genuine intellectual power suggested by the simple force of her language on such occasions as when, after Willoughby's desertion, she so grandly exclaims to Elinor: "The Middletons and Palmers—how am I to bear their pity?"

The very words of Jane Austen's title require some explanation. In modern usage, *Sense and Sensibility* can be paraphrased as meaning something like "Common Sense and Sensitiveness"; and its original reviewer in *The British Critic* interpreted it fairly enough: "The object of the work is to represent the effects on the conduct of life, of discreet quiet good sense on the one hand, and an over-refined and excessive susceptibility on the other." Yet behind the two terms there is also a complex historical and literary tradition which helps us to understand both why Jane Austen thought the problem important and why she presented it in the way she did.

Some forty years ago T. S. Eliot gave wide currency to the phrase "the dissociation of sensibility," and, through the phrase, to the idea that since the end of the metaphysical school of Donne and Herbert English poetry had suffered from a growing divorce between feeling and intellect. The very term "sensibility," however, is itself a product of the process he deplores; and this process has much to do, not only with the background of *Sense and Sensibility*, but with the development of the novel in general.

In the seventeenth century, no doubt because the Renaissance had begun to undermine the traditional order in man's social, intellectual, and religious outlook, philosophers became much preoccupied with the problem of whether man is a wholly self-centered and self-seeking being. Hobbes argued that he was; and this also seemed to be a possible consequence of Locke's theory of the *tabula rasa*, the notion that at birth the individual had no innate propensities, and that his moral and social being must therefore be regarded merely as the result of the impressions inscribed by the external environment on the originally "clean slate" of his mind during the process of growing up. As a result a great deal of attention in the eighteenth century was focused on the problem of how the sensations in man's mind were connected with the people and the world outside it; and since these sensations involved the feelings as well as the intellect, great attention was paid to the process of emotional identification, or sympathy. One very influential group of philosophers, headed by Lord Shaftesbury and Francis Hutcheson, maintained that Hobbes and Locke were wrong, and that man was naturally benevolent; that he had an innate moral sense, in the meaning of a specific ethical faculty, and that this faculty spontaneously led the individual to satisfy his impulses of sympathetic good will through his personal relationships.

This doctrine of natural benevolence, and of the innate moral sense, was taken up by many of the writers of the eighteenth century. It had important political implications: if man was naturally good, then society must be at fault, and this idea led towards Rousseau and the French Revolution. The revolt against Hobbes also had other and more directly literary consequences. For one thing, man's outgoing impulses obviously included the sensations of imaginative and aesthetic pleasure; these also were unselfish feelings, and as a result an intense love both of nature and art somehow became indicators of the individual's moral superiority in general. Eventually, with the Romantic movement, "sensibility" became one of the terms which reflected a radical change in the view of man's essential nature by embodying a historically new emphasis on the domain of feeling and imagination, as opposed to that of reason, will and fact.

Jane Austen's particular target was one of the extreme literary consequences of the doctrine of benevolence—the sentimental novel. Its most characteristic emphasis was on the sympathetic tear. Hobbes had said we enjoyed the misfortune of others; but Henry Mackenzie's *Man of Feeling* (1771) so completely identified himself with the sentiments of others that he spent his whole life weeping at them—and so did nearly two generations of popular heroes and heroines. The word "sentimental," as in the title of Sterne's *The Sentimental Journey* (1768), was originally used in a wholly favorable sense; like "sensibility" it denoted a strong capacity for sympathetic identification; but since the staple form of fiction during the last decades of the eighteenth century set out to portray intense emotional reactions to situations, reactions that demonstrated the depth of the character's "sensibility," the novels of the school of sensibility inevitably tended to be "sentimental" in the modern sense of "showing feeling in excess of the demands of the situation."

Many of Jane Austen's youthful writings were parodies of the popular sentimental fiction of the day; and *Sense and Sensibility* contains some evidence that it was originally prompted by a primarily satiric, as opposed to novelistic, impulse. The quality of Marianne's sensibility in general is shown by the intensity of her feeling for poetry and landscape. She rejoices that she does not love Edward Ferrars, for example, when she hears him read Cowper because "it would have broke *my* heart had I loved him, to hear him read with so little sensibility." Later, Jane Austen is obviously parodying the sentimental heroine's stock reactions to places that remind her of lost love when she writes: "in such moments of precious, of invaluable misery, [Marianne] rejoiced in tears of agony to be at Cleveland."

For the most part, however, Jane Austen takes Marianne more seriously, and makes her a study of a person who lives according to the general tenets of the Moral Sense philosophers, with their idea of an innate and spontaneous ethical sense. When, for example, Elinor reproves her for accepting the horse from Willoughby, Marianne retorts: "If there had been any real impropriety in what I did, I should have been sensible of it at the time, for we always know when we are acting wrong, and with such a conviction I could have had no pleasure."

Jane Austen, of course, does not agree. A more traditional school of moralists had taught her that we must beware of how our moral judgment, and indeed our whole consciousness, can be colored by our self-regarding impulses; even pride in one's own sensibility might well be a form of selfishness. This criticism is found in one of her hilarious early parodies, *Love and Freindship,* where Jane Austen's heroine Laura

proudly confesses that "a sensibility too tremblingly alive to every affliction of my friends, my acquaintance and particularly to every affliction
of my own, was my only fault, if a fault it could be called." The cooing
note of self-approving pleasure at one's susceptibility to the afflictions of
others had in fact been rather conspicuous both in the Moral Sense
philosophers and in their literary analogues, the sentimental novelists:
Sterne for example, proudly exclaimed: "Praised be God for my sensibility!" Jane Austen, on the other hand, makes us observe that Marianne's
selfish indulgence of her own sufferings makes her insensitive to Elinor's;
and indeed the criticism goes deeper, since the narrative shows such indulgence resulting in a parasitical exploitation of others. Marianne forces
Elinor to take over all the unpleasant tasks of practical life, while at
the same time scorning her sister's steady self-command because it demonstrates the inferiority of her sensibility.

Sensibility is also shown to be self-interested in a more directly economic sense. Marianne thinks no more than her mother about the need
for economy, and despises Elinor for allowing herself to worry about
such gross practical matters. But just as in *Love and Freindship* Laura's
lover, Augustus, assumes an innate right to the material goods he despises,
and "gracefully purloins" money "from his unworthy father's escritoire,"
so Marianne is made to attack Elinor for holding that "wealth has much
to do with happiness," although she herself assumes that "a family cannot very well be maintained" on less than two thousand pounds a year—
twice what Elinor sees as the prerequisite of happiness. This point, of
course, is later underlined by the plot; Marianne marries Colonel Brandon who indeed has two thousand a year, while Elinor marries Edward
Ferrars, who has a third of that income. Not only so: Marianne's first
love, Willoughby, whose taste and spirit in everything from poetry to
passion was of the requisite intensity, actually relinquishes Marianne
for a mercenary marriage merely because it is the price of continued self-
indulgence; while Edward, whose defective sensibility has been exhaus-
tively diagnosed by Marianne, is now called "unfeeling" by John Dashwood because he unhesitatingly endures disinheritance so that he can
marry for love.

The case against the various sorts of selfishness associated with sensibility is pushed home relentlessly—too relentlessly, certainly, unless we
appreciate that Jane Austen does not do this merely to build up a case
for its opposite quality, "sense." Actually, the manifestations of "sense"
in the novel are equally varied and ambiguous. Elinor's "sense," for
example, obviously includes a prudent regard for economic reality; but
it is soon made clear that not all kinds of economic "sense" are laudable.
Elinor, for example, "soon allowed" the Steele girls "credit for some kind
of sense when she saw with what constant and judicious attentions they
were making themselves agreeable to Lady Middleton." We must, there-

fore, abandon any attempt to view the book as based on an unqualified and diametrical opposition between sense and sensibility, and see instead that Jane Austen requires us to make much more complex discriminations between the two terms.

The opening scene, with the John Dashwoods' coolly disengaging themselves from their solemn family obligations to support Mrs. Dashwood and her daughters, begins the book, it must be noted, with an attack on the abuses, not of sensibility, but of sense, in its prudential economic meaning. John Dashwood is much more a caricature of a narrow view of sense than Marianne is of sensibility; while his wife, as Jane Austen tells us, is a "strong caricature" of him. When we come to the Middletons, however, we have a less obvious thematic contrast. Sir John is a caricature of some aspects of sensibility—he is prompt in relieving the distress of his homeless female relatives, and his whole nature is an epitome of man as a benevolent social animal. His wife, on the other hand, is a parallel case of Fanny Dashwood's conventional "sense." "There was a kind of cold hearted selfishness on both sides," we are told, "which mutually attracted them; and they sympathised with each other in an insipid propriety of demeanour, and a general want of understanding."

The Middleton duality is repeated, in turn, by the Palmers: Mrs. Palmer is a ludicrously optimistic expression of her brother-in-law's jovial gregariousness, while her husband flaunts his rudeness as if it were an emblem of social distinction, a masculine variant of Lady Middleton's inarticulate and insensitive elegance.

The similarity between the two villains completes the picture, since Lucy Steele's pretense at sensibility, though less convincing than Willoughby's, is a mere surface veneer to hide her basic cruelty and selfishness. We are thus in a position to see almost the whole of Jane Austen's *dramatis personae* as highly unsatisfactory representatives of the two concepts which she has aligned against each other. Her moral judgment of their relative merits, however, becomes fairly clear when we consider that the characters on the side of sensibility, as equated with unselfish benevolence, are obviously superior to the protagonists of sense, in its selfish prudential form.

Thus Sir John Middleton clearly lacks sense in the finer meaning of judgment; he is easily taken in by the surface politeness of the Misses Steele. He is also deficient in the finer aspects of sensibility; quite apart from his lack of aesthetic interests, he completely fails to understand the importance of emotional and intellectual rapport in personal relationships, thinking nothing "more [is] required" for intimacy between people than "sitting an hour or two together in the same room almost every day." Still, Middleton is much closer to a desirable human norm than his wife, and only the intransigent perfectionism of youth would

take violent offense at the promiscuity of his benevolence; and this "ir-
ritable refinement" of the adolescent sensibility, which Elinor diagnoses
in Marianne, but which she herself partly shares, is eventually humbled.

Interestingly enough, the main agent of this educative process is the
vulgar Mrs. Jennings. She has all Sir John's indiscriminate cheerfulness;
her tactless curiosity and thoughtless gossip begin by offending Elinor
and Marianne even more deeply; yet by the end of the novel they have
learned that the uncultivated Mrs. Jennings has the essence of what
really matters as regards both sense and sensibility. Once her intellectual
judgments are made, and her benevolent feelings are engaged, she acts
disinterestedly and energetically, siding with Elinor and Marianne against
the wealth and the family connections of the Dashwoods and the Ferrars.
Even before then her "naturalness" and her "blunt sincerity" have implicitly corrected Marianne's erroneous assumptions about the proper
relationship between marriage and money, for she at once assumes that
the very modest income of Edward Ferrars' living at Delaford will not
and should not be any obstacle to the marriage of lovers: her head and
her heart combine to point out that the lovers must merely make do with
less.

Elinor and Marianne, of course, come to look back with shame on their
early superciliousness about Mrs. Jennings; indeed they even learn to
be grateful to the later kindness of the Palmers. This is part of a general
softening of the thematic oppositions between sense and sensibility in
the last chapters; even Willoughby's rather stagy confession to Elinor
underlines the suffering that comes from letting economic sense dominate the dictates of sensibility; reason and experience have brought him,
by a devious route, towards a sorrowful understanding of the need to
reconcile the two claims. The fact that Elinor responds to him with great
sympathy also serves to remind us that just as Jane Austen does not intend any flat opposition between sense and sensibility, so she does not
intend any diametrical opposition between her heroines either, since one
major emphasis in the narrative is on how differences between them are
eventually removed.

. . . It would not have been easy to make Elinor as attractive as her
sister. For it is not only in this book, and it is not only in Jane Austen,
that grave difficulties arise in making sensible characters vivid and attractive. Every novelist, surely, must feelingly echo the old prayer
that the bad may be made good, the good nice, and the nice—interesting.

Elinor is good and nice, but she is only intermittently interesting. Yet
her general functions in the narrative are clear enough, and some of
them have occasionally been overlooked. For, just as it is evident that
Marianne has sense, has an excellent "understanding both natural and
improved," so Elinor is by no means deficient in sensibility. She shares
all the tastes of her sister, if with a lesser intensity, but, perhaps because

she is older, she consistently tries to relate her imagination and her feelings to her judgment and to the moral and social tradition on which the order of society is based. Almost the whole course of the book, in fact, presents us with a picture of the everyday heroism of Elinor struggling to control the anguish of disappointed love so that she can fulfill her obligations as a daughter, a sister, and member of society. For this, of course, she is rewarded; and, in no very oblique criticism of the tearful tendency of the cult of sensibility, Jane Austen shows Elinor nearly overcome by joyful emotion when she hears that Edward Ferrars is, after all, going to be free to marry her: she "almost ran out of the room, and as soon as the door was closed, burst into tears of joy."

The joy was not less intense because Elinor remembered that ladies do not run, and that they always shut the door. But Elinor's sense involves much more than prudent reticence and a regard for the forms of social decorum; these may be its surface expression, but its essence is fidelity to the inward discriminations of both the head and the heart. As Jane Austen so assuredly puts it, after the lovers have at last been united Edward is "the happiest of men . . . not only in the rapturous profession of the lover, but in the reality of reason and truth."

Edward Ferrars and Colonel Brandon have found even fewer admirers than Elinor. It is clear that both heroes are intended to combine the prudence, responsibility, and practical intelligence of sense with the goodheartedness and emotional delicacy of sensibility. That they are also both rather dull fellows is perhaps in accord with the sad truth that in real life the attempt to combine the qualities of sense and sensibility often leads to a certain timidity in speech and action, presumably because the pressure of the dual set of considerations tends to inhibit or at least retard full intellectual or emotional commitment. Even so, there is certainly an unconvincing quality about Brandon, especially when he tells all to Elinor; and the final marriage to Marianne is hurriedly presented and psychologically unconvincing. One of the best of Jane Austen's modern critics, Marvin Mudrick, indeed goes much further, and charges that "Marianne, the life and center of the novel, has been betrayed; and not by Willoughby."

This position, however, depends upon our accepting Marianne as an admirable example of the gallant struggle of the individual sensibility against a hostile world. But, as we have seen, that was not Jane Austen's view of the matter. Like T. S. Eliot, she was, in her own way, an opponent of the dissociation of sensibility: she knew very well that in life both the heart and the mind often came up against all but insurmountable obstacles; and, charming as she found Marianne, she thought her tactics unwise. Silent rather than open suffering sometimes seemed both the more prudent and the more dignified course; society often had to be met with its own despicable weapons, since it was idle to pretend and futile to expect that the "realities of reason and truth" could be widely shared. With the complacent loquacity of the Robert Ferrars of this world, for example, Jane Austen certainly endorsed Elinor's tactics when she merely "agreed to it all, for she did not think he deserved the compliment of rational opposition."

It is an immortal phrase for a perennial predicament—and before we condemn such venial dishonesties we must consider the alternatives. When Marianne, for example, was asked a boring or awkward question in company, "she was silent; it was impossible for her to say what she did not feel, however trivial the occasion." But the consequence was instructive: "Upon Elinor, therefore, the whole task of telling lies when politeness required it, always fell."

Jane Austen, one may hazard, thought that in life sensibility would founder if it were not directed by sense, because its course would take no account of what she thought were the actual, and assumed to be the unalterable, configurations of society. Marianne had been lucky, not only to find Colonel Brandon waiting to take her in, but also to have a sister like Elinor who took a more realistic view of what the individual can concede without losing his integrity. When Marianne accused her of advocating being "subservient to the judgments of our neighbours," Elinor replied, "My doctrine has never aimed at the subjection of understanding." The question is how far one can afford to be either intellectually or emotionally sincere, and under what conditions. There will always be many views about this, and Jane Austen was perhaps essentially closer than she would have cared to the position of Joyce's Stephen Dedalus who, a century later, thought the price of individual integrity not less than "silence, exile, and cunning." With this difference, that, unlike Marianne—or Dedalus—Jane Austen was not a Romantic; she did not visualize the course of the individual life as a process of climbing to higher and yet higher planes of aesthetic perfection and moral insight. More classical, and more pessimistic, she saw the individual life less as a series of pinnacles to be scaled than as, and in many senses, a set position to be maintained against the forces of selfishness, unreason, and emotional excess; nor, all things considered, were silence and cunning too high a price to pay for maintaining it at home.

As regards her treatment of Marianne, then, we can, with R. W. Chapman, say of Jane Austen that "the hostile criticism amounts to . . . little more than this, that she was not a poet." Jane Austen was, indeed, the inheritor of the eighteenth century, the age of Prose and Reason, as Matthew Arnold called it. But that was only one side of her age, and she learned from the other side too, the side which has been labelled sentimental and pre-romantic, and which, after all, gave us much of our modern way of looking at the individual's consciousness of himself and of his personal and social relationships. The primary importance of *Sense and Sensibility* in the history of the novel—and for us—is that in it Jane Austen developed for the first time a narrative form which fully articulated the conflict between the contrary tendencies of her age: between reason and rapture, between the observing mind and the feeling heart, between being sensible and being sensitive. The dissociation of sensibility may or may not have been all but mortal for poetry, but in splitting the human mind into its component parts, and so making them available for inspection, both in themselves and in relation to the outside world, it brought life to the novel. So, in addition to the timeless relevance of its general theme, great historical importance attaches to the novel in which, despite a certain amount of awkwardly obtrusive manipulation, Jane Austen nevertheless brought off her supreme coup as a matchmaker, and triumphantly introduced Sense to Sensibility.

Critical Realism in *Northanger Abbey*

by Alan D. McKillop

For the purposes of this discussion we may disregard the fact that Jane Austen's *Susan* (the original *Northanger Abbey*) came after *First Impressions* (the original *Pride and Prejudice*) and after both *Elinor and Marianne* and its revision as *Sense and Sensibility*. As it stands *Northanger Abbey* must contain more untouched early work than either *Pride and Prejudice* or *Sense and Sensibility*. The present study considers *Northanger Abbey* as the comprehensive result of Jane Austen's early reactions to and exercises in prose fiction.

At the beginning of her career Jane Austen could easily have drawn up an elaborate burlesque "Plan of a Novel" of the kind she actually wrote in 1814. Such a program underlies *Love and Freindship,* dated at the end June 13, 1790. This piece caricatures what Jane Austen later calls the "desultory novel," with rapid changes of place, sudden introduction of new characters, accidents, recognitions, and reversals. "My Father was a native of Ireland and an inhabitant of Wales; my Mother was the natural Daughter of a Scotch Peer by an Italian Opera-girl—I was born in Spain and received my Education at a Convent in France. When I had reached my eighteenth Year I was recalled by my Parents to my paternal roof in Wales." The heroine is excessively accomplished, learns everything without effort, and shows extreme sensibility at every turn. The prominence given to the theme of instantaneous love and friendship explains the title: "We flew into each others arms and after having exchanged vows of mutual Freindship for the rest of our Lives, instantly unfolded to each other the most inward secrets of our Hearts." The sentimental novel had already reduced to absurdity the principle set forth in one of Richardson's favorite quotations:

> Great souls by instinct to each other turn,
> Demand alliance, and in friendship burn.

With the first appearance of the young man Edward we have another cluster of novelistic devices, beginning with the knocking at the door and the appearance of the interesting stranger (as, for example, at the opening of Mrs. Helme's *Louisa; or, The Cottage on the Moor*). The actual presentation of the incident, with the knocking twice repeated and the situation prolonged by Father's deliberate comment, is probably a little independent exercise in the manner of Sterne. Then follow the instantaneous friendship and prompt rehearsal of previous history, introducing a *non sequitur* which delightfully hits off the emergence of such situations in the "desultory novel": "My Father's house is situated in Bedfordshire, my Aunt's in Middlesex, and tho' I flatter myself with being a tolerable proficient in Geography, I know not how it happened, but I found myself entering this beautiful Vale which I find is in South Wales, when I had expected to have reached my Aunts."

The basic method of the early burlesques is the direct inflation of the novel style, together with the *non sequitur*. It would be useless to list many instances of such mockery, but especially significant is the burlesque of didactic comment: after a phaeton is upset, "what an ample subject for reflection on the uncertain Enjoyments of this World, would not that Phaeton and the Life of Cardinal Wolsey afford a thinking Mind!" But there is also the deflationary comment, by writer or characters, to point up absurdity: thus when Edward, in the scene just mentioned, makes a high-flown speech his father replies: "Where, Edward in the name of wonder did you pick up this unmeaning gibberish? You have been studying Novels I suspect." Or again, inflation and deflation appear together in such a passage as this:

> Isabel had seen the World. She had passed 2 Years at one of the first Boarding-schools in London; had spent a fortnight in Bath and had supped one night in Southampton.
>
> "Beware my Laura (she would often say) Beware of the insipid Vanities and idle Dissipations of the Metropolis of England; Beware of the unmeaning Luxuries of Bath and of the stinking fish of Southampton."
>
> "Alas! (exclaimed I) how am I to avoid those evils I shall never be exposed to? What probability is there of my ever tasting the Dissipations of London, the Luxuries of Bath, or the stinking Fish of Southampton? I who am doomed to waste my Days of Youth and Beauty in an humble Cottage in the Vale of Uske."

Here is the theme of seeing the world later to be developed in *Northanger Abbey*, "all the difficulties and dangers of a six weeks' residence in Bath," treated with mock-didacticism and a mock-heroic attitude toward adventure. Similarly in the first of *A Collection of Letters* an anxious mother supervises her girls' *"entrée* into Life" by taking them out to pay visits and drink tea; the girls return "in raptures with the World, its Inhab-

itants, and Manners." This is the lighter side of the *Grandison* tradition
as transmitted by Fanny Burney and now treated playfully, though not
with utter contempt. *A Collection* and *The Three Sisters* begin to give
something like Richardson's long reports of dialogue and social detail,
and present situations in which young girls display their patience, folly,
disappointment, or impudence. The point of view of the girl is sometimes
used to provide irresponsible humor, but the dialogue lends some social
credibility to the extravagance. Playful exaggeration remains, but irony
and deflation tend to become central, and the more extravagant burlesque devices tend to become marginal or incidental. We are at the
beginning of a development which will assign the pompous didactic
comment to a Mary Bennet, or the utterly preposterous letter to a Mr.
Collins.

The heroine may be said to emerge in *Catharine, or the Bower,* dated
August 1792. "Catharine had the misfortune, as many heroines have had
before her, of losing her Parents when she was very young, and of being
brought up under the care of a Maiden Aunt, who while she tenderly
loved her, watched over her conduct with so scrutinizing a severity, as
to make it very doubtful to many people, and to Catharine amongst the
rest, whether she loved her or not." This is the moderated isolation and
persecution of the heroine as it derived from the patterns of Richardson
and Burney. We learn that "Kitty," as she is called henceforth, is an
heiress, the daughter of a merchant; this too connects with the Burney
pattern, but might raise the issue of social distinctions too sharply to fit
Jane Austen's maturer plots. The opening immediately refers to characters to be introduced later: the friend who was sent to the East Indies
to find a husband (a contemporary real-life situation never used elsewhere by Jane Austen); this friend's sister, serving as companion to the
daughters of the Dowager Lady Halifax; the haughty Dudley family,
who look down on Kitty. This cast might have proved to be unmanageable, but with the actual entrance of the Stanley family we find ourselves
perhaps for the first time established in Jane Austen's social milieu.
Kitty's opening conversation with Camilla Stanley uses the stock device
of discussing novels in a fresh and effective way:

> You have read Mrs. Smith's Novels, I suppose?" said she to her Compan-
> ion—. "Oh! Yes, replied the other, and I am quite delighted with them—
> They are the sweetest things in the world—" "And which do you prefer
> of them?" "Oh! dear, I think there is no comparison between them—Em-
> meline is *so much* better than any of the others—" "Many people think
> so, I know; but there does not appear so great a disproportion in their
> Merits to *me;* do you think it is better written?" "Oh! I do not know any-
> thing about *that*—but it is better in *everything*—Besides, Ethelinde is so
> long—" "That is a very common Objection I believe, said Kitty, but for
> my own part, if a book is well written, I always find it too short." "So

do I, only I get tired of it before it is finished." "But did not you find
the story of Ethelinde very interesting? And the Descriptions of Grasmere,
are not the[y] Beautiful?" "Oh! I missed them all, because I was in such a
hurry to know the end of it—Then from an easy transition she added, We
are going to the Lakes this Autumn, and I am quite Mad with Joy."

In 1792 Jane Austen is evidently taking the novels of Charlotte Smith
seriously, and we may bear in mind the manifest connection of this little
scene with the dialogue between Catherine Morland and Isabella Thorpe
in *Northanger Abbey* concerning "horrid books." [1] The appearance of
Camilla's brother Edward leads to episodes in which his "address and
Vivacity" appeal to "the good natured lively Girl," but arouse the distrust
of her aunt; his sudden departure troubles Kitty, though she still has
hopes of gaining his affection. The fragment breaks off with the young
novelist evidently perplexed about her next move. The heroine is still at
her aunt's house near Exeter, corresponding with various friends, some of
whom have not yet been brought on stage; evidently, it appears, she is
to go to London, where Edward may disappoint her still further. We
can find in *Catherine* some analogies with *Northanger Abbey*, though
the earlier Kitty is more vivacious and independent than Catherine Morland in *Northanger Abbey*. Kitty talks of novels and other feminine concerns with a more sophisticated but silly acquaintance who no doubt
turns out to be no true friend (Camilla Stanley = Isabella Thorpe); the
brother of this girl appears as a possible suitor, though the gay Edward
is otherwise utterly unlike the boorish John Thorpe; and the sister reports on the supposed state of this brother's mind. In their quick acquaintance and separation Kitty and Edward may remind us of Marianne
Dashwood and Willoughby in *Sense and Sensibility*, though they are
much gayer.

Northanger Abbey develops from the deflationary vein in the early
writings and begins on the plan of introducing into a novel frequent
references belittling the conventions of novels. In a crude and sporadic
form this device was quite common: "Let it be remembered that our
heroine has neither been in sea-storms nor land storms; she has never
been interred in caverns, nor bewildered in the corridors of a haunted
castle; no assassin has lifted his dagger against her innocent bosom; no
ravisher has hung on her peaceful walks." [2] Maria Edgeworth's *Belinda*
(1801) must have been read by Jane Austen about the time when she finished *Northanger Abbey* in its original form, and is mentioned with praise
in the defense of novels and novelists as we now have it (I, v). In Miss
Edgeworth's story Lady Delacour offers comments of this kind: "My dear,

[1] See Alan D. McKillop, "Allusions to Prose Fiction in Jane Austen's 'Volume the
Third,' " *Notes and Queries*, CXCVI (1951), 428-429.
[2] Mrs. Rachel Hunter, *Letitia: or, The Castle without a Spectre*, 1801.

you will be woefully disappointed, if in my story you expect any thing like a novel. I once heard a general say, that nothing was less like a review than a battle; and I can tell you, that nothing is more unlike a novel than real life." In *Northanger Abbey* Jane Austen keeps saying in effect, "Catherine is not a story-book heroine, and things do not happen to her as they do in novels," and alternately, "Nevertheless she must be a heroine, and this *is* a novel after all."

In dwelling on these points the novelist interposes herself as in no other of her works. The scope of her satire appears in a mere listing of the conventions and formulas glanced at in the first few chapters: Catherine Morland's father was not a victim of misfortune or a domestic tyrant; her mother did not die at her birth; she was not a beautiful girl, versatile and prodigiously accomplished. Miss Lascelles aptly points out the contrast with Charlotte Smith's Emmeline, and though the theme was common—many a heroine brought up in obscurity astonishes fashionable people by her skill in music, embroidery, and languages—it is very likely that Jane Austen did have Charlotte Smith's heroine in mind here. No amiable youth appears in the neighborhood for Catherine to fall in love with—no young lord, foundling, squire's son, or ward brought up in her family. The "difficulties and dangers of a six weeks' residence in Bath," into which she is launched, call forth no presentiments, lengthened good advice, or warnings about the danger of abduction by some nobleman. Catherine did not promise to send her sister long letters from Bath full of characters and conversation. There was no tearful parting, no generous gift from her father, no storm, robbery, or carriage accident "to introduce them to the hero." The passage in *Northanger Abbey* on the uneventful journey to Bath may be compared with Jane Austen's account of her own journey to Bath in 1801:

> Our journey here was perfectly free from accident or event; we changed horses at the end of every stage, and paid at almost every turnpike. We had charming weather, hardly any dust, and were exceedingly agreeable, as we did not speak above once in three miles. Between Luggershall and Everley we made our grand meal, and then with admiring astonishment perceived in what a magnificent manner our support had been provided for. We could not with the utmost exertion consume above the twentieth part of the beef.

According to rule, Catherine's companion Mrs. Allen should prove to be an imprudent, vulgar, or jealous guardian, and thus "promote the general distress of the work." But she is merely passive and colorless. Catherine at first made no impression in the public rooms at Bath; no young man "started with rapturous wonder on beholding her, no whisper of eager inquiry ran round the room, nor was she once called a divinity by any body." (I, ii) This sustained satire of novelistic formulas comes to a close when Jane Austen says of the Thorpes:

> This brief account of the family is intended to supersede the necessity of a long and minute detail from Mrs. Thorpe herself, of her past adventures and sufferings, which might otherwise be expected to occupy the three or four following chapters; in which the worthlessness of lords and attornies might be set forth, and conversations which had passed twenty years before, be minutely repeated. (I, iv)

In the preceding chapter the criticism had been lightly varied by playful slurs on the Richardson tradition, to be detected in Henry Tilney's remarks on young ladies' "delightful habit of journalizing" and their "talent of writing agreeable letters," and in Jane Austen's own reference to Richardson's severe standards of propriety. Throughout the early part of the story Jane Austen is careful to point out that Catherine has nothing of the conscious correctness and sententiousness to be found in the ideal heroine of a didactic novel. After some playful remarks on the vanity of dress, the novelist adds, "But not one of these grave reflections troubled the tranquillity of Catherine" (I, x). The device of rejecting the novel formula continues to be used now and then, as in the long passage at the end on the heroine's return. "A heroine in a hack post-chaise, is such a blow upon sentiment, as no attempt at grandeur or pathos can withstand" (II, xiv). Thus the novelist conducts the story by acknowledging the defeat of the heroic and the ideally correct. Less frequently she professes to be keeping up the novel formula: "Monday, Tuesday, Wednesday, Thursday, Friday and Saturday have now passed in review before the reader; the events of each day, its hopes and fears, mortifications and pleasures have been separately stated, and the pangs of Sunday only now remain to be described, and close the week" (I, xiii). This mocks the day by day and hour by hour chronicle of Richardson's important sequences, with an echo perhaps of Fanny Burney's solemn indications of time in *Camilla*: "Thus passed the first eight days of the Tunbridge excursion, and another week succeeded without any varying event." "Thus again lived and died another week."

So far Catherine has been only *a* heroine or anti-heroine, not *the* heroine; Jane Austen has spoken not so much about her as about her role. But when Catherine develops as an individual two possibilities appear, and Jane Austen's difficulties come from trying to develop both possibilities at the same time. In a sharp opposition between fiction and ordinary life, common sense should have the upper hand, and Catherine by virtue of being commonplace is on the side of common sense. But in the quixotic mode Catherine is to illustrate, not merely to negate, romantic folly. The reader might expect to find her carried away from the outset by poetry and romance, well versed in the literature of the subject, and eager to find a romantic lover and to meet him more than halfway. We are told in the first chapter, "But from fifteen to seventeen she was in training for a heroine; she read all such works as heroines must read to supply their memories with quotations which are so serviceable and so soothing in the vicissitudes of their eventful lives." Yet Catherine does not oblige us with a single quotation, and her romantic dreaming is but slightly touched on, as when Henry Tilney's disappearance from Bath is translated into novelistic terms: "This sort of mysteriousness, which is always so becoming in a hero, threw a fresh grace in Catherine's imagination around his person and manners, and increased her anxiety to know more of him" (I, v).

Though it is playfully assumed that the novelist and the reader expect romance in Catherine's adventures at Bath, Catherine herself looks for nothing of the kind; her expectations are so inarticulate that they can hardly be put into words; she is denied a vocabulary even of "novel slang." She is docile and receptive, but unassuming good sense keeps her from a prompt and extreme adoption of romantic follies. For her, as for many young people, the value of a suggestion must depend on the value of the person who offers it, and she is chiefly susceptible to suggestions from people of her own age. But though she accepts to a degree the instantaneous friendship offered by Isabella Thorpe, she is never completely duped by it. This friendship leads directly to the introduction of novel-reading as part of the action of the story. Henceforth we are to have the characters talking, not too seriously and not always very sensibly, about novels. But before Jane Austen hands over the subject to her characters, she tries to make her own position clear. The passage (I, v) is too familiar for quotation, but we may note that Jane Austen wishes to suggest that her satire is directed not against the novel as such, but against silly novelists and novel-readers. She singles out the absurdity of complete condemnation of the novel in a novel, but even here she presents the theme lightly. Why shouldn't the heroine of one novel patronize another? We novelists must stick together. The defense is serious, but we still have the playful assumption, almost in the spirit of the *juvenilia,* that writing and reading novels is a kind of game.

What follows is an informal survey of novel-readers, whether silly, stupid, naïve, affected, or, as we now say, "sophisticated." The famous conversation about "horrid books" (I, vi) is perhaps the best remembered passage in *Northanger Abbey.* Its relation to the conversation in *Catherine* has been noted above. But the earlier passage contrasted the sensible Kitty with the foolish Camilla, whereas we now have the active folly of Isabella Thorpe and the naïve docility of Catherine. Isabella is twenty-two to Catherine's eighteen, more knowing in the ways of the world. She takes the initiative in reading and planning to read the Gothic novels; for Catherine such reading is part of her new social experiences, and the playful anti-Gothic satire is thus connected with and subordinated to the Burney theme. The ordinary didactic novelist of the time would have built up Catherine's reference to *Sir Charles Grandison* into a contrast between sensible and silly readers, and good and bad books; but though *Grandison* was one of Jane Austen's favorite novels, she is here interested in using the references to novels for purposes of characterization, rather than in building up a case against Mrs. Radcliffe and in favor of Richardson.

Talk about novels is less successfully used in Catherine's discussion with John Thorpe, who seems to refer to *Tom Jones* and *Camilla* chiefly because Jane Austen wants him to do so (I, vii). Catherine is soon comparing the uncertain weather at Bath with the beautiful weather at Udolpho, and thinks of Mrs. Radcliffe's towers and galleries as they plan a visit to Blaize Castle (I, xi). A little later *Udolpho* is wittily put in its place by Henry Tilney in the long discussion of Mrs. Radcliffe, the reading of history, and the principles of the picturesque (I, xiv). Here again Catherine is completely docile, accepting ideas from the Tilneys. Jane Austen takes occasion to comment that whereas "a sister author" (Fanny Burney in *Camilla*?) has praised "the advantages of natural folly in a beautiful girl," there are some people, among them Henry, who prefer simple ignorance to imbecility. Thus far Catherine's education at Bath, conducted without the solemnity of the didactic novelist, has gone well. Neither novelist nor heroine has been forced into absurdity or extravagance. Though Catherine has gone along with Isabella's reading of Gothic novels, she is carefully dissociated from Isabella's use of sentimental and romantic clichés. " 'Had I the command of millions, were I mistress of the whole world, your brother would be my only choice.' This charming sentiment, recommended as much by sense as novelty, gave Catherine a most pleasing remembrance of all the heroines of her acquaintance" (I, xv). Isabella, professing to be all for female friendship, sublime disregard of money, and love in a cottage, usually betrays her insincerity before she reaches the end of a sentence.

In all this Jane Austen certainly has in mind routine performances on the Richardson pattern, inferior imitations of Fanny Burney, current effusions of sensibility, the staple wares of the circulating library. But she names only Gothic novels, and this has obscured the actual relation of the story to contemporary fiction. As Catherine and the Tilneys approach the Abbey we have the last of the light conversations about fiction, in which Henry outlines to Catherine the supposed adventures of the Radcliffian kind that will befall her there. Henry playfully imputes Gothic quixotism to Catherine; her fantasies have at first to be devised for her, and even so she knows that Henry, as we say, is "kidding" her. No one is as yet seriously mixing up romance and real life. The approach to the Abbey, we are told, offers no landscapes in the manner of Mrs. Radcliffe, and Catherine enters without foreboding or suspicion. Things are still as they were at Bath. "Her passion for ancient edifices was next in degree to her passion for Henry Tilney—and castles and abbies made usually the charm of those reveries which his image did not fill" (II, ii). There is a nice hint here, a possible connection between her growing affection for Henry and her Gothic fixation, but I am not sure that we can emphasize this without reading too much into the story.

But once Catherine's quixotism becomes so active that she suspects General Tilney of being a Montoni, and tries to ferret out dark family secrets, the tone of the story changes for a time. In the Bath chapters it was the novelist who was pointing out the disparities between literature and life; now it is Catherine herself who is illustrating these disparities by trying to find Gothic romance in the Midlands. The narrative is still interesting, and remarkably documentary; Jane Austen is more explicit than usual in her descriptions of the Abbey and the details of life there; her plan requires her to match in a way Mrs. Radcliffe's elaborate descriptions. But Catherine's active pursuit of Gothic illusions, culminating in Henry's gentle rebuke, jolts the story rather violently and for a time takes us back to the earlier mode of crude burlesque in which heroines were made to behave outrageously in order to reduce romance to absurdity. By 1800 Gothic burlesque had become commonplace, though it was still felt to be timely. As early as 1785 we can find in Elizabeth Blower's *Maria* a fair reader of *The Castle of Otranto* who anticipates "delightful horrors" in a Gothic castle. Jane Austen herself certainly enjoyed both the absurdities of Gothic fiction and, some fifteen years later, a burlesque like Eaton Stannard Barrett's *Heroine,* which is too broad and obvious for our taste. It is true that one of her favorite themes continues to be the illusions of her heroine; in *Emma,* more truly than in *Northanger Abbey,* the story turns on the heroine's eagerness to misunderstand, but such illusions are more natural in a spirited and eager girl (in Marianne Dashwood, Elizabeth Bennet, and Emma Woodhouse, rather than in Catherine Morland, Fanny Price, or Anne Elliot), and even when they are obstinately cherished they never, save in the Abbey sequence, pass the bounds of social probability.[3]

Though this breach in the imaginative continuity of *Northanger Abbey* is never fully repaired, another change in the conduct of the story goes some way toward mending the flaw. We now get, instead of a blank opposition between romance and real life, a kind of surrogate romance in real life. After all, there is no fixed rule that things should never happen as they do in novels. Eleanor Tilney has already proved herself a true friend, who more than makes up for the loss of the pseudo-romantic

---

[3] For a brief comparison of the quixotism of Catherine and Marianne, see McKillop, "The Context of *Sense and Sensibility,*" *Rice Institute Pamphlet,* XLIV (1957), 67, 72.

Isabella. Henry at last appears as a lover in good earnest, and indeed the very qualities of docility and ignorance that had led to Catherine's quixotic reveries were the substantial ground of her attraction for him. Thus a reversal is brought about. "I must confess that his affection originated in nothing better than gratitude, or, in other words, that a persuasion of her partiality for him had been the only cause of giving her a serious thought. It is a new circumstance in romance, I acknowledge, and dreadfully derogatory of an heroine's dignity; but if it be as new in common life, the credit of a wild imagination will at least be all my own" (II, xv). If Catherine had dreamed of being a charmer, she could not have done better. When General Tilney abruptly and rudely sends Catherine home, he gives a pretty good imitation of Montoni in real life, the British domestic sub-variety of the Gothic tyrant. Catherine's intuitions about Henry and his father are confirmed. At the same time, Jane Austen concedes that she is writing a novel, and the pretense that Catherine is a heroine is more than mere pretense. "The anxiety, which in this state of their attachment must be the portion of Henry and Catherine, and of all who loved either, as to its final event, can hardly extend, I fear, to the bosom of my readers, who will see in the tell-tale compression of the pages before them, that we are all hastening together to perfect felicity." "To begin perfect happiness at the respective ages of twenty-six and eighteen, is to do pretty well" (II, xvi). Maria Edgeworth at the conclusion of *Belinda* likewise gives us a playful but more elaborate acceptance of novel conventions after having been at some pains to repudiate those conventions. "'And now, my good friends,' continued Lady Delamere, 'shall I finish the novel for you?'" Jane Austen's conclusion may appear to be the light dismissal of the ending which is characteristic of the tradition of comedy; but taken in relation to the rest of the story, it implies also that one can come to terms with real life and still play the novel-writing game, still enjoy the heightened consciousness of making up a story which is so prominent in the *juvenilia*. Jane Austen even offers in the last sentence of the book to make a playful truce with the strictly didactic novel: "I leave it to be settled by whomsoever it may concern, whether the tendency of this work be altogether to recommend parental tyranny, or reward filial disobedience."

Light and Bright and Sparkling:
Irony and Fiction in *Pride and Prejudice*

by Reuben A. Brower

> The work is rather too light, and bright, and sparkling; it wants shade; it wants to be stretched out here and there with a long chapter of sense, if it could be had; if not, of solemn specious nonsense. . . .
>
> JANE AUSTEN

Many pages of *Pride and Prejudice* can be read as sheer poetry of wit, as Pope without couplets. The antitheses are almost as frequent and almost as varied; the play of ambiguities is certainly as complex; the orchestration of tones is as precise and subtle. As in the best of Pope, the displays of ironic wit are not without imaginative connection; what looks most diverse is really most similar, and ironies are linked by vibrant reference to basic certainties. There are passages too in which the rhythmical pattern of the sentence approaches the formal balance of the heroic couplet:

> Mr. Bennet was so odd a mixture of quick parts, sarcastic humour, reserve, and caprice, that the experience of three and twenty years had been insufficient to make his wife understand his character. *Her* mind *was less difficult* to develope. She was a woman of mean understanding, little information, and uncertain temper. When she was discontented she fancied herself nervous. The business of her life was to get her daughters married; its solace was visiting and news.

The triumph of the novel—whatever its limitations may be—lies in combining such poetry of wit with the dramatic structure of fiction. In historical terms, to combine the traditions of poetic satire with those of the sentimental novel, that was Jane Austen's feat in *Pride and Prejudice*.

For the "bright and sparkling," seemingly centrifugal play of irony is dramatically functional. It makes sense as literary art, the sense with which a writer is most concerned. The repartee, while constantly amusing, delineates characters and their changing relations and points the way to a climactic moment in which the change is most clearly recognized. Strictly speaking, this union of wit and drama is achieved with complete success only in the central sequence of *Pride and Prejudice,* in the presentation of Elizabeth's and Darcy's gradual revaluation of each other. Here, if anywhere, Jane Austen met James's demand that the novel should give its readers the maximum of "fun"; at the same time she satisfied the further standard implied in James's remark that the art of the novel is "above all an art of preparations." That she met these demands more continuously in *Emma* does not detract from her achievement in *Pride and Prejudice.*

Her blend of ironic wit and drama may be seen in its simplest form in the first chapter of the novel, in the dialogue between Mr. and Mrs Bennet on the topic of Mr. Bingley's leasing Netherfield Park. Every remark which each makes, Mrs. Bennet petulantly, and Mr. Bennet perversely, bounces off the magnificent opening sentence:

> It is a truth universally acknowledged, that a single man in possession of a good fortune, must be in want of a wife.

The scene that follows dramatizes the alternatives implied in "universally," Mrs. Bennet reminding us of one; and Mr. Bennet, of the other:

> "My dear Mr. Bennet," said his lady to him one day, "have you heard that Netherfield Park is let at last?"
>
> Mr. Bennet replied that he had not.
>
> "But it is," returned she; "for Mrs. Long has just been here, and she told me all about it."
>
> Mr. Bennet made no answer.
>
> "Do not you want to know who has taken it?" cried his wife impatiently.
>
> "*You* want to tell me, and I have no objection to hearing it."
>
> This was invitation enough.
>
> "Why, my dear, you must know, Mrs. Long says that Netherfield is taken by a young man of large fortune from the north of England; that he came down on Monday in a chaise and four to see the place, and was so much delighted with it that he agreed with Mr. Morris immediately; that he is to take possession before Michaelmas, and some of his servants are to be in the house by the end of next week."
>
> "What is his name?"
>
> "Bingley."
>
> "Is he married or single?"
>
> "Oh! single, my dear, to be sure! A single man of large fortune; four or five thousand a year. What a fine thing for our girls!"
>
> "How so? how can it affect them?"

"My dear Mr. Bennet," replied his wife, "how can you be so tiresome! You must know that I am thinking of his marrying one of them."

"Is that his design in settling here?"

"Design! nonsense, how can you talk so!"

A parallel appears in the opening of Pope's Epistle, "Of the Characters of Women":

> Nothing so true as what you once let fall,
> "Most Women have no Characters at all,"

a pronouncement immediately followed by a series of portraits showing that women have "characters" in one sense if not in another. It is also easy to find counterparts in Pope's satirical mode for Mr. Bennet's extreme politeness of address, his innocent queries, and his epigrammatic turns. The character that emerges from this dialogue is almost that of a professional satirist: Mr. Bennet is a man of quick parts and sarcastic humor, altogether a most unnatural father. Mrs. Bennet speaks another language; *her* talk does not crackle with irony and epigram; *her* sentences run in quite another mold. They either go on too long or break up awkwardly in impulsive exclamations; this is the talk of a person of "mean understanding" and "uncertain temper."

But though the blended art of this scene is admirable, a limitation appears. Mr. and Mrs. Bennet are so perfectly done that little more is left to be expressed. Variety or forward movement in the drama will almost surely be difficult, which obviously proves to be the case. The sequences that depend most closely on the opening scene—those concerned with the business of getting the Bennet daughters married—are all amusingly ironic, but relatively static as drama. As Mrs. Bennet contrives to join Jane and Bingley, to marry one daughter to Mr. Collins, and to further Lydia's exploits with the military, father, mother, and daughters remain in very nearly the same dramatic positions. True enough, the last of these sequences ends in a catastrophe. But the connection between Lydia's downfall and the earlier scenes of ironic comedy in which Mr. and Mrs. Bennet are opposed is not fully expressed. Lydia's behavior "leads to this" in a Richardsonian moral sense, but Lydia is too scantly presented in relation to her parents or to Wickham to prepare us adequately for her bad end. We accept it if at all as literary convention. Incidentally, we might conjecture that the marriage-market sequences belong to the early version of *Pride and Prejudice,* or at least that they are examples of Jane Austen's earlier manner. In the central sequence of *Pride and Prejudice,* especially in its more complex blend of ironic and dramatic design, we can see anticipated the more mature structure of both *Mansfield Park* and *Emma.*

In portraying the gradual change in Elizabeth's estimate of Darcy and in his attitude to her, Jane Austen achieves a perfect harmony between the rich ambiguity of ironic dialogue and the movement toward the climactic scenes in which the new estimate is revealed. I shall limit my discussion to scenes from the Elizabeth-Darcy narrative through the episode in which Elizabeth recognizes her "change in sentiment." Let us first read Jane Austen's dialogue as poetry of wit, disregarding for the time being any forward movement in the drama, and observing the variety of the irony and the unity of effect achieved through recurrent patterns and through assumptions shared by writer and reader. As in our reading of Pope, we may in this way appreciate the extraordinary richness of ironic texture and the imaginative continuity running through the play of wit. In analyzing the ironies and the assumptions, we shall see how intensely dramatic the dialogue is, dramatic in the sense of defining characters through the way they speak and are spoken about.

The aura of implications which surrounds many of the dialogues between Elizabeth and Darcy is complex enough to delight the most pure Empsonian. Take for example the dialogue in which Sir William Lucas attempts to interest Mr. Darcy in dancing:

. . . Elizabeth at that instant moving towards them, he was struck with the notion of doing a very gallant thing, and called out to her,

"My dear Miss Eliza, why are not you dancing?—Mr. Darcy, you must allow me to present this young lady to you as a very desirable partner.— You cannot refuse to dance, I am sure, when so much beauty is before you." And taking her hand, he would have given it to Mr. Darcy, who, though extremely surprised, was not unwilling to receive it, when she instantly drew back, and said with some discomposure to Sir William,

"Indeed, Sir, I have not the least intention of dancing.—I entreat you not to suppose that I moved this way in order to beg for a partner."

Mr. Darcy with grave propriety requested to be allowed the honour of her hand; but in vain. Elizabeth was determined; nor did Sir William at all shake her purpose by his attempt at persuasion.

"You excel so much in the dance, Miss Eliza, that it is cruel to deny me the happiness of seeing you; and though this gentleman dislikes the amusement in general, he can have no objection, I am sure, to oblige us for one half hour."

"Mr. Darcy is all politeness," said Elizabeth, smiling.

"He is indeed—but considering the inducement, my dear Miss Eliza, we cannot wonder at his complaisance; for who would object to such a partner?"

Elizabeth looked archly, and turned away.

"Mr. Darcy is all politeness": the statement, as Elizabeth might say, has a "teazing" variety of meanings. Mr. Darcy is polite in the sense indicated by "grave propriety," that is, he shows the courtesy appropriate to a gentleman—which is the immediate, public meaning of Elizabeth's compliment. But "grave propriety," being a very limited form of politeness, reminds us forcibly of Mr. Darcy's earlier behavior. His "gravity" at the ball had been "forbidding and disagreeable." "Grave propriety" may also mean the bare civility of "the proudest, most disagreeable man in the world." So Elizabeth's compliment has an ironic twist: she smiles and looks "archly." "All politeness" has also quite another meaning. Mr. Darcy "was not unwilling to receive" her hand. He is polite in more than the public proper sense; his gesture shows that he is interested in Elizabeth as a person. Her archness and her smile have for the reader an added ironic value: Elizabeth's interpretation of Darcy's manner may be quite wrong. Finally, there is the embracing broadly comic irony of Sir William's action. "Struck with the notion of doing a very gallant thing," he is pleasantly unconscious of what he is in fact doing and of what Elizabeth's remark may mean to her and to Darcy.

A similar cluster of possibilities appears in another conversation in which Darcy asks Elizabeth to dance with him:

> . . . soon afterwards Mr. Darcy, drawing near Elizabeth, said to her—
> "Do not you feel a great inclination, Miss Bennet, to seize such an opportunity of dancing a reel?"
> She smiled, but made no answer. He repeated the question, with some surprise at her silence.
> "Oh!" said she, "I heard you before; but I could not immediately determine what to say in reply. You wanted me, I know, to say 'Yes,' that you might have the pleasure of despising my taste; but I always delight in overthrowing those kind of schemes, and cheating a person of their premeditated contempt. I have therefore made up my mind to tell you, that I do not want to dance a reel at all—and now despise me if you dare."
> "Indeed I do not dare."
> Elizabeth, having rather expected to affront him, was amazed at his gallantry; but there was a mixture of sweetness and archness in her manner which made it difficult for her to affront anybody; and Darcy had never been so bewitched by any woman as he was by her. He really believed, that were it not for the inferiority of her connections, he should be in some danger.
> Miss Bingley saw, or suspected enough to be jealous; and her great anxiety for the recovery of her dear friend Jane, received some assistance from her desire of getting rid of Elizabeth.
> She often tried to provoke Darcy into disliking her guest, by talking of their supposed marriage, and planning his happiness in such an alliance.

Again Mr. Darcy's request may be interpreted more or less pleasantly, depending on whether we connect it with his present or past behavior. Again Elizabeth's attack on Darcy and her archness have an irony beyond the irony intended by the speaker. But the amusement of this dialogue lies especially in the variety of possible tones which we detect in Darcy's speeches. Elizabeth hears his question as expressing "premeditated contempt" and scorn of her own taste. But from Mr. Darcy's next remark and the comment which follows, and from his repeating his question and showing "some surprise," we may hear in his request a tone expressive of some interest, perhaps only gallantry, perhaps, as Elizabeth later puts it "somewhat of a friendlier nature." We could take his "Indeed I do not dare" as pure gallantry (Elizabeth's version) or as a sign of conventional "marriage intentions" (Miss Bingley's interpretation), if it were not for the nice reservation, "He really believed, that were it not for the inferiority of her connections, he should be in some danger." We must hear the remark as spoken with this qualification. This simultaneity of tonal layers can be matched only in the satire of Pope, where, as we have seen, the reader feels the impossibility of adjusting his voice to the rapid changes in tone and the difficulty of representing by a single sound the several sounds he hears as equally appropriate and necessary. Analysis such as I have been making shows clearly how arbitrary and how thin any stage rendering of *Pride and Prejudice* must be. No speaking voice could possibly represent the variety of tones conveyed to the reader by such interplay of dialogue and comment.

It would be easy enough to produce more of these dialogues, especially on the subject of music or dancing, each with its range of crisply differentiated meanings. Similar patterns of irony recur many times. Mr. Darcy makes his inquiries (polite or impolite), asking with a smile (scornful or encouraging) questions that may be interpreted as pompous and condescending or gallant and well-disposed. So Mr. Darcy cross-examines Elizabeth in the scene in which their "superior dancing" gives such pleasure to Sir William:

> "What think you of books?" said he, smiling.
>
> "Books—Oh! no.—I am sure we never read the same, or not with the same feelings."
>
> "I am sorry you think so; but if that be the case, there can at least be no want of subject.—We may compare our different opinions."
>
> "No—I cannot talk of books in a ball-room; my head is always full of something else."
>
> "The *present* always occupies you in such scenes—does it?" said he, with a look of doubt.

When connected with a hint of Darcy's changing attitude, that "look of doubt," Elizabeth's arch comments take on the added ironic value we have noted in other conversations.

Earlier in this dialogue, Darcy and Elizabeth run through the same sort of question and answer gamut, and with very nearly the same ironic dissonances:

> He smiled, and assured her that whatever she wished him to say should be said.
>
> "Very well.—That reply will do for the present.—Perhaps by and bye I may observe that private balls are much pleasanter than public ones.—But *now* we may be silent."
>
> "Do you talk by rule then, while you are dancing?"
>
> "Sometimes. One must speak a little, you know. It would look odd to be entirely silent for half an hour together, and yet for the advantage of *some,* conversation ought to be so arranged as that they may have the trouble of saying as little as possible."
>
> "Are you consulting your own feelings in the present case, or do you imagine that you are gratifying mine?"
>
> "Both," replied Elizabeth archly; "for I have always seen a great similarity in the turn of our minds.—We are each of an unsocial, taciturn disposition, unwilling to speak, unless we expect to say something that will amaze the whole room, and be handed down to posterity with all the eclat of a proverb."
>
> "This is no very striking resemblance of your own character, I am sure," said he.

When Darcy himself is being quizzed he frequently remarks on his own behavior in a way that may be sublimely smug or simply self-respecting, as for example in his comment on his behavior at the first of the Hertford-shire balls:

> "I certainly have not the talent which some people possess," said Darcy, "of conversing easily with those I have never seen before. I cannot catch their tone of conversation, or appear interested in their concerns, as I often see done."

But these conversations are not simply sets of ironic meanings; they are in more than a trivial sense *jeux d'esprit,* the play of an adult mind. (The sophistication they imply is of a kind which, as John Jay Chapman once remarked, is Greek and French, rather than English.) The fun in Jane Austen's dialogue has a serious point; or rather, the fun *is* the point. The small talk is the focus for her keen sense of the variability of character, for her awareness of the possibility that the same remark or action has very different meanings in different relations. What most satisfies us in reading the dialogue in *Pride and Prejudice* is Jane Austen's awareness that it is difficult to know any complex person, that knowledge of a man like Darcy is an interpretation and a construction, not a simple absolute. Like the characters of Proust, the chief persons in *Pride and Prejudice* are not the same when projected through the conversation of different people. The *snobisme* of Darcy's talk, like Swann's, is measured according to the group he is with. Mr. Darcy is hardly recognizable as the same man when he is described by Mr. Wickham, by his housekeeper, or Elizabeth, or Mr. Bingley.

But it is only the complex persons, the "intricate characters," that require and merit interpretation, as Elizabeth points out in the pleasant conversation in which she tells Bingley that she "understands him perfectly":

> "You begin to comprehend me, do you?" cried he, turning towards her.
> "Oh! yes,—I understand you perfectly."
> "I wish I might take this for a compliment; but to be so easily seen through I am afraid is pitiful."
> "That is as it happens. It does not necessarily follow that a deep, intricate character is more or less estimable than such a one as yours."
> "Lizzy," cried her mother, "remember where you are, and do not run on in the wild manner that you are suffered to do at home."
> "I did not know before," continued Bingley immediately, "that you were a studier of character. It must be an amusing study."
> "Yes; but intricate characters are the *most* amusing. They have at least that advantage."
> "The country," said Darcy, "can in general supply but few subjects for such a study. In a country neighbourhood you move in a very confined and unvarying society."
> "But people themselves alter so much, that there is something new to be observed in them for ever."

Elizabeth's remark with its ironic application to Darcy indicates the interest that makes the book "go" and shows the type of awareness we are analyzing. "Intricate characters are the *most* amusing," because their behavior can be taken in so many ways, because they are not always the same people. The man we know today is a different man tomorrow. Naturally, we infer, people will not be equally puzzling to every judge. Mr. Bingley and Jane find Mr. Darcy a much less "teazing" man than Elizabeth does. It is only the Elizabeths, the adult minds, who will observe something new in the "same" people.

Such are the main assumptions behind the irony of *Pride and Prejudice,* as they are expressed through conversation studies of Darcy's character. In marked contrast with the opening scene of the novel, there is in these dialogues no nondramatic statement of the ironist's position, a further sign that in shaping the Elizabeth-Darcy sequence Jane Austen was moving away from the modes of satire toward more purely dramatic techniques.

While Jane Austen's irony depends on a sense of variability and intricacy of character, her vision is not one of Proustian relativity. The sense of variability is balanced by a vigorous and positive belief. Elizabeth, in commenting on Charlotte Lucas' choice of Mr. Collins, expresses very emphatically this combination of skepticism and faith:

> "My dear Jane, Mr. Collins is a conceited, pompous, narrow-minded silly man; you know he is, as well as I do; and you must feel, as well as I do, that the woman who marries him, cannot have a proper way of thinking. You shall not defend her, though it is Charlotte Lucas. You shall not, for the sake of one individual, change the meaning of principle and integrity, nor endeavour to persuade yourself or me, that selfishness is prudence, and insensibility of danger, security for happiness."

Though as usual Elizabeth's affirmations have an ironic overtone for the reader, they express a belief that is implied throughout *Pride and Prejudice*. There are persons such as Mr. Collins and Mrs. Bennet and Lady Catherine, about whom there can be no disagreement among people who "have a proper way of thinking." These fixed characters make up a set of certainties against which more intricate exhibitions of pride and prejudice are measured. They are the "fools" which James says are almost indispensable for any piece of fiction. For Jane Austen there can be no doubt about the meaning of "principle and integrity" and similar terms of value. Right-thinking persons know what pride is and when to apply the term. In common with her contemporaries Jane Austen enjoys the belief that some interpretations of behavior are more reasonable than others. The climactic scene of the novel, in which Elizabeth arrives at a new view of Darcy, shows us what is meant by a more reasonable interpretation: it is a reasoned judgment of character reached through long experience and slow weighing of probabilities. The certainty is an achieved certainty.

So the local ironies in Jane Austen, as in Pope, are defined and given larger significance through assumptions shared by the writer and public. The trivial dialogues are constantly being illuminated by a fine sense of the complexity of human nature and by a steady belief in the possibility of making sound judgments. At the same time the playfulness is always serving for "the illustration of character." (The term is Elizabeth's, though in applying it to Darcy, she is as usual unaware of its aptness to her own behavior.) Both she and Darcy are "illustrated" by their ambiguous questions and answers and the alternate interpretations which are so deftly indicated: the poetry of wit in *Pride and Prejudice* is completely dramatic. Certainly nothing could be more dramatic than the assumptions we have been describing: they reflect the practical dramatist's interest in human beings and their behavior, his awareness that character is expressed by what men say and do. The assumption that more reasonable interpretations of conduct are attainable provides for the movement toward a decisive change in relationships at the climax of the novel. It also lays the ground for the resolution of ambiguities and the cancellation of irony at the same moment.

We can now appreciate how beautifully the ironies of the dialogue function in the curve of the main dramatic sequence. The conversations have been skilfully shaped to prepare us for Elizabeth's revised estimate of Darcy, for her recognition that Darcy regards her differently, and for her consequent "change of sentiment" toward him. The preparation for this climax is made mainly through the controlled use of ambiguity that we have been observing. Though we are always being led to make double interpretations, we are never in confusion about what the alternatives are. It is important also that in these ironic dialogues no comment is included that makes us take Darcy's behavior in only an unpleasant sense. When there is comment, it is mainly used to bring out the latent ambiguity without in any way resolving it. So in general the earlier Darcy scenes are left open in preparation for a fresh estimate of his character. The pleasanter interpretation of one of Darcy's or Elizabeth's remarks or of one of the author's comments allows for the later choice and for the consequent recognitions. The pleasanter possibility also gives in passing a hint of Darcy's changing attitude to Elizabeth. For instance, the more favorable meaning of Elizabeth's "Mr. Darcy is all politeness" or of the comment on his "grave propriety" points forward to Darcy's perfect courtesy at Pemberley and to Elizabeth's admission that he was right in objecting to her family's "impropriety of conduct."

This exquisite preparation pays wonderfully at the climactic moment of the novel, when Elizabeth reconsiders the letter in which Darcy justified his conduct toward Bingley and Jane and Wickham. Since more kindly views of Darcy have been introduced through the flow of witty talk, Darcy does not at that point have to be remade, but merely reread. (The tendency to remake a character appears in an obvious form only in the later and lesser scenes of the novel.)

The passages in which Elizabeth reviews the letter present an odd, rather legalistic process. After the more obvious views of Darcy's behavior and the possible alternatives are directly stated, the evidence on both sides is weighed and a reasonable conclusion is reached:

> After wandering along the lane for two hours, giving way to every variety of thought; re-considering events, determining probabilities, and reconciling herself as well as she could, to a change so sudden and so important, fatigue, and a recollection of her long absence, made her at length return home. . . .

To illustrate her manner of "determining probabilities" we might take one of several examples of Darcy's pride. Immediately after Darcy has proposed to her, she describes his treatment of Jane in rather brutal language:

> . . . his pride, his abominable pride, his shameless avowal of what he had done with respect to Jane, his unpardonable assurance in acknowledging, though he could not justify it.

A little later, she rereads the passage in which Darcy explains that Jane had shown no "symptom of peculiar regard" for Bingley. A second perusal reminds Elizabeth that Charlotte Lucas had a similar opinion, and she acknowledges the justice of this account of Jane's outward behavior. In much the same way she reviews other charges, such as Darcy's unfairness to Wickham or his objection to her family's "want of importance," and she is forced by the new evidence to draw "more probable" conclusions.

Jane Austen does not make us suppose that Elizabeth has now discovered the real Darcy or that an intricate person is easily known or known in his entirety, as is very clearly shown by Elizabeth's reply to Wickham's ironic questions about Darcy:

> "I dare not hope," he continued in a lower and more serious tone, "that he is improved in essentials."
>
> "Oh, no!" said Elizabeth. "In essentials, I believe, he is very much what he ever was."
>
> While she spoke, Wickham looked as if scarcely knowing whether to rejoice over her words, or to distrust their meaning. There was a something in her countenance which made him listen with an apprehensive and anxious attention, while she added,
>
> "When I said that he improved on acquaintance, I did not mean that either his mind or manners were in a state of improvement, but that from knowing him better, his disposition was better understood."

It is wise not to be dogmatic about "essentials," since in any case they remain "as they were." A sensible person contents himself with "better understanding."

This process of judgment is not merely odd or legalistic, because it is dramatically appropriate. It fits exactly the double presentation of Darcy's character through ironic dialogue and comment, and it fits perfectly the picture of Elizabeth as "a rational creature speaking the truth from her heart," one who adapts her statements to her knowledge. She is quite clear about the meaning of "pride" and "vanity," and she judges herself with complete honesty:

> "Had I been in love, I could not have been more wretchedly blind. But vanity, not love, has been my folly.—Pleased with the preference of one, and offended by the neglect of the other, on the very beginning of our acquaint-

ance, I have courted prepossession and ignorance, and driven reason away, where either were concerned. Till this moment, I never knew myself."

We feel that Elizabeth's judgment of Darcy and of herself is right because the preparation for it has been so complete. The foundations for Elizabeth's choices and her acknowledgment of error were laid in the ambiguous remarks of the earlier scenes of the novel.

The dialogue has been preparing us equally well and with perhaps greater refinement for Elizabeth's realization that she and Darcy now regard one another with very different feelings. The ironic remarks and commentary have included hints that revealed ever so gradually Darcy's developing interest in Elizabeth. Mr. Darcy's "politeness," his "repeated questions," his "gallantry," his "look of doubt," if interpreted favorably, indicate his increasing warmth of feeling. Elizabeth's pert remarks and impertinent questions bear an amusing relation to this change in Darcy's sentiments. Besides being more ambiguous than she supposes, they backfire in another way, by increasing Darcy's admiration. Her accusation of "premeditated contempt" brings out his most gallant reply, and her "mixture of sweetness and archness" leaves him more "bewitched" than ever. In this and other ways the repartee provides local "amusements" while pointing forward to the complete reversal of feeling that follows the meeting at Pemberley.

The judicial process by which Elizabeth earlier "determined probabilities" in judging Darcy's past conduct is matched by the orderly way in which she now "determines her feelings" toward him:

> . . . and the evening, though as it passed it seemed long, was not long enough to determine her feelings towards *one* in that mansion; and she lay awake two whole hours, endeavouring to make them out. She certainly did not hate him. No; hatred had vanished long ago, and she had almost as long been ashamed of ever feeling a dislike against him, that could be so called. The respect created by the conviction of his valuable qualities, though at first unwillingly admitted, had for some time ceased to be repugnant to her feelings; and it was now heightened into somewhat of a friendlier nature, by the testimony so highly in his favour, and bringing forward his disposition in so amiable a light, which yesterday had produced. But above all, above respect and esteem, there was a motive within her of good will which could not be overlooked. It was gratitude.—Gratitude, not merely for having once loved her, but for loving her still well enough, to forgive all the petulance and acrimony of her manner in rejecting him, and all the unjust accusations accompanying her rejection. He who, she had been persuaded, would avoid her as his greatest enemy, seemed, on this accidental meeting, most eager to preserve the acquaintance, and without any indelicate display of regard, or any peculiarity of manner, where their two selves only were concerned, was soliciting the good opinion of her friends, and bent on making her known to his sister. Such a change in a man of so much pride,

excited not only astonishment but gratitude—for to love, ardent love, it must be attributed; and as such its impression on her was of a sort to be encouraged, as by no means unpleasing, though it could not be exactly defined. She respected, she esteemed, she was grateful to him, she felt a real interest in his welfare. . . .

In this beautifully graded progress of feeling, from "hatred" or any "dislike" to "respect" to "esteem" to "gratitude" and "a real interest" in Darcy's "welfare," each sentiment is defined with an exactness that is perfectly appropriate to Elizabeth's habit of mind as presented earlier in the novel. She defines her sentiments as exactly as her moral judgments.

As all ambiguities are resolved and all irony is dropped, the reader feels the closing in of a structure by its necessary end, the end implied in the crude judgment of Darcy in the first ballroom scene. The harsh exhibit of the way character is decided in this society prepares us to view Mr. Darcy's later actions as open to more than one interpretation:

. . . Mr. Darcy soon drew the attention of the room by his fine, tall person, handsome features, noble mien; and the report which was in general circulation within five minutes after his entrance, of his having ten thousand a year. The gentlemen pronounced him to be a fine figure of a man, the ladies declared he was much handsomer than Mr. Bingley, and he was looked at with great admiration for about half the evening, till his manners gave a disgust which turned the tide of his popularity; for he was discovered to be proud, to be above his company, and above being pleased; and not all his large estate in Derbyshire could then save him from having a most forbidding, disagreeable countenance, and being unworthy to be compared with his friend.

. . . His character was decided. He was the proudest, most disagreeable man in the world, and everybody hoped that he would never come there again.

These comments convey above all the aloof vision of the ironist, of Jane Austen herself, who had been described years before as a little girl "who is a judge of character and who remains silent." In the very grammar of the sentences (the passive voice, the *oratio obliqua*), there is an implication of a detached and superior mind that reports both judgments of Darcy, knowing quite well which is the more true, and fully aware that true judgment is considerably more difficult than most people suppose. The display of alternatives in ironic dialogue, the projection by this means of intricate characters, and the movement toward a sounder evaluation of first impressions—all this and more is implicit in the initial view of Darcy and his judges.

Once we have reached the scenes in which the promise of the introduction is fulfilled, the literary design both ironic and dramatic is complete.

Thereafter, it must be admitted, *Pride and Prejudice* is not quite the same sort of book. There are fewer passages of equally bright and varied irony and consequently rarer exhibitions of intricacy of character. Mr. Darcy now appears as "humble," not "proud," and even as "perfectly amiable." There are single scenes of a broadly satiric sort, in which Mr. and Mrs. Bennet express characteristic opinions on their daughters' alliances and misalliances. But the close and harmonious relation between ironic wit and dramatic movement is disturbed. A great deal happens, from seductions and mysterious financial transactions to reunions of lovers and weddings. But these events seem to belong to a simpler world where outright judgments of good and bad or of happy and unhappy are in place. The double vision of the ironist is more rarely in evidence.

Occasionally, we feel a recovery of the richer texture of amusement and of the more complex awareness of character revealed in the central sequence. One glancing remark suggests that the final picture of Darcy might have been less simply ideal (Darcy has just been commenting on how well Bingley had taken his confession of having separated Bingley and Jane):

> Elizabeth longed to observe that Mr. Bingley had been a most delightful friend; so easily guided that his worth was invaluable; but she checked herself. She remembered that he had yet to learn to be laught at, and it was rather too early to begin. In anticipating the happiness of Bingley, which of course was to be inferior only to his own, he continued the conversation till they reached the house.

It is perhaps not "rational," as Elizabeth would say, to expect the same complexity when a drama of irony has once arrived at its resolution. But it is probably wise for the novelist to finish up his story as soon as possible after that point has been reached. In *Emma,* the crucial scene of readjustment comes very near the end of the novel. Jane Austen does not run the risk of presenting many scenes in which Emma appears as a wiser and less fanciful young woman. To be sure, the risk is lessened somewhat because the initial and governing vision in Emma is less purely ironic than in *Pride and Prejudice.*

The triumph of *Pride and Prejudice* is a rare one, just because it is so difficult to balance a purely ironic vision with credible presentation of a man and woman undergoing a serious "change of sentiment." Shakespeare achieves an uneasy success in *Much Ado About Nothing,* and Fielding succeeds in *Tom Jones* because he does not expect us to take "love" too seriously. The problem for the writer who essays this difficult blend is one of creating dramatic speech which fulfils his complex intention. In solving this problem of expression, Jane Austen has her special triumph.

Irony as Discrimination: *Pride and Prejudice*

by Marvin Mudrick

In *Pride and Prejudice,* for the first time, Jane Austen allows her heroine to share her own characteristic response to the world. Elizabeth Bennet tells Darcy:

> ". . . Follies and nonsense, whims and inconsistencies do divert me, I own, and I laugh at them whenever I can. . . ." (p. 57)

The response is not only characteristic of Elizabeth and her author, but consciously and articulately aimed at by both of them. Both choose diversion; and both, moreover, look for their diversion in the people about them. Elizabeth, despite her youth and the limitations of a rural society, is a busy "studier of character," as Bingley leads her to affirm:

> "You begin to comprehend me, do you?" cried he, turning towards her.
>
> "Oh! yes—I understand you perfectly."
>
> "I wish I might take this for a compliment; but to be so easily seen through I am afraid is pitiful."
>
> "That is as it happens. It does not necessarily follow that a deep, intricate character is more or less estimable than such a one as yours."
>
> "Lizzy," cried her mother, "remember where you are, and do not run on in the wild manner that you are suffered to do at home."
>
> "I did not know before," continued Bingley immediately, "that you were a studier of character. It must be an amusing study."
>
> "Yes; but intricate characters are the *most* amusing. They have at least that advantage." (p. 42)

"Character" gains a general overtone: with Elizabeth's qualifying adjective, it becomes not only the summation of a single personality, but the summation of a type, the fixing of the individual into a category. So Elizabeth sets herself up as an ironic spectator, able and prepared to judge and classify, already making the first large division of the world into two sorts of people: the simple ones, those who give themselves away out of shallowness (as Bingley fears) or perhaps openness (as Elizabeth implies) or an excess of affectation (as Mr. Collins will demonstrate); and the intricate ones, those who cannot be judged and classified so easily, who are "the most amusing" to the ironic spectator because they offer the most formidable challenge to his powers of detection and analysis. Into one of these preliminary categories, Elizabeth fits everybody she observes.

Elizabeth shares her author's characteristic response of comic irony, defining incongruities without drawing them into a moral context; and, still more specifically, Elizabeth's vision of the world as divided between the simple and the intricate is, in *Pride and Prejudice* at any rate, Jane Austen's vision also. This identification between the author and her heroine establishes, in fact, the whole ground pattern of judgment in the novel. The first decision we must make about anyone, so Elizabeth suggests and the author confirms by her shaping commentary, is not moral but psychological, not whether he is good or bad, but whether he is simple or intricate: whether he may be disposed of as fixed and predictable or must be recognized as variable, perhaps torn between contradictory motives, intellectually or emotionally complex, unsusceptible to a quick judgment.

Once having placed the individual in his category, we must proceed to discriminate him from the others there; and, in the category of simplicity at least, Elizabeth judges as accurately as her author. Jane Austen allows the "simple" characters to have no surprises for Elizabeth, and, consequently, none for us. They perform, they amuse; but we never doubt that we know what they are, and why they act as they do.

We know Mrs. Bennet, for example, at once, in her first conversation with her husband, as she describes the newcomer at Netherfield Park:

". . . A single man of large fortune; four or five thousand a year. What a fine thing for our girls." (pp. 3-4)

And the author curtly sums her up at the end of the first chapter:

She was a woman of mean understanding, little information, and uncertain temper. When she was discontented, she fancied herself nervous. The business of her life was to get her daughters married; its solace was visiting and news. (p. 5)

Two subjects dominate her life and conversation: the injustice of the entail by which Mr. Bennet's estate will descend to his closest male relative rather than to his immediate family, and the problem of getting her daughters married. Out of these fixed ideas, untempered by any altruism, circumspection, wit, or intellect, derive all of her appearances and her

total function in the story. The matter of the entail serves mainly to introduce Mr. Collins and to complicate the second and stronger fixed
idea; it also provides Mr. Bennet with opportunities to bait his wife:

> "About a month ago I received this letter . . . from my cousin, Mr. Col-
> lins, who, when I am dead, may turn you all out of the house as soon as he
> pleases."
> "Oh! my dear," cried his wife, "I cannot bear to hear that mentioned.
> Pray do not talk of that odious man. I do think it is the hardest thing in the
> world, that your estate should be entailed away from your own children;
> and I am sure if I had been you, I should have tried long ago to do some-
> thing or other about it." (pp. 61-2)

The problem of getting her daughters married, however, involves her
much more directly in the tensions and progress of the narrative. It is
her irrepressible vulgarity in discussing Jane's prospective marriage to
Bingley which convinces Darcy that any alliance with Mrs. Bennet's
family—for his friend or for himself—would be imprudent and degrad-
ing:

> . . . Mrs. Bennet seemed incapable of fatigue while enumerating the ad-
> vantages of the match. His being such a charming young man, and so rich,
> and living but three miles from them, were the first points of self-gratula-
> tion. . . . It was, moreover, such a promising thing for her younger daugh-
> ters as Jane's marrying so greatly must throw them in the way of other rich
> men. . . .
> In vain did Elizabeth endeavour to check the rapidity of her mother's
> words, or persuade her to describe her felicity in a less audible whisper;
> for to her inexpressible vexation, she could perceive that the chief of it
> was overheard by Mr. Darcy, who sat opposite to them. Her mother only
> scolded her for being nonsensical!
> "What is Mr. Darcy to me, pray, that I should be afraid of him? I am
> sure we owe him no such particular civility as to be obliged to say nothing
> *he* may not like to hear." (p. 99)

Having decided that Darcy is too haughty to pursue any of her daughters,
she goes out of her way, in fact, to offend him.

Her feeling toward Mr. Collins swings between extremes of deference
and indignation, according as she must consider him a profit or a loss: a
suitor, or the holder of the entail. When he is quite unknown to her
except as the latter, she detests him. When, in his letter, he barely hints
at courting one of the Bennet girls during his coming visit, she thaws
almost at once:

> "There is some sense in what he says about the girls however; and if he
> is disposed to make them any amends, I shall not be the person to dis-
> courage him." (p. 83)

When, on appearing, he seems quite bent on marriage,

> Mrs. Bennet . . . trusted that she might soon have two daughters married; and the man whom she could not bear to speak of the day before, was now high in her good graces. (p. 71)

After Elizabeth, in spite of Mrs. Bennet's strenuous pleading, has turned him down and he marries Charlotte Lucas instead, she can see him only as she saw him at first, gloating—and with a wife now to help him gloat —over the entail:

> ". . . And so, I suppose, they often talk of having Longbourn when your father is dead. They look upon it as quite their own, I dare say, whenever that happens." (p. 228)

An inadequate mind to begin with, marriage to a man who treats her with contempt only, preoccupation with the insistent material concerns imposed by society upon a woman of her class—they have all combined in Mrs. Bennet's single continuously operating motive: to be herself secure and comfortable, and to fortify her own security by getting her daughters settled in prudent marriage, that condition symbolic of material well-being. For Mrs. Bennet, everything in life reduces itself to the dimensions of this motive; everything except her daughter Lydia.

Lydia is, of course, Mrs. Bennet as she must remember herself at the same age:

> Lydia was a stout, well-grown girl of fifteen, with a fine complexion and good-humoured countenance; a favourite with her mother, whose affection had brought her into public at an early age. She had high animal spirits, and a sort of natural self-consequence, which the attentions of the officers, to whom her uncle's good dinners and her own easy manners recommended her, had increased into assurance. (p. 45)

The coming of a militia regiment to Meryton has determined the course of her life, as far ahead as she cares to look. When the regiment is ordered to Brighton, her world seems ready to collapse, and Mrs. Bennet is scarcely less despairing; but Lydia, at least, is spared by receiving an invitation from her good friend, the colonel's wife, to accompany the regiment to Brighton. Parting from Lydia, Mrs. Bennet

> . . . was diffuse in her good wishes for the felicity of her daughter, and impressive in her injunctions that she would not miss the opportunity of enjoying herself as much as possible; advice, which there was every reason to believe would be attended to. . . . (p. 235)

One of Jane Austen's triumphs in *Pride and Prejudice* is her refusal to
sentimentalize Lydia (as well as Mrs. Bennet) once she has fashioned her
to a hard and simple consistency. Lydia is a self-assured, highly sexed,
wholly amoral and unintellectual girl. When she runs off with Wickham,
nothing can lower her spirits or drive her to shame—not all the disapproval of society, not the horror and shame of her family (though her
mother, of course, is neither horrified nor ashamed). She has done what
she wanted to do; and if her uncle or father or someone else must pay
Wickham to persuade him to legalize the union, that is their worry, not
hers. She is not defiantly, but simply, impenitent: she recognizes no authority to which penitence or concealment is due. If marriage is valued
by some, so much the better; if, for no effort on her part, it gives her a
social precedence and dignity, she will take these, though she did not ask
for them and could have lived without them. What Elizabeth designates
as Lydia's "susceptibility to her feelings" (p. 317), what the author has
called her "high animal spirits" (p. 45), is Lydia's only motive, as it must
once have been Mrs. Bennet's also; but Lydia has not abandoned it out
of prudence or fear, has even seen it assume the unanticipated respectability of marriage:

> "Well, mamma . . . and what do you think of my husband? Is not he a
> charming man? I am sure my sisters must all envy me. I only hope they may
> have half my good luck. They must all go to Brighton. That is the place
> to get husbands. What a pity it is, mamma, we did not all go."
> "Very true; and if I had my will, we should. . . ." (p. 317)

And Lydia never repents; neither mother nor daughter even recognizes
that there is anything to repent.

Mr. Collins and Lady Catherine, though "simple" also, differ from
Lydia and Mrs. Bennet at least to the extent that Elizabeth can observe
them more freely, without the sense of shame and responsibility she must
feel toward her mother and sister. Mr. Collins is, indeed, so remote from
Elizabeth's personal concerns that she and the reader can enjoy him as a
pure fool, unweighted by moral import. The fact that he is a clergyman
underscores his foolishness and moral nullity:

> ". . . I have been so fortunate as to be distinguished by the patronage
> of the Right Honourable Lady Catherine de Bourgh, widow of Sir Lewis de
> Bourgh, whose bounty and beneficence has preferred me to the valuable rec-
> tory of this parish, where it shall be my earnest endeavour to demean myself
> with grateful respect towards her Ladyship, and be ever ready to perform
> those rites and ceremonies which are instituted by the Church of England."
> (pp. 62-3)

" '. . . Can he be a sensible man, sir?' " Elizabeth asks; and her father replies:

> "No, my dear; I think not. I have great hopes of finding him quite the reverse. There is a mixture of servility and self-importance in his letter, which promises well. I am impatient to see him." (p. 64)

Mr. Bennet's expectation of amusement is fulfilled many times over. "Mr. Collins was not a sensible man," (p. 70) as the author begins a superfluous descriptive paragraph; and his fatuity, sycophancy, conceit, and resolutely unprejudiced wife-hunting are given ample range. Wherever he goes, whatever he does, he remains unshakably foolish. Elizabeth's declining his proposal, once he can believe that it is not to be ascribed to the "usual practice of elegant females," (p. 108) clouds his jauntiness for a moment; but he recovers soon enough to propose as fervently to Charlotte Lucas three days later, and when he leaves Longbourn he wishes his "fair cousins . . . health and happiness, not excepting my cousin Elizabeth" (p. 124). As he likes to be useful to Lady Catherine, so he is useful to the plot: he provides a place for Elizabeth to visit, where she can observe Lady Catherine and see Darcy again; he draws out his "affable and condescending" patroness for Elizabeth's edification; he serves as a medium through which Lady Catherine's opinions on events in the Bennet family are graciously transmitted to the Bennets. And always he remains firm in the conviction of his importance and dignity, of his place at the center— or a little off the matriarchal center—of the universe.

Like Mr. Collins, Lady Catherine is chiefly amusing because of the incongruity between the importance she assumes to herself and the actual influence she exercises upon the story. At first glance, she is, of course, far more formidable than Mr. Collins; yet, in the story at least, she never does what she thinks she is doing or wishes to do. It is true—as Elizabeth remarks—that "Lady Catherine has been of infinite use, which ought to make her happy, for she loves to be of use" (p. 381). She is useful to the story; but only in ways she is unaware of and would repudiate with outrage if she knew of them. By her insulting condescension toward Elizabeth, she helps Darcy to balance off his distaste of Mrs. Bennet's not dissimilar shortcomings. She provokes Elizabeth into asserting her own independence of spirit, even to the point of impertinence. In her arrogant effort to dissuade Elizabeth from accepting Darcy, she gives Elizabeth the opportunity to set her own proud value upon herself as an individual, and later, having angrily brought the news to Darcy, encourages him to believe that Elizabeth may not refuse him a second time. Lady Catherine is a purely comic figure, not because she is not potentially powerful and dangerous in the authority that rank and wealth confer upon her, but because she is easily known for what she is, and because the lovers are in a position—Darcy by his own rank and wealth, Elizabeth by her spirit and intelligence—to deny her power altogether.

This quality of powerlessness is, indeed, peculiar to Elizabeth's, and the author's, whole category of simplicity: not merely in Mrs. Bennet, Lydia, Mr. Collins, and Lady Catherine, but in the predictably malicious Miss Bingley, in single-postured simpletons like Sir William Lucas and Mary Bennet, down to an unrealized function like Georgiana Darcy. They are powerless, that is, at the center of the story. They cannot decisively divert Elizabeth's or Darcy's mind and purpose because they cannot cope with the adult personality that either of the lovers presents. They are powerless, ultimately, because they are not themselves adult. They convince us of their existence (except, perhaps, Georgiana and Mary), sometimes even brilliantly; but they are not sufficiently complex or self-aware to be taken at the highest level of seriousness. Elizabeth's judgment of them is, then, primarily psychological, not moral: they have not grown to a personal stature significantly measurable by moral law. However Elizabeth may console Bingley that a "deep, intricate character" may be no more "estimable than such a one as yours" (p. 42), the fact is that though she finds simplicity comfortable or amusing, it is only intricacy, complexity of spirit, that she finds fascinating, deserving of pursuit and capture, susceptible to a grave moral judgment.

It may be objected that Jane Bennet belongs in the category of simplicity also, and that Elizabeth, nonetheless, loves and admires her sister above anyone else. Both statements are true; but the latter is true only in a very special sense. There is something maternal, something affectionately envious, something of the nature of a schoolgirl passion in Elizabeth's feeling for Jane.

The difference between her natural, uncomplex, unintuitive, almost unseeing goodness and Elizabeth's conscious, reasoned, perpetual examination into motive—this is a difference not merely between individuals, but between altogether different orders of mind. Elizabeth loves Jane as Jane is a kind and loving sister, she envies Jane her facile solution—or her plain ignorance—of the problems of interpreting personality, she even plays the schoolgirl to her older sister as confidante; but Elizabeth never doubts that Jane's opinions of others have no objective value, and that Jane's response toward people and society is much too simple, even too simple-minded, to be hers. So Elizabeth, as Jane defends Bingley's sisters against her charge of snobbery,

. . . listened in silence, but was not convinced; their behaviour at the assembly had not been calculated to please in general; and with more quickness of observation and less pliancy of temper than her sister, and with a judgment too unassailed by any attention to herself, she was very little disposed to approve them. (p. 15)

The surest proof of Elizabeth's, and the author's, attitude toward Jane is the lover they are both delighted to supply her with. Bingley is a person of secondary order far more obviously than Jane. He is handsome, very amiable and courteous,. lively, properly smitten by Jane almost at first glance. That, and his considerable wealth, make up the extent of his charms. It is significant that Elizabeth never has a twinge of feeling for him, except as he seems a fine catch for her sister. In his conversation with Elizabeth at Netherfield, he fears that he gives himself away out of shallowness (p. 42); and, despite Elizabeth's graceful denial, he does. There is nothing below the surface. His strong-willed friend, Darcy, leads him about by the nose. Though he is supposed to have fallen seriously in love with Jane, the merest trick of Darcy's and his sister's is enough to send and keep him away from her. As Darcy explains:

". . . Bingley is most unaffectedly modest. His diffidence had prevented his depending on his own judgment in so anxious a case, but his reliance on mine, made every thing easy. . . ." (p. 371)

"Modest" is a charitable word here. Darcy has been equally successful, moreover, in turning about and persuading Bingley that Jane *is* in love with him; whereupon

Elizabeth longed to observe that Mr. Bingley had been a most delightful friend; so easily guided that his worth was invaluable. . . . (p. 371)

It is true that Jane pines over Bingley for a long time. She is a sincere and faithful lover; but our admiration of this trait tends to diminish as we think about the object of her love. Jane and Bingley provide us, then, with one of the book's primary ironies: that love is simple, straightforward, and immediate only for very simple people. Jane and Bingley could, of course, have served very well as a pair of story-book lovers, tossed romantically on a sea of circumstances not only beyond their control but beyond their understanding. In the pattern of the novel, however, they have their adult guardians and counterparts—Jane in her sister, Bingley in his friend—to haul them in when the sea gets too rough; and though, like the standard lovers of romance, they will never have to worry about growing up, we are obliged, by the presence of Elizabeth at least, to admit that it *is* possible—perhaps even preferable—for lovers to be complex and mature.

To this point Elizabeth's judgment is as acute and ironic as her author's. Elizabeth, indeed, is far more aware of distinctions in personality than any of the author's previous heroines: Catherine Morland, Elinor or Marianne Dashwood. In *Northanger Abbey,* the author could not allow her heroine to be aware from the outset since her story developed precisely out of Catherine's unawareness of distinctions (a quality suggested, perhaps, by Jane Austen's early tendency to assert an arbitrary omniscience over the objects of her irony). In *Sense and Sensibility,* Jane Austen, yielding for the first time to the moral pressures inevitable upon a woman of her time and class, allowed Elinor only the solemn and easy discriminations of bourgeois morality, and finally smothered the threatening spark of Marianne's much livelier and more observing consciousness. In *Pride and Prejudice,* however, there is no compulsion—personal, thematic, or moral—toward denying the heroine her own powers of judgment. There is, on the contrary, a thematic need for the heroine to display a subtle, accurate, a perceiving mind. In *Pride and Prejudice,* as in the previous novels, Jane Austen deals with the distinction between false moral values and true; but she is also dealing here with a distinction antecedent to the moral judgment—the distinction between the simple personality, unequipped with that self-awareness which alone makes choice seem possible, and the complex personality, whose most crucial complexity is its awareness, of self and others. This distinction, which in her youthful defensive posture Jane Austen has tended to make only between her characters and herself, she here establishes internally, between two categories of personality within the novel. The distinction is, in fact, one that every character in *Pride and Prejudice* must make if he can; and the complex characters—Elizabeth and Darcy among them—justify their complexity by making it, and trying to live by its implications, through all their lapses of arrogance, prejudice, sensuality, and fear. Elizabeth is aware because, in the novel's climate of adult decision, she must be so to survive with our respect and interest.

Yet the distinction must be made in a social setting, by human beings fallible, if for no other reason, because of their own social involvement. The province of *Pride and Prejudice*—as always in Jane Austen's novels —is marriage in an acquisitive society. Elizabeth herself, being young, attractive, and unmarried, is at the center of it; and it is this position that sets her off from such an external and imposed commentator as Henry Tilney. Her position of personal involvement subjects her, moreover, to a risk of error never run by the detached Mr. Tilney. She can tag and dismiss the blatantly simple persons very well; it is when she moves away from these toward ambiguity and self-concealment, toward persons themselves aware enough to interest and engage her, that her youth and inexperience and emotional partiality begin to deceive her.

They deceive her first with Charlotte Lucas. The two girls have been good friends. Charlotte, according to the author, is a "sensible, intelligent

young woman" (p. 18), and she shares Elizabeth's taste for raillery and
social generalization. Even when Charlotte offers her altogether cynical
views on courtship and marriage, Elizabeth refuses to take her at her
word:

> ". . . Happiness in marriage is entirely a matter of chance. If the disposi-
> tions of the parties are ever so well known to each other, or ever so similar
> before-hand, it does not advance their felicity in the least. They always con-
> tinue to grow sufficiently unlike afterwards to have their share of vexation;
> and it is better to know as little as possible of the defects of the person with
> whom you are to pass your life."
>   "You make me laugh, Charlotte; but it is not sound. You know it is not
> sound, and that you would never act in this way yourself." (p. 23)

It is not that Elizabeth misjudges Charlotte's capabilities, but that she
underestimates the strength of the pressures acting upon her. Charlotte
is twenty-seven, unmarried, not pretty, not well-to-do, living in a society
which treats a penniless old maid less as a joke than as an exasperating
burden upon her family. But Elizabeth is inexperienced enough, at the
beginning, to judge in terms of personality only. She recognizes Mr. Collins' total foolishness and Charlotte's intelligence, and would never
have dreamed that any pressure could overcome so natural an opposition.
Complex and simple, aware and unaware, do not belong together—except that in marriages made by economics they often unite, however
obvious the mismatching. Living under a pall of economic anxiety has
withered every desire in Charlotte except the desire for security:

> ". . . I am not romantic. . . . I never was. I ask only a comfortable home;
> and considering Mr. Collins's character, connections, and situation in life, I
> am convinced that my chance of happiness with him is as fair, as most
> people can boast on entering the marriage state." (p. 125)

What Charlotte has resolved, finally, is to grow progressively unaware, to
reduce herself to simplicity; and, in the meantime, while that is not yet
possible, to close her eyes and ears. Her decision is clear when Elizabeth
visits Hunsford:

> When Mr. Collins said any thing of which his wife might reasonably be
> ashamed, which certainly was not unseldom, she involuntarily turned her
> eye on Charlotte. Once or twice she could discern a faint blush; but in gen-
> eral Charlotte wisely did not hear. (p. 156)

So the natural antithesis which separates simple from complex, and
which should separate one from the other absolutely in the closest human
relationship, can be upset and annulled by economic pressure.

Elizabeth's continual mistake is to ignore, or to set aside as uninfluential, the social context. It is a question not merely of individuals and marriage, but of individuals and marriage in an acquisitive society. Elizabeth expects nothing except comfort or amusement from simplicity; but she likes to believe that complexity means a categorically free will, without social distortion or qualification.

When complexity and a pleasing manner combine, as they do in Wickham, Elizabeth is at her least cautious. Wickham is clever and charming, a smooth social being, and for these qualities Elizabeth is ready to believe his long, unsolicited tale of being wronged and even to imagine herself falling in love with him. What she never allows, until much later, to cast a doubt upon his testimony is the fact that he is a dispossessed man in an acquisitive society.

It is with Wickham, nevertheless, that Jane Austen's directing and organizing irony—which functions doubly, at the same time through and upon Elizabeth—begins to fail; and the area of failure is the sexual experience outside marriage.

The first flattening of tone occurs in Darcy's letter (pp. 195ff.), in which Wickham's infamy is revealed. Wickham has attempted to seduce Darcy's sister, Georgiana; and it is this specific attempt, beyond any other evidence of profligacy, that automatically makes him a villain from Darcy's point of view, and from Elizabeth's also as soon as she can accept the truth of the letter. The curious fact is, not that Elizabeth and, here at least, Jane Austen regard seduction as infamous, but that, into an ironic atmosphere elaborated and intensified out of the difficulty of interpreting motive, Jane Austen pushes a standard black-and-white seduction-scene, with all the appurtenances of an ingenuous young girl, a scheming profligate, a wicked governess, and an outraged brother, and with no trace of doubt, shading, or irony. It is hardly enough to say, with Miss Lascelles,[1] that Jane Austen clings to this novelistic convention through almost all her work as to a usable climax, which she met in Richardson and for which she could find no adequate substitute. *Why* she retained this threadbare revelation when, as early as *Pride and Prejudice,* she could demonstrate the most subtle and resourceful skill in representing every other particular of the action, remains a question.

The answer seems to be that, though the nature of her subject makes an approach to the sexual experience inevitable, Jane Austen will not allow herself (as she did in *Love and Freindship* and continues to do in her letter) to assimilate extra-marital sex to her characteristic unifying irony, and that her only other possible response is conventional. She must truncate, flatten, falsify, disapprove, all in the interests of an external

---

[1] M. Lascelles, *Jane Austen and Her Art,* Oxford, 1939, 72f.

morality; and the process in *Pride and Prejudice* is so out of key with its surroundings as to be immediately jarring.

Lydia is the outstanding victim. Not that Lydia is not throughout a wholly consistent and living character. On the solid and simple foundations of her personality she works up to her triumphant end in marriage to Wickham. If she acts from her sensual nature, it is Elizabeth and the author themselves who have proved to us that Lydia, being among the simple spirits who are never really aware and who act only upon their single potentiality, cannot do otherwise. The irony is, or should be, in her unawareness, in her powerlessness to change, in the incongruity between her conviction of vitality and her lack of choice. This irony, though, Jane Austen quite cuts off. She is herself silent, but it is clear that she allows Elizabeth to define the proper attitude toward Lydia. Elizabeth can feel, at first, no sympathy for Lydia at all. Later, however, when the moment of shame is long past, her attitude has not changed except to harden into sarcastic resentment: when Lydia offers to give Elizabeth an account of the wedding,

> "No really," replied Elizabeth; "I think there cannot be too little said on the subject." (p. 318)

Elizabeth's ill-tempered efforts to shame Lydia are fruitless, as Elizabeth should have known they would be while Lydia is Lydia still. What they amount to is a kind of floating moral judgment. It seems that both Jane Austen and her heroine feel uneasily that a moral lesson must be taught, though they have already proved that Lydia is incapable of learning it:

> . . . how little of permanent happiness could belong to a couple who were only brought together because their passions were stronger than their virtue, she could easily conjecture. (p. 312)

So Jane Austen suspends her irony, suspends her imagination altogether, while Wickham is engaged in seducing Georgiana or Lydia. Yet, apart from this temporary suspension, Wickham fits admirably into the large pattern of Elizabeth's social education. Not only is he, like Charlotte, an example of the complex personality discarding scruples, discarding candor, making the wrong choice under economic pressure; he is also an evil agent, quite willing to corrupt others as well, to involve them in public disgrace if he can thereby assure his own security. What he uses deliberately is what Mrs. Bennet used, much less deliberately, in her conquest of her husband: sexual attractiveness. It is, then, Wickham who by exploiting sex sets off that other intricate character who passively succumbed to it—Mr. Bennet.

It is, in fact, easy to imagine that when Mr. Bennet calls Wickham his favorite son-in-law (p. 379) he is not merely indulging in habitual paradox, but ironically recognizing the painful contrast between Wickham's awareness, however directed, and his own self-delusion, in the same emotional circumstance. Mr. Bennet made his mistake many years before, and must now stand by it because his class recognizes no respectable way out:

> . . . captivated by youth and beauty, and that appearance of good humour, which youth and beauty generally give, he had married a woman whose weak understanding and illiberal mind, had very early in their marriage put an end to all real affection for her. Respect, esteem, and confidence, had vanished for ever; and all his views of domestic happiness were overthrown. But Mr. Bennet was not of a disposition to seek comfort for the disappointment which his own imprudence had brought on, in any of those pleasures which too often console the unfortunate for their folly or their vice. He was fond of the country and of books; and from these tastes had arisen his principal enjoyments. To his wife he was very little otherwise indebted, than as her ignorance and folly had contributed to his amusement. This is not the sort of happiness which a man would in general wish to owe to his wife; but where other powers of entertainment are wanting, the true philosopher will derive benefit from such as are given. (p. 236)

Mr. Bennet has become an ironic spectator almost totally self-enclosed, his irony rigidly defensive, a carapace against the plain recognition of his own irrevocable folly. He observes, he stands apart "in silence . . . enjoying the scene" (p. 103), he likes to make blunt comments on the silliness of his daughters, especially of Lydia and Kitty:

> "From all that I can collect by your manner of talking, you must be two of the silliest girls in the country. I have suspected it some time, but I am now convinced." (p. 29)

and, equally, when Charlotte accepts Mr. Collins:

> . . . it gratified him, he said, to discover that Charlotte Lucas, whom he had been used to think tolerably sensible, was as foolish as his wife, and more foolish than his daughter! (p. 127)

He likes to upset, in small ways, the social decorum which has overwhelmed him in its massive and permanent way, he enjoys pointing the contrast between what he ought to think and what he does think. It is a very minor social victory, but the only one now possible for him.

It is true that Lydia's elopement shocks him into exposing himself for as long as it takes him to transact the unpleasant business. When he returns from his futile search in London, in acknowledgment of Elizabeth's

> . . . briefly expressing her sorrow for what he must have endured, he replied, "Say nothing of that. Who should suffer but myself? It has been my own doing, and I ought to feel it."
> "You must not be too severe upon yourself," replied Elizabeth.
> "You may well warn me against such an evil. Human nature is so prone to fall into it! No, Lizzy, let me once in my life feel how much I have been to blame. I am not afraid of being overpowered by the impression. It will pass away soon enough." (p. 299)

It does soon enough, or at least the impulse to articulate it. With Lydia and Wickham safely married, Mr. Bennet restores himself to what he has been—rather, to what he has seemed. He needs only another letter from Mr. Collins to reaffirm all his amused detachment, to make explicit the only code by which he can tolerate the vacuity, the hopeless failure of sympathy, in his life.

> ". . . For what do we live, but to make sport for our neighbours, and laugh at them in our turn?" (p. 364)

If Elizabeth cannot answer, it is because she recognizes that there is nothing else left for her father, that his choice was made long ago, that he cannot withdraw or alter it, that he must live by it in the only way endurable for him. Of course his mistake and his despair might be decently masked; things would be better, for his children at least, if he could put up a front of quiet respectability concerning his relations with his wife:

> Elizabeth . . . had never been blind to the impropriety of her father's behaviour as a husband. She had always seen it with pain; but respecting his abilities, and grateful for his affectionate treatment of herself, she endeavoured to forget what she could not overlook, and to banish from her thoughts that continual breach of conjugal obligation and decorum which, in exposing his wife to the contempt of her children, was so highly reprehensible. (p. 236)

But the damage to himself is done and cannot be remedied. Elizabeth knows her father: of the complex characters in the story, he is the only one whom she has known long and well enough to judge accurately from the outset. She has learned from his example that a complex personality may yield to the pressure of sensuality; that marriages made by sex—as well as those made by economics—represent, for the free individual, an abdication of choice, an irremediable self-degradation and defeat.

In his social context, in his status as a gentleman of independent means, Mr. Bennet was lulled into believing that choice was easy, a matter of simple and unexamined inclination; and in the same society Mrs. Bennet could not believe otherwise than that any gentleman of means must make a desirable husband. This much Elizabeth recognizes about the pressures of an acquisitive society, even upon a free individual like her father. The shock of Charlotte's marriage to a fool makes Elizabeth recognize that these pressures act decisively upon other free individuals as well. In spite of examples, however, it takes a long series of vexations and misunderstandings before she can be convinced that the imposed pride of rank and wealth, perhaps the strongest pressure in an acquisitive society, may act, not yet decisively—for the area of decision is marriage—but conditionally upon a free individual like Darcy, to make him behave with an overconfident and unsympathetic obstinacy, to make him seem far different from what he is capable of being behind the façade of pride.

It is the social façade of the complex person that deceives Elizabeth. She can penetrate her father's, out of sympathetic familiarity and concern; but Charlotte's has deceived her. Wickham's takes her in altogether; and by contrast with Wickham's, by the contrast which Wickham himself takes care to emphasize in his own support, Darcy's façade seems disagreeable indeed, or rather a clear window on a disagreeable spirit.

Darcy's function as the character most difficult for the heroine to interpret, and yet most necessary for her to interpret if *she* is to make a proper decision in the only area of choice her society leaves open, his simultaneous role as the heroine's puzzle and her only possible hero, is clearly marked out during the action. From Elizabeth's point of view, in fact, the process of the interpretation of Darcy's personality from disdain through doubt to admiration is represented with an extraordinarily vivid and convincing minuteness.[2] Nevertheless, Darcy himself remains unachieved: we recognize his effects upon Elizabeth, without recognizing that he exists independently of them.

Mrs. Leavis has persuasively documented her belief that *Pride and Prejudice* is an effort to "rewrite the story of *Cecilia* in realistic terms";[3] and she observes, more particularly, that Darcy fails because he does not transcend his derivation: he is a character out of a book, not one whom Jane Austen created or reorganized for her own purpose. But why Darcy

---

[2] In "The Controlling Hand: Jane Austen and *Pride and Prejudice*," *Scrutiny*, XIII (September 1945) [an earlier form of the essay included in this volume], R. A. Brower brilliantly analyzes the process by means of which Elizabeth comes to an understanding of Darcy.

[3] Q. D. Leavis, "A Critical Theory of Jane Austen's Writings," *Scrutiny*, X (June, 1941), 71ff.

alone: why is he, among the major figures in *Pride and Prejudice,* the only one disturbingly derived and wooden?

The reason seems to be the same as that which compelled Jane Austen to falsify her tone and commentary concerning Wickham's seductions and to supply Elinor and Marianne Dashwood with such nonentities for husbands. The socially unmanageable, the personally involving aspects of sex, Jane Austen can no longer treat with irony, nor can she as yet treat them straightforwardly. Darcy is the hero, he is the potential lover of a complex young woman much like the author herself; and as such Jane Austen cannot animate him with emotion, or with her characteristic informing irony. She borrows him from a book; and, though she alters and illuminates everything else, she can do nothing more with him than fit him functionally into the plot.

Even here the author is so uncharacteristically clumsy as to rely on inconsistencies of personality to move her story along. However difficult Elizabeth's task of interpreting Darcy, it is clear from the beginning that, in his consistent functional impact upon the story, he is a proud man with a strong sense of at least external propriety and dignity, and with no taste whatever for his aunt's vulgar condescension or the kind of sarcasm dispensed by Mr. Bennet. Yet on his first appearance he initiates Elizabeth's prejudice by speaking with a simple vulgarity indistinguishable from his aunt's, and in a voice loud enough to be overheard by the object of his contempt:

> . . . turning round, he looked for a moment at Elizabeth, till catching her eye, he withdrew his own and coldly said, "She is tolerable; but not handsome enough to tempt *me;* and I am in no humour at present to give consequence to young ladies who are slighted by other men. . . ." (pp. 11-12)

In spite of his rigid and principled reserve, in spite of Elizabeth's having just turned down his arrogant proposal, he makes his explanation to Elizabeth in a thoroughly frank and unreserved letter, which—more appropriate to a Richardsonian correspondent than to Darcy as he has been presented—seems an author's gesture of desperation to weight the scales in favor of her predetermined hero.

Out of inconsistency, Darcy emerges into flatness. Only in his sparring with Elizabeth, and then only occasionally, does he establish himself with a degree of solidity, of independent reference, as when Elizabeth tries to tease him into communicativeness while they are dancing:

> ". . . One must speak a little, you know. It would look odd to be entirely silent for half an hour together, and yet for the advantage of *some,* conversation ought to be so arranged as that they may have the trouble of saying as little as possible."

"Are you consulting your own feelings in the present case, or do you imagine that you are gratifying mine?"

"Both," replied Elizabeth archly, "for I have always seen a great similarity in the turn of our minds.—We are each of an unsocial, taciturn disposition, unwilling to speak, unless we expect to say something that will amaze the whole room, and be handed down to posterity with all the éclat of a proverb."

"This is no very striking resemblance of your own character, I am sure," said he. "How near it may be to *mine,* I cannot pretend to say.—*You* think it a faithful portrait undoubtedly." (p. 91)

In dialogue, at least when Elizabeth is an enlivening participant, Jane Austen seems able now and then to overcome her awkwardness in handling Darcy. Otherwise, however, she can only make him serve: he interests us chiefly because he is the center of Elizabeth's interest; and because, in a book in which the individual must choose and in which marriage is the single area of choice, Darcy represents Elizabeth's only plausible, or almost plausible, mate. And when Darcy is ironed out into the conventionally generous and altruistic hero, making devoted efforts to shackle Wickham to Lydia, expending thousands of pounds to restore peace of mind to Elizabeth's family, and all for the love of Elizabeth—when he does all this, with no more of personal depth than Jane Austen allows of moral depth in the whole Lydia-Wickham episode, he comes very close to forfeiting even the functional plausibility that Elizabeth's interest lends him.

The last third of the book, as R. A. Brower has pointed out,[4] does in fact diminish suddenly in density and originality: that is, beginning with Lydia's elopement. We get a conventional chase by an outraged father, a friendly uncle, and a now impeccable hero; we get outbursts of irrelevantly directed moral judgment, and a general simplification of the problems of motive and will down to the level of the Burneyan novel. Jane Austen herself, routed by the sexual question she has raised, is concealed behind a fogbank of bourgeois morality; and the characters, most conspicuously Darcy, must shift for themselves, or, rather, they fall automatically into the grooves prepared for them by hundreds of novels of sentiment and sensibility.

Only Elizabeth does not. She may yield temporarily to a kind of homeless moralizing on Lydia's disgrace, she may be rather obvious and stiff in acquainting herself with Darcy's virtues at last; but the lapses are minor, and they never seriously dim her luminous vigor, her wit, curiosity, discrimination, and independence. If the novel does not collapse in the predictabilities of the denouement, it is because Elizabeth has from the outset been presented in a depth specific and vital enough to resist

[4] *Op. cit.,* Brower.

flattening, because she remains what she has been—a complex person in search of conclusions about people in society, and on the way to her unique and crucial choice.

She observes, and her shield and instrument together is irony. Like Mary Crawford later, Elizabeth is a recognizable and striking aspect of her author; but, unlike Mary's, her sins are all quite venial, her irony unclouded by the author's disapproval and—after a few detours—grandly vindicated in its effect. Jane Austen has not yet made her first unqualified capitulation to the suspicious sobriety of her class, and surrendered her values in exchange for its own. She can, in fact, embody her personal values in her heroine and be delighted with the result; so she writes to her sister about Elizabeth: "I must confess that I think her as delightful a creature as ever appeared in print, and how I shall be able to tolerate those who do not like *her* at least I do not know." (*Letters,* ii, 297, 29 Jan. 1813)

Elizabeth's third dimension is irony; and it is her irony that fills out and sustains the action. Her slightest perception of incongruity reverberates through the scene, and from it out into the atmosphere of the book. When Lydia, having informed Elizabeth that Wickham's wealthy catch has got away, adds:

". . . he never cared three straws about her. Who *could* about such a nasty little freckled thing?"
Elizabeth was shocked to think that, however incapable of such coarseness of *expression* herself, the coarseness of the *sentiment* was little other than her own breast had formerly harboured and fancied liberal! (p. 220)

At Pemberley, she listens as the housekeeper eulogizes Darcy, until her uncle asks:

"Is your master much at Pemberley in the course of the year?"
"Not so much as I could wish, sir; but I dare say he may spend half his time here; and Miss Darcy is always down for the summer months."
"Except," thought Elizabeth, "when she goes to Ramsgate." (p. 248)

recalling by this most astonishing economy of means—like a flashback in intent but with none of its deadening machinery—the whole charged atmosphere of Wickham's earlier attempt at seduction (more successfully than Darcy's letter, our original source of information, had created it at first), recalling the tension of Darcy's insulting and rejected proposal, the excitement of his letter and the depression and change of heart it inevitably brought: and all this richness and clarity of reference out of a single and immediately irrelevant ironic thought.

There is, above all, the perpetual exuberant yet directed irony of her conversation, especially as she uses it to sound Darcy. When Miss Bingley assures her that Darcy cannot be laughed at, Elizabeth exclaims:

> "That is an uncommon advantage, and uncommon I hope it will continue, for it would be a great loss to *me* to have many such acquaintance. I dearly love a laugh."
>
> "Miss Bingley," said he, "has given me credit for more than can be. The wisest and the best of men, nay, the wisest and best of their actions, may be rendered ridiculous by a person whose first object in life is a joke."
>
> "Certainly," replied Elizabeth—"there are such people, but I hope I am not one of them. I hope I never ridicule what is wise or good. Follies and nonsense, whims and inconsistencies *do* divert me, I own, and I laugh at them when I can.—But these, I suppose, are precisely what you are without." (p. 57)

Darcy protests that his failings are not of understanding, but of temper:

> ". . . My temper would perhaps be called resentful.—My good opinion once lost is lost for ever."
>
> "*That* is a failing indeed!" cried Elizabeth. "Implacable resentment *is* a shade in a character. You have chosen your fault well.—I really cannot *laugh* at it. You are safe from me."
>
> "There is, I believe, in every disposition a tendency to some particular evil, a natural defect, which not even the best education can overcome."
>
> "And *your* defect is a propensity to hate every body." (p. 58)

Whether Elizabeth is teasing him about his silence at dancing (p. 271), or, in Lady Catherine's drawing room, explaining her lack of skill at the piano to refute Darcy's claim of having no talent for sociability (p. 175), she draws him out in the only ways in which he can be drawn out at all, by a challenging indirection just short of impudence, by the appeal of an intelligence as free and aware as that on which he prides himself, by the penetration of a wit which makes its own rules without breaking any significant ones, which even establishes its priority over simple truth:

> "You mean to frighten me, Mr. Darcy, by coming in all this state to hear me? But I will not be alarmed. . . ."
>
> "I shall not say that you are mistaken," he replied, "because you could not really believe me to entertain any design of alarming you; and I have had the pleasure of your acquaintance long enough to know that you find great enjoyment in occasionally professing opinions which in fact are not your own." (p. 174)

If Darcy, finally sounded and known, hardly differs from the stiff-jointed Burneyan aristocratic hero, except as Darcy is provided with a somewhat more explicit personality, the fault is not Elizabeth's, but her author's.

Elizabeth has learned what can be learned about him; she has even learned, with Miss Bingley, that Darcy is *not* to be laughed at—not, at least, in the matter of his influence over Bingley:

> Elizabeth longed to observe that Mr. Bingley had been a most delightful friend; so easily guided that his worth was invaluable; but she checked herself. She remembered that he had yet to learn to be laught at, and it was rather too early to begin. (p. 371)

In the process of interpretation, moreover—with its deflections, its spurious evidence, its shocks of awareness and repentance—she has brought to a focus at last all the scattered principles which her overconfidence and lack of experience continually obliged her to underestimate, forget, or abandon.

She never gives up her first principle: to separate the simple personality from the complex, and to concentrate her attention and interest on the latter. Her point of reference is always the complex individual, the individual aware and capable of choice. Her own pride is in her freedom, to observe, to analyze, to choose; her continual mistake is to forget that, even for her, there is only one area of choice—marriage—and that this choice is subject to all the powerful and numbing pressures of an acquisitive society.

The central fact for Elizabeth remains the power of choice. In spite of social pressures, in spite of the misunderstandings and the obstacles to awareness that cut off and confuse the individual, in spite of the individual's repeated failures, the power of choice is all that distinguishes him as a being who acts and who may be judged. There are, certainly, limitations upon his choice, the limitations of an imposed prudence, of living within a social frame in which material comfort is an article of prestige and a sign of moral well-being: since even Elizabeth, though an acute and critical observer, is no rebel, she cannot contemplate the possibility of happiness outside her given social frame. The author is, likewise, pointedly ironic in contrasting Elizabeth's charitable allowances, first for Wickham, and then for Colonel Fitzwilliam, an "Earl's younger son" (p. 184), when her relative poverty obliges them to regard her as ineligible. Yet the irony does not go so far as to invalidate choice or distinctions in choice. Fitzwilliam, no rebel, is prudent in the hope that both prudence and inclination may be satisfied together in the future; but Wickham's "prudence," rather than merely limiting his choice, has deprived him of it entirely. In Elizabeth's feeling, upon touring Darcy's estate, "that to be mistress of Pemberley might be something!" (p. 245) the irony is circumscribed with an equal clarity: Darcy gains by being a rich man with a magnificent estate; but Pemberley is an expression of Darcy's taste as well as of his wealth and rank, and the image of Pemberley cannot divert Elizabeth from her primary concern with Darcy's motives and the meaning of his façade. Pemberley with Mr. Collins, or even with Bingley, would not do at all.

The focus is upon the complex individual; the only quality that distinguishes him from his setting, from the forms of courtship and marriage in an acquisitive society, which otherwise standardize and absorb him, is also his unique function—choice. What Elizabeth must choose, within the bounds set by prudence, is an individual equally complex, and undefeated by his social role. The complex individual is, after all, isolated by his freedom, and must be seen so at the end; for even if pressures from without, from the social system and the social class, deflect or overwhelm him, they demonstrate not that he is indistinguishable from his social role, but that he is vulnerable to it. The fact of choice makes him stand, finally, alone, to judge or be judged.

In *Pride and Prejudice,* Jane Austen's irony has developed into an instrument of discrimination between the people who are simple reproductions of their social type and the people with individuality and will, between the unaware and the aware. The defensive—and destructive—weapon of *Northanger Abbey* and *Sense and Sensibility* has here been adapted directly to the theme through the personality of Elizabeth Bennet, who reflects and illustrates her author's vision without ever becoming (except in her malice toward Lydia) merely her author's advocate. The irony is internal, it does not take disturbing tangents toward the author's need for self-vindication: even self-defensive, it is internal and consistent— Mr. Bennet's shying from the consequences of his disastrous mistake, Elizabeth's provocative parrying of Darcy. And if this new control over her irony permits Jane Austen only to be more clever (and not particularly more persuasive) in avoiding a commitment, by Elizabeth in love, for example:

"... Will you tell me how long you have loved him?"

"It has been coming on so gradually, that I hardly know when it began. But I believe it must date from my first seeing his beautiful grounds at Pemberley."

Another intreaty that she would be serious, however, produced the desired effect; and she soon satisfied Jane by her solemn assurances of attachment. (p. 373)

the characteristic block of Jane Austen's against direct emotional expression has occasion only very rarely to operate in *Pride and Prejudice*: above all, in the talk and atmosphere of Darcy's proposals, and in his letter—passages which most nearly reproduce the flat or melodramatic textures of *Cecilia,* without any lift of emotion or of irony either. The moment is soon over; and irony is not only back, but back at its proper task of discrimination.

In *Pride and Prejudice,* the flaw of an irrelevant defensiveness has almost vanished; and the flaw of a too obvious personal withdrawal before a moral or emotional issue, as with Lydia and Darcy, is not obtrusive enough, to annul or seriously damage the sustained and organizing power of Jane Austen's irony. Irony here rejects chiefly to discover and illuminate; and, though its setting is the same stratified, materialistic, and severely regulated society, its new text and discovery—its new character, in fact, whom Jane Austen has hitherto allowed only herself to impersonate—is the free individual.

The Humiliation of Emma Woodhouse

by Mark Schorer

Jane Austen's *Emma*, 1816, stands at the head of her achievements, and, even though she herself spoke of Emma as "a heroine whom no one but myself will much like," discriminating readers have thought the novel her greatest. Her powers here are at their fullest, her control at its most certain. As with most of her novels, it has a double theme, but in no other has the structure been raised so skillfully upon it. The novel might have been called *Pride and Perception*, or *Perception and Self-Deception*, for the comedy is concerned with a heroine who must be educated out of a condition of self-deception brought on by the shutters of pride into a condition of perception when that pride had been humbled through the exposure of the errors of judgment into which it has led her. No novel shows more clearly Jane Austen's power to take the moral measurement of the society with which she was concerned through the range of her characters.

Morality in the novel lies not in spread but in scale, in the discrimination of values on scale and the proportion that is held between values within scale. In *Emma*, the word *scale* has a special meaning, for its subject is a fixed social scale in need of measurement by moral scale. As the social scale is represented by the scene as a whole, by all the characters, so the chief characters establish, in addition, the moral scale. The story is the progress of the heroine on this second scale toward her position on the first. *Emma* gives us the picture of an externally balanced society which the novel itself readjusts, or puts in perspective, through the internal balance that is the root of moral, not social, judgment.

Can we permit the notion that Jane Austen is capable of making a moral judgment on that social world which she herself accepts and from which her novels emerge? I have argued elsewhere that our surest way of knowing the values out of which a novel comes lies in an examination of style, more particularly, of metaphor. Jane Austen's style is, of course, remarkably nonmetaphorical, if we are thinking of explicit metaphor, the

"The Humiliation of Emma Woodhouse" by Mark Schorer. From *The Literary Review* (Teaneck, N.J.: Fairleigh Dickinson University), II, No. 4 (Summer 1959), pp. 547-563. Reprinted by permission of the author and the editors of *The Literary Review*.

stated analogy, but it is no less remarkable in the persistency with which the buried or dead metaphors in her prose imply one consistent set of values. These are the values of commerce and property, of the counting house and the inherited estate. I will divide this set of values rather arbitrarily into five categories. First of all, of *scale* itself, all that metaphor of high and low, sink and rise, advance and decline, superior and inferior, rank and fortune, power and command; as "held below the level," "raise her expectations too high," "materially cast down," "the intimacy between her and Emma must sink." Second, of *money:* credit, value, interest, rate, reserve, secure, change and exchange, alloy, resources, gain, want, collect (for "assume"), reckon, render, account claim, profit, loss, accrue, tax, due, pay, lose, spend, waste, fluctuate, dispense, "precious deposit," appropriate, commission, safety. Third, of *business and property:* inherit, certify, procure, solicit, entitle, business, venture, scheme, arrangement, insure, cut off, trust, charge, stock. Fourth, of *number and measure:* add, divide, multiply, calculate, how much and how little, more and less. And fifth, of *matter:* incumbrance, weight, substance, material (as, material change, or material alteration), comfort.

These terms are constantly appearing, both singly and in clusters. One or two illustrations must suffice:

> She listened, and found it well *worth* listening to. That very *dear* part of Emma, her fancy, *received* an amusing *supply* . . . it became henceforth her *prime object of interest;* and during the ten days of their stay at Hartfield it was not to be expected—she did not herself expect—that anything beyond occasional fortuitous assistance could be *afforded by her* to the lovers. They *might advance* rapidly if they would, however; they *must advance* somehow or other, whether they would or no. She hardly wished to have more leisure for them. They are people, who *the more you do* for them, *the less they will do* for themselves. Mr. and Mrs. John Knightley . . . were exciting, of course, rather *more than the usual interest.* Till this year, every long vacation since their marriage had been *divided* between Hartfield and Donwell Abbey.

This language, as a functioning element in the novel, begins to call attention to itself when we discover it in clusters where moral and material values are either juxtaposed or equated: "no material injury *accrued* either to body or mind"; "glad to have *purchased* the mortification of having loved"; "except in a moral light, as a penance, a lesson, a source of *profitable humiliation* to her own mind, she would have been thankful to be *assured* of never seeing him again . . . his welfare twenty miles off would *administer* most satisfaction."

It would seem that we are in a world of peculiarly *material* value, a world of almost instinctive material interests in its basic, intuitive response to experience. The style has created a texture, the "special feel" of that world. At the same time, on the surface of the action, this is usually a world of refined sensibility, of concern with moral propriety, and in Emma's case, presumably at least, of intelligent clarity of evaluation. A large portion of Jane Austen's comedy arises from the discrepancy that we see here, from the tension between these two kinds of value, these different *scales,* material and moral, which the characters, like the metaphors, are all the time juxtaposing and equating. But when we say that, we have moved from considerations of language alone, into the function of the language in the whole.

How do we transfer ourselves from one to the other? Notice, first of all, that in some very impressive details, the implicit stylistic values erupt every now and then into explicit evaluation in the action, explicit evaluations that are, of course, ironical illuminations of the characters in their special situations. "You were very popular before you came, because you were Mr. Weston's son; but lay out half a guinea at Ford's, and your popularity will stand upon your own virtues."

> "No—I cannot call them gifts; but they are things that I have valued very much."
> She held the parcel towards her, and Emma read the words *Most Precious treasures* on the top.

Emma's charity: "Emma was very compassionate; and the distress of the poor were as sure of relief from her personal attention and kindness, her counsel and her patience, as from her purse."

Emma's judgment of Mr. Martin:

> ". . . He will be a completely gross, vulgar farmer, totally inattentive to appearances, and thinking of nothing but profit and loss."
> "Will he, indeed? That will be very bad."
> "How much his business engrosses him already, is very plain from the circumstances of his forgetting to inquire for the book you recommended. He was a great deal too full of the market to think of anything else—which is just as it should be, for a thriving man. What has he to do with books? And I have no doubt that he *will* thrive, and be a very rich man in time; and his being illiterate and coarse need not disturb *us.*"

Most impressive, because most central to the theme of the book, this passage:

> Emma perceived that her taste was not the only taste on which Mr. Weston depended, and felt that to be the favourite and intimate of a man who had so many intimates and confidantes, was not *the very first distinction in the scale of vanity.* She liked his open manners, but a little less of openheartedness would have made him a higher character.

We may summarize this much as follows:

(1) The language itself defines for us, and defines most clearly, that area of available experience and value from which this novel takes its rise, and on which the novel itself must place the seal of its value. The texture of the style itself announces, therefore, the subject, and warns us, suggesting that we not be deceived by the fine sentiments and the moral scruples of the surface; that this is a material world where property and rank are major and probably as important as "character." More specifically, that this is not simply a novel of courtship and marriage, but a novel about the economic and social significance of courtship and marriage. (The basic situation in all the novels arises from the economics of marriage.) There is other evidence that Jane Austen knew marriage, in her world, to be a market; in her *Letters,* she wrote, "Single women have a dreadful propensity for being poor—which is one very strong argument in favor of matrimony."

(2) The implicit textural values created by language become explicit thematic statements in important key phrases such as "the scale of vanity" and "their intimacy must sink." In such phrases we detect the novel's themes (what it has to say about its subject) and its tone, too (how Jane Austen feels about it). We are led now, from language merely, to structure, to observe the particularized dramatic expression, the actualization, of this general narrative material, this "world."

Let us consider structure from the two points of view of architectural and thematic development. The two are of course interdependent, but we may see the novel more clearly, finally, if we make the separation.

From an architectural point of view, *Emma* seems to consist of four movements, or of four intermeshing blocks, each larger than the preceding. Emma is always the focus for us, but her own stature is altered as one block gives way to the next—that is, she bulks less large in the whole action of each as one follows upon another. The first block is the "Harriet Smith" block, and here Emma's dimensions are nearly coextensive with the block itself; this gives way to the Eltons' block (and that includes, of course, others); that, in turn, gives way to the Frank Churchill-Jane Fairfax block; and that, finally, to the Knightley block, where Emma is completely absorbed. John Knightley observes at one point, "Your neighborhood is increasing and you mix more with it." That is, of course, precisely what happens in the structure: an "increasing neighborhood" diminishes Emma. This development is perhaps best represented by the Cole's dinner party, where she finds herself in danger of exclusion and is herself alarmed, and it is completely dramatized in Frank Churchill's casual readiness to use—to abuse—her for his own purposes. Thus, as the plot becomes more intricate, and even as we view it through Emma eyes, she actually plays a less and less central or relevant part in it.

Now on these blocks of increasing size we must imagine another figure, a cone, to represent Knightley. Its point would lie somewhere near the end of the first—the Harriet—block, and through each of the following blocks it would widen, until, in the final block, it would be nearly coextensive with the limits of the block itself. It is important to see that the movement from block to block is accomplished not only by new elements in the action (the arrival of Mrs. Elton; of Jane Fairfax; the death of Mrs. Churchill) but by scenes between Emma and Mr. Knightley himself, scenes in which he usually upbraids her for an error of judgment and scenes out of which she emerges with an altered awareness, a dim alteration in the first, a slightly clearer alteration in the second and third, and at last, in the fourth, as full an awareness as she is capable of. The first of these is in Chapter 8, and the subject is Harriet; the second, Chapter 18, and the subject is Frank Churchill; the third, Chapter 33, the subject Jane Fairfax; and the last, Chapter 43, the subject Miss Bates. These scenes are debates between moral obstinacy and moral wisdom, and the first is slowly brought up to the proportion of the second. In the last scene, when Knightley takes Emma to task for her cruelty to Miss Bates, she fully recognizes and bitterly repents her fault. She *alters* at last: "could he *even* have seen into her heart," she thinks, "he would not, on this occasion, have found anything to reprove." Only then is she prepared to know that it is only Knightley that she can love, and with that the movement of awareness swells: "Every other part of her mind was disgusting." And then, before his declaration, the movement comes to rest:

> When it came to such a pitch as this, she was not able to refrain from a start, or a heavy sigh, or even from walking about the room for a few seconds; and the only source whence anything like consolation or composure could be drawn, was in the resolution of her own better conduct, and the hope that, however inferior in spirit and gaiety might be the following and every future winter of her life to the past, it would yet find her more rational, more acquainted with herself, and leave her less to regret when it were gone.

Thus we have a double movement in the architecture—the diminution of Emma in the social scene, her reduction to her proper place in the whole scale of value (which is her expiation), and the growth of Emma in the moral scheme (which is her enlargement). It is very beautiful. Now most of this we are never told, and of Emma's diminution, not at all. We are made to experience this double development through the movement of the plot itself. This fact calls attention to Jane Austen's method, and makes us ask what her reasons were for developing it. The method consists of an alteration of narration conducted almost always through the heroine's eyes, with dramatic scenes illustrative of the narrative material. There is almost no direct statement of the significance of the material, and there is a minimum of reported action. The significance of the material comes to us through two chief sources: the dramatized scene itself, and the play of irony through the narration. Of Jane Austen's skill in making scene speak, I will say nothing, except to point out our awareness of the significance of Emma's silence—she says not a word—in the scene in Chapter 12 where her sister is praising Jane Fairfax and explaining why Jane and Emma had always seemed to everyone to be perfectly suited for an equal friendship; and that later scene, in Chapter 21, where we are made so acutely aware of the presence of the others and their several emotions, as Miss Bates blunders along on the matter of how some people had mistakenly felt that Mr. Elton might have married a certain person—well, clearly, it is Miss Woodhouse herself, who is there, again stonily silent. Now just as the dramatic values of scene are left to speak for themselves, so the moral values are left, implicit *in* the scenes, not discussed through them.

Such a method, intermingling as it does dramatic scene with narrative observations of the heroine, requires from the author a constant irony that at all times transcends the ironic habit of mind of the heroine herself. Sometimes Jane Austen achieves this simply by seeming to accept the scene as the characters pretend that it was; as, for example, following on Emma's silence when Isabella praises Jane, the narrative proceeds: "This topic was discussed very happily, and others succeeded of similar moment, and passed away with similar harmony." Sometimes she achieves it through an unobtrusive verbal pointing, as: "Poor Mr. Woodhouse was silent from consternation; but everybody else had something to say; everybody was either surprised, or not surprised, and had some question to ask, or some comfort to offer." Could the triviality of the situation find a more effective underlining? On still other occasions, Jane Austen achieves this necessary irony simply by shifting her point of view a fraction away from the person who presumably holds it. This is shown nowhere more effectively than in the passage I have already cited, in which we begin with Emma's observation, then shift to that phrase, "the scale of vanity," which cannot possibly be hers, and then return at once to her.

> Emma perceived that her taste was not the only taste on which Mr. Weston depended, and felt that to be the favourite and intimate of a man who had so many intimates and confidantes, was not the very first distinction in the scale of vanity. She liked his open manners, but a little less of open-heartedness would have made him a higher character. General benevolence, but not general friendship, made a man what he ought to be. She could fancy such a man.

I am pressing this matter of the method of scene and the method of irony not only because it is through this method that the significance of the architectural structure of the work is brought home to us, that double movement I have described, but because it reveals an important fact about Jane Austen's relation to her audience, then and now, and because, unless we understand this relation, we cannot see as much as we should see in that thematic structure to which I will presently turn, or see at all that relationship of social and moral scale that is the heart of the book. Jane Austen was in an ambiguous situation in relation to her readers, a situation in which she was committed simultaneously to cherish and abominate her world. Within the framework of what is presumably a happy story, where everyone gets married off properly in the end, she must still make her comment, from her deepest moral evaluations, on the misery of this happiness. The texture of her style already has suggested that the world she pictures is hardly founded on the highest values. But that is not enough. She must besides develop a technique which could both reveal and conceal, that would give only as much as the reader wished to take. (That is why she can still be read in both the most frivolous and the most serious spirit.) Her problem—and perhaps this is the problem of every novelist of manners, at least if he is a satirist, who criticizes the society within which he yet wishes to remain and, indeed, whose best values are his own—her problem was to develop a novelistic technique that would at once conceal and reveal her strongest feelings, her basic observation of her heroine and her heroine's world, and that would express with sufficient clarity, if one looks at that technique closely, the ultimate values here involved.

For those who do not read while they run, the range of Jane Austen's irony, from the gentlest to the most corrosive, will suggest that she was perfectly able to see with absolute clarity the defects of the world she used. I will not trouble with the mild examples, but only with the gradation at the extreme:

> "It was a delightful visit—perfect, in being much too short." And she leaned back in the corner to indulge her murmurs, or to reason them away; probably a little of both—such being the commonest process of a not ill-disposed mind.

Surely a mind that throws out observations such as these is not an entirely well-disposed one. But to go on—

> "I am persuaded that you can be as insincere as your neighbours, when it is necessary."

Still further: Emma on Miss Bates:

> ". . . and nobody is afraid of her—that is a great charm."

Consider next the bitter violence of the verb, in that comment on boarding schools, where young women are *"screwed* out of health and into vanity." And come last to the extreme, an amazing irruption into this bland social surface of what has been called her "regulated hatred"—

> Miss Bates stood in the very worst predicament in the world for having much of the public favour; and she had no intellectual superiority to make atonement to herself, or *frighten those who might hate her into outward respect.*

Surely there is no failure here to judge the values of the social scale. We, in turn, are enabled to recognize these values, to judge the material, in other words, to place our evaluation upon it, not only by these oblique uses of irony, but by two other means: first, the dramatization of Emma's diminution in the community as we see more and more of it; second, by judging the real significance of her end.

The first, the dramatization of value, or moral scale, is achieved through what I have been calling "thematic structure," a structure that supports and unifies the architectural structure, the thematic integration of characters. Thematic structure exists, first of all, in the selection and disposal of characters around the heroine, and the relationship in moral traits which we are meant to observe between the heroine and the others. Emma is in many ways a charming heroine, bright and attractive and energetic, but Jane Austen never lets us forget that if she is superior to the Eltons, for example, the author (or, if you wish, Knightley) is superior to her. Emma's vanity is of no trivial kind. She is not "personally vain," Knightley tells us; "her vanity lies another way." It lies, for example, in her very charity. "Harriet would be loved as one to whom she could be useful. For Mrs. Weston there was nothing to be done; for Harriet everything." It is the vanity of giving, and brings to mind E. M. Forster's remark that, for many people indeed, it is better to receive than to give. It is the vanity, next, of power, for through the exercise of her charity, she succeeds in the imposition of her will. It is the vanity of abstract intellect. That Emma is capable of sound judgment is evident in her recognition of the real Elton even as she is urging him upon Harriet; it is evident again in her analysis of the real relation that probably pertains between Frank Churchill and his step-mother, even as she is herself about to fall in love with him. It is evident again in some of her self-studies, when, for example, after the Elton-Harriet fiasco, she resolves, in tears, that, since it is too late to be "simpleminded and ignorant," like Harriet, she will be at least "humble and discreet." In the next chapter she reveals herself incapable of acting on her own self-judgment, and Mr. Knightley again points up the discrepancy for us.

Emma: "He may have as strong a sense of what would be right as you can have, without being so equal, under particular circumstances, to act up to it."

Knightley: "Then it would not be so strong a sense. If it failed to produce equal exertion, it could not be an equal conviction."

Emma's intellectual judgments do not relate sufficiently to her conduct; in short, she is immoral. And we are not to be surprised when, rather early in the novel, she announces her own values: "those pleasantest feelings of our nature—eager curiosity and warm prepossession." The novel shows us the disastrous moral consequences of such insufficient standards.

This is Emma in her vanity. Let us observe, now, the kind of symbolic relationships in which her vanity is placed: First, of contrast, the contrast being with Miss Bates, and none in the novel more explicit:

Emma Woodhouse, handsome, clever and rich, with a comfortable home and happy disposition seemed to unite some of the best blessings of existence; and had lived nearly twenty-one years in the world with very little to distress her.

Ten pages later:

Miss Bates . . . a woman neither young, handsome, rich, nor married. Miss Bates stood in the very worst predicament in the world for having much of the public favour . . . and yet she was a happy woman.

That Emma unites with "some of the best blessings of existence," some of the worst possibilities of human society, is all too soon quite evident, but nowhere more evident than when she says of Miss Bates, "so silly, so satisfied, so smiling. . . ."

The second kind of symbolic relationship is not contrasting but comparative, and is evident in Harriet and Mrs. Elton. Of Harriet we need only point out that she is a silly but harmless girl educated by Emma into exactly the same sort of miscalculations, only to be abused by Emma for her folly. The comparison with Mrs. Elton is more fully developed: Emma's judgment on the Coles, who are struggling to rise above the stigma of trade, is exactly duplicated by Mrs. Elton's judgment on a family living near Maple Grove, called Tupman: ". . . very lately settled there, and encumbered with many low connections, but giving themselves immense airs, and expecting to be on a footing with the old established families. . . . They came from Birmingham. . . . One has not great hopes for Birmingham." The analogy with Emma is detailed: Mrs. Elton, like Emma, has an almost aggressive determination to "do" for other people, and to ride over their wishes; on the "scale of vanity," she is precisely where we begin with Emma: "a vain woman, extremely well satisfied with herself, and thinking much of her own importance; that she meant to shine and be very superior; but with manners which had been formed in a bad school; pert and familiar; that all her notions were drawn from one set of people, and one style of living; that, if not foolish, she was ignorant. . . ." And Emma makes this analysis: Emma, who herself is "amused by such a picture of another set of beings"—the Martins; who broods on the inferior society of Highbury; who makes one test only, the class test, except when she judges creations of her own, like Harriet, and even Harriet's high-born antecedents, as Emma fancies them, are apparent in her face; Emma, whose manners at one point, at any rate, are not merely pert and familiar, but coldly cruel, which even Mrs. Elton never is.

The third kind of symbolic relationship is the contrasting-comparative kind that is evident in Jane Fairfax. This is a crucial relationship in the thematic structure. We are told that they are alike in many ways—age, station, accomplishments. They are alike, furthermore, in that Emma *thinks* of Jane as complacent and reserved, whereas we *know* Emma to be both. Her reserve with Jane Fairfax is complete from the beginning, and stoney. Her complacency is nearly admitted: she "could not quarrel with herself"; "I cannot really change for the better." What a contrast, then, in actuality. Jane, whom we see through Emma's eyes as complacent, cold, tiresome, and in some ways rather disgusting, is, really, as much an antithesis to Emma as Miss Bates, and a much more difficult antithesis for Emma ever to deal with, to really admit. She is a woman capable of rash and improper behavior, a genuine commitment to passion, a woman torn by feeling, and feeling directed at an object not entirely worthy. She is hardly prudent. In short, she is quite different from what Emma sees, and quite different from what Emma is—all too complacent and perhaps really cold—and she stands in the novel as a kind of symbolic rebuke to Emma's emotional deficiencies, just as Knightley stands as a rebuke to her moral deficiencies. That Emma has emotional deficiencies is perhaps sufficiently apparent in her attachment to her father, and in her use of that attachment. Jane Fairfax is the blurred threat to Emma's complacency, the threat that Emma herself has never brought into focus in her own life and character, and at the end of the novel still has not, and so still has not achieved it for herself, or any radical reform of her qualities. They have merely moved on the scale.

So much for the heroine and the female characters. If we look now at the men, we can consider them as variations, or gradations, on the two traits, egotism and sociability, or "Candor," which is the positive virtue sought by Mr. Knightley. These characters run from Mr. Elton, the vain social snob, all egotism; through Frank Churchill, the man whose candor conceals a treacherous egotism; through Mr. Weston, so thoroughly amiable as to be nearly without judgment, and yet an egotist himself, the egotism of parenthood; to Mr. Knightley, who is the pivot, the middleman, moderate and sound, balanced and humane, neither an egotist nor a gadabout. From him, we shade off into his brother, the dour social egotist, to Mr. Woodhouse, the destructive (though comic, of course) malingering egotist.

Emma's relationships to them are revealing: she patronizes and then scorns Elton, of course; she "loves" Frank Churchill; she is fond of Weston; toward Knightley she holds a friendly animosity; she has tolerance for John; she adores her father. These relationships or emotional responses are Jane Austen's way of dramatizing Emma, of showing us her value. We see her through them, even as we are seeing them through her. It is a process of reciprocal illumination. And so in both the men and women, we come to see her above and beyond her presentation of herself, and at the same time, of course, we come to see the community at large through them—they represent Jane Austen's social "analysis," her breakdown of a community into its major traits, its two poles. If we study the bulking up at one end or the other of the scale, we can hardly conclude that the analysis is entirely friendly.

Thus we begin to see the real accomplishment of this objective technique, how deep it can go, how much subtle work it can do, how it defines its interpretations and analysis of the material, how it separates the material (which is trivial) and the effect (which is grave). Most remarkable, perhaps, how it holds together, makes one, the almost bland, comic tone, appropriate to the kind of society, too brittle for a severer tone, and a really bitter, sometimes acrid theme.

To define the theme completely we have to look closely at the real history of Emma. For all her superiority, Emma's values are really the values of the society she patronizes, and although she partially resolves her personal dilemma (hers really is a "profitable humiliation"), she *retains* those qualities: complacency, a kind of social cruelty, snobbery (Harriet must sink), and even greed (little Henry, who must inherit Donwell). Emma's self-study has always been partially mistaken; will it always be correct henceforth? Except for her final moment of awareness, her others have always exempted herself from judgment; can we believe that that is never to happen again? Does the final comment not come from Knightley, when Emma says, "Poor child! . . . what will become of her?" and he replies, "Nothing very bad. The fate of thousands. She will be disagreeable in infancy, and correct herself as she grows older. I am losing all my bitterness against spoilt children, my dearest Emma." The modification is minor. Does Jane Austen say less? Near the end she tells us:

Seldom, very seldom does complete truth belong to any human disclosure; seldom can it happen that something is not a little disguised, or a little mistaken; but where, as in this case, though the conduct is mistaken, the feelings are not, it may not be very material. Mr. Knightley could not impute to Emma a more relenting heart than she possessed or a heart more disposed to accept of his.

How severely does Jane Austen "chasten" Emma? "Do not physic them," says Isabella of her children; are we not left to "physic" Emma, to chasten her and her world together, with all necessary guidance from the style and the basic motives that analysis reveals in the work itself?

When we say that Emma is diminished at the end, as her world is, in a way, for us—the bright, easy society put in a real shade—we are really saying that she has been absorbed into that world, and has become inseparable from it. This observation suggests that we look again at the end of the novel. There is something apparently aimless and long-winded about it. Of *Pride and Prejudice* the author said, "The work is rather too light, bright, and sparkling; it wants shade; it wants to be stretched out here and there, with a long chapter of sense, if it could be had." In *Pride and Prejudice* and *Sense and Sensibility*, Jane Austen's heroines were superior to their world. Then, in *Mansfield Park*, her dull Fanny was completely submissive to the conventional pieties of this same world, somewhat white-washed. In *Emma*, Jane Austen seems to do what the remark about *Pride and Prejudice* aims at. Emma is finally nearly at the top of the moral scale, with Knightley, but the moral scale still has its relation to the social scale. The entire end of *Emma* is such a "shade" (even as it busily gets its characters happily married off, it is creating the shade, the moral shade, in which they will live) and the only justification for that long ending, once the Emma-Knightley arrangements have been made, is that it is needed there, as a kind of decrescendo into the social twilight that lies at the heart of the book. And so the end remains "open" —a question, in a way. It is Emma who at one point near the end exclaims, "I like everything decided and open"; everything here is at once decided and, in another sense, open.

How completely resolved are these strains of feeling? Emma and Jane, for example? Emma and Frank? How much "candor" is there? And how "happy" is this marriage, with Knightley having to move into old Mr. Woodhouse's establishment? Isn't it all, perhaps, a little superficial—not the writing but the self-avowals of the characters? A little perfunctory, as comedy may be, telling us thereby that this *is* comedy? One is reminded of the end of *Mansfield Park*:

I purposefully abstain from dates on this occasion, that everyone may be at liberty to fix their own, aware that the cure of unconquerable passions, and the transfer of unchanging attachments, must vary as to time in different people. I only entreat everybody to believe that exactly at the time when it was quite natural that it should be so, and not a week earlier, Edmund did cease to care about Miss Crawford, and became as anxious to marry Fanny as Fanny herself could desire.

Emma, then, is a complex study of self-importance and egotism and malice, as these are absorbed from a society whose morality and values are derived from the economics of class; and a study, further, in the mitigation of these traits, as the heroine comes into partial self-recognition, and at the same time sinks more completely into that society. Just as with Elizabeth Bennet, her individual being, as she has discovered it, will make that society better, but it will not make it different. This is moral realism, and it shows nowhere more clearly than in the very end, when the pilfering of a poultry house is given us as the qualification of "the perfect happiness of the union." The irresolution of the book gives it its richness, and its tautness and precision of structure and style give it its clarity. The two together make it great.

We have not said enough about Knightley, and if we are to see Jane Austen's values as they positively underlie her drama, we must look at him. Only a little pompous, he is the humanely civilized man; it is he whose judgments move beyond class; only he seems to breathe deeply; only he, certainly, ventures out impervious to that "weather" that is always keeping the others in a state of alarm and inside their littleness; it is he who wants complete candor and no mystery; it is he who makes Jane Austen's demand that awareness and conduct be brought into the relationship which is morality. In the only unclear speech in the novel (a haunting speech, in Chapter 33) he observes the separation: "her own comparative littleness in action, if not in consciousness." This is likewise Jane Austen's demand, although she lets Emma speak it: "faith engaged . . . and manners so *very* disengaged." But if there were a complete congruity between profession and conduct, there would be no comedy in the world; and Jane Austen wants comedy.

That comedy was sufficient for her purposes she certainly knew, just as she knew the size of the world her comedy measures. John Knightley says, "Business, you know, may bring money, but friendship hardly does." Frank Churchill says, "I would have given worlds—all the worlds one ever has to give—for another half-hour." And chiefly that phrase "a crowd in a little room," varied four times in a dozen lines:

> Emma demurred. "It would be a crowd—a sad crowd; and what could be worse than dancing without space to turn in? . . . Nothing can be further from pleasure than to be dancing in a crowd—and a crowd in a little room."
> "There is no denying it," he replied. "I agree with you exactly. A crowd in a little room—Miss Woodhouse, you have the art of giving pictures in a few words."

Miss Woodhouse has, in fact, given us a picture of Jane Austen's art. And it suggests that a narrow scene, like a good plot, is the occasion of pressure on the characters, to squeeze out their moral essence.

> Their being fixed, so absolutely fixed, in the same place, was bad for each, for all three. Not one of them had the power of removal, or of effecting any material change of society. They must encounter each other, and make the best of it.

And again:

> When she considered how peculiarly unlucky poor Mr. Elton was in being in the same room at once with the woman he had just married, the woman he had wanted to marry, and the woman whom he had been expected to marry, she must allow him to have the right to look as little wise . . . as could be.

The weather, so much a part of this book as of the others, is a double device for Jane Austen: it keeps these characters on the narrow social stage where they enact their moral drama; and it underlines, for us, the fact of their enclosure, their narrowness. It is only in Christmas weather, in the season of love, we are told, that everyone ventures boldly out. In Highbury, as elsewhere, it comes, alas, only once a year. We may conclude then, that the scene may be narrow, the action trivial, the feelings (from the point of view of other kinds of novels) thin—but the condition is the human condition, and the problem is nothing less than original sin—the dry destructiveness of egotism. And so the novel, if one is pressed to say so, is really about the narrowness of a wholly "secularized" life— in Eliot's meaning—no prevailing spiritual awareness, no prevailing emotional fullness, no prevailing gravity except in the author's construction, in the character she allows to speak for her, in her own oblique comment. We are reminded of all this in one of the few metaphorical outbursts of the novel. Jane Fairfax, resigning herself to the life of a schoolteacher, is thrown into the posture of religious renunciation:

> With the fortitude of a devoted novitiate, she had resolved at one-and-twenty to complete the sacrifice, and retire from all the pleasures of life, of rational intercourse, equal society, peace and hope, to penance and mortification for ever.

And her motive? The deplorable absence of a fortune!

Emma

by Arnold Kettle

"My strong point is those little things which are more important
than big ones, because they make up life. It seems that big ones do
not do that, and I daresay it is fortunate. . . ."

I. COMPTON-BURNETT: *A Family and a Fortune*

The subject of *Emma* is marriage. Put that way the statement seems
ludicrously inadequate, for *Emma*—we instinctively feel—is not about
anything that can be put into one word. And yet it is as well to begin
by insisting that this novel does have a subject. There is no longer,
especially after Mrs. Leavis's articles, any excuse for thinking of Jane
Austen as an untutored genius or even as a kind aunt with a flair for
telling stories that have somehow or other continued to charm. She was
a serious and conscious writer, absorbed in her art, wrestling with its
problems. Casting and re-casting her material, transferring whole novels
from letter to narrative form, storing her subject-matter with meticulous
economy, she had the great artist's concern with form and presentation.
There is nothing soft about her.[1]

Emma is about marriage. It begins with one marriage, that of Miss
Taylor, ends with three more and considers two others by the way. The
subject is marriage; but not marriage in the abstract. There is nothing
of the moral fable here; indeed it is impossible to conceive of the subject
except in its concrete expression, which is the plot. If, then, one insists
that the subject of *Emma* is important it is not in order to suggest that
the novel can be read in the terms of *Jonathan Wild,* but rather to
counteract the tendency to treat plot or story as self-sufficient. If it is not

"Emma." (Originally entitled "Jane Austen: *Emma* (1816).") From *An Introduction
to the English Novel* by Arnold Kettle, Volume I. Copyright 1951 by Hutchinson's
University Library; published in America by Torchbooks (Harper & Row, Inc.). Reprinted by permission of Hutchinson & Company, Ltd.

[1] Mrs. Leavis has emphasized, too, how strong a part in Jane Austen's novels is played
by her conscious war on the romance. She did to the romance of her day (whether the
domestic romance of Fanny Burney or the Gothic brand of Mrs. Radcliffe) what Cervantes had done in his. *Pride and Prejudice* is as much an anti-*Cecilia* as *Northanger
Abbey* is an anti-*Udolpho.*

quite adequate to say that *Emma* is about marriage it is also not adequate to say it is about Emma.

The concrete quality of the book, that is what has to be emphasized. We have no basic doubts about *Emma*. It is there, a living organism, and it survives in the vibrations of its own being. In *Clarissa* time and again our attention is shifted in a particular direction not because it *must* be so directed but because Richardson wishes to give his reader an "exquisite sensation"; in *Tom Jones* the happenings are too often contrived, so that we sense Fielding's presence behind the scenes, pulling a string. But *Emma* lives with the inevitable, interlocking logic of life itself; no part of it is separable from any other part. Even those episodes of the plot which seem at first mere contrivances to arouse a little suspense and keep the story going (such as the mystery of the pianoforte, Jane's letters at the post office, the confusion as to whether Harriet referred to Mr. Knightley or to Frank Churchill), such passages all have a more important purpose. They reveal character, or they fail to reveal it. This latter function is subtle and important.

Jane Austen, like Henry James, is fascinated by the complexities of personal relationships. What is a character *really* like? Is Frank Churchill *really* a bounder? She conveys the doubt, not in order to trick, but in order to deepen. The more complex characters in *Emma*, like people in life, reveal themselves gradually and not without surprises. Putting aside for the moment certain minor faults which we will return to, it is not an exaggeration to say that *Emma* is as convincing as our own lives and has the same kind of concreteness.

It is for this reason that the subject of *Emma*, its generalized significance, is not easily or even usefully abstracted from the story. Just as in real life "marriage" (except when we are considering it in a very theoretical and probably not very helpful way) is not a problem we abstract from the marriages we know, so marriage in *Emma* is thought of entirely in terms of actual and particular personal relationships. If we learn more about marriage in general from Jane Austen's novel it is because we have learned more—that is to say experienced more—about particular marriages. We do, in fact, in reading *Emma* thus enrich our experience. We become extremely closely involved in the world of Hartfield so that we experience the precise quality of, say, Mr. Woodhouse's affection for his daughters, or Harriet's embarrassment at meeting the Martins in the draper's. When Emma is rude to Miss Bates on Box Hill we *feel* the flush rise to Miss Bates's cheek.

The intensity of Jane Austen's novels is inseparable from their concreteness and this intensity must be stressed because it is so different from the charming and cosy qualities with which these novels are often associated. Reading *Emma* is a delightful experience but it is not a soothing one. On the contrary our faculties are aroused, we are called upon to participate in life with an awareness, a fineness of feeling, and a moral concern more intense than most of us normally bring to our everyday experiences. Everything matters in *Emma*. When Frank Churchill postpones his first visit to Randalls it matters less finely to Mr. Weston than to his wife, but the reader gauges precisely the difference in the two reactions and not only appreciates them both but makes a judgment about them. We do not "lose ourselves" in *Emma* unless we are the kind of people who lose ourselves in life. For all the closeness of our participation we remain independent.

Jane Austen does not demand (as Richardson tends to) that our subjective involvement should prejudice our objective judgment. On the contrary a valid objective judgment is made possible just because we have been so intimately involved in the actual experience. This seems to me a very valuable state of mind. How can we presume to pass judgment on the Emma Woodhouses of the world unless we have known them, and how can we valuably know them without bringing to bear our critical intelligence?

Because the critical intelligence is everywhere involved, because we are asked continuously, though not crudely, to judge what we are seeing, the prevailing interest in *Emma* is not one of mere "aesthetic" delight but a moral interest. And because Jane Austen is the least theoretical of novelists, the least interested in Life as opposed to living, her ability to involve us intensely in her scene and people is absolutely inseparable from her moral concern. The moral is never spread on top; it is bound up always in the quality of feeling evoked.

Even when a moral conclusion is stated explicitly, as Mr. Knightley states it after the Box Hill incident or while he reads Frank Churchill's letter of explanation, its force will depend not on its abstract "correctness" but on the emotional conviction it carries, involving of course our already acquired confidence in Mr. Knightley's judgment and character. Some of Mr. Knightley's remarks, out of their context, might seem quite intolerably sententious.

"My Emma, does not everything serve to prove more and more the beauty of truth and sincerity in all our dealings with one another?" (III, xv)

The sentiment, abstracted, might serve for the conclusion of one of Hannah More's moral tales. In fact, in the novel, it is a moment of great beauty, backed as it is (even out of context the "my Emma" may reveal something of the quality) by a depth of feeling totally convincing.

How does Jane Austen succeed in thus combining intensity with precision, emotional involvement with objective judgment? Part of the answer lies, I think, in her almost complete lack of idealism, the delicate and unpretentious materialism of her outlook. Her judgment is based never on some high-falutin irrelevancy but always on the actual facts and aspirations of her scene and people. The clarity of her social observation (the Highbury world is scrupulously seen and analysed down to the exact incomes of its inmates) is matched by the precision of her social judgments and all her judgments are, in the broadest sense, social. Human happiness not abstract principle is her concern. Such precision—it is both her incomparable strength and her ultimate limitation—is unimaginable except in an extraordinarily stable corner of society. The precision of her standards emerges in her style. Each word—"elegance," "humour," "temper," "ease"—has a precise unambiguous meaning based on a social usage at once subtle and stable. Emma is considering her first view of Mrs. Elton:

> She did not really like her. She would not be in a hurry to find fault, but she suspected that there was no elegance;—ease, but no elegance—she was almost sure that for a young woman, a stranger, a bride, there was too much ease. Her person was rather good; her face not unpretty; but neither feature, nor air, nor voice, nor manner, were elegant. Emma thought at least it would turn out so. (II, xiv)

The exquisite clarity, the sureness of touch, of Jane Austen's prose cannot be recaptured because in a different and quickly changing society the same sureness of values cannot exist.

But to emphasize the stability and, inevitably too, the narrowness of Jane Austen's society may lead us to a rather narrow and mechanical view of the novels. *Emma* is *not* a period-piece. It is *not* what is sometimes called a "comedy of manners." We read it not just to illuminate the past, but also the present. And we must here face in both its crudity and its importance the question: exactly what relevance and helpfulness does *Emma* have for us today? In what sense does a novel dealing (admittedly with great skill and realism) with a society and its standards dead and gone for ever have value in our very different world today? The question itself—stated in such terms—is not satisfactory. If *Emma* today captures our imagination and engages our sympathies (as in fact it does) then either it has some genuine value for us, or else there is something wrong with the way we give our sympathy, and our values are pretty useless.

Put this way, it is clear that anyone who enjoys *Emma* and then remarks "but of course it has no relevance today" is in fact debasing the novel, looking at it not as the living work of art which he has just enjoyed, but as something he does not even think it is—a mere dead picture of a past society. Such an attitude is fatal both to art and to life. The more helpful approach is to enquire why it is that this novel does in fact still have the power to move us today.

One has the space only to suggest one or two lines of consideration.

The question has, I hope, been partly answered already. An extension of human sympathy and understanding is never irrelevant and the world of *Emma* is not presented to us (at any rate in its detail) with complacency. Emma faced (I, xvi) with what she has done to Harriet, the whole humiliating horror of it, or Emma finding—the words are not minced—that, save for her feeling for Mr. Knightley, "every other part of her mind was disgusting" (III, xi): these are not insights calculated to decrease one's moral awareness. And in none of the issues of conduct arising in the novel is Jane Austen morally neutral. The intensity with which everything matters to us in *Emma* is the product of this lack of complacency, this passionate concern of Jane Austen for human values. Emma is the heroine of this novel only in the sense that she is its principal character and that it is through her consciousness that the situations are revealed; she is no heroine in the conventional sense. She is not merely spoilt and selfish, she is snobbish and proud, and her snobbery leads her to inflict suffering that might ruin happiness. She has, until her experience and her feeling for Mr. Knightley brings her to a fuller, more humane understanding, an attitude to marriage typical of the ruling class. She sees human relationships in terms of class snobbery and property qualifications: Harriet, for the sake of social position, she would cheerfully hand over to the wretched Elton and does in fact reduce to a humiliating misery; her chief concern about Mr. Knightley is that his estate should be preserved for little Henry. It is only through her own intimate experiences (which we share) that she comes to a more critical and more fully human view.

The question of Jane Fairfax is relevant here. Many readers find her and her relationship with Frank Churchill less than fully convincing. Does she quite bear the full weight of admiration which clearly we are supposed to feel for her? If she is indeed the person she is intended to be, would she love Frank Churchill? Has not Jane Austen here failed, perhaps, completely to reconcile the character she has created and the plot and pattern to which she is committed?

I think it is worth pausing for a moment on these criticisms, in order to consider not only their justice (which can be fairly objectively tested by careful reading) but their relevance. May we not here be slipping into the undisciplined habit of judging a novel according to rather vague criteria of "probability" or "character"? We all know the old lady who doesn't like *Wuthering Heights* because it's so improbable and the old gentleman who reads Trollope for the characters (not to mention the "Janeites" whose chief interest in *Emma* is to determine how many nursemaids Isabella Knightley brought with her to Hartfield); and we all know how unsatisfactory such criteria are when it comes to the point.

It is worth emphasizing, therefore, that a just criticism of Jane Fairfax has nothing to do with the question of whether we should like to meet her at dinner or even whether we think she acted rightly or wrongly. Jane Fairfax is a character in a novel. We know nothing of her except what we gather in the course of the novel. What we learn while we read (and we learn, of course, more than mere "facts"), is that, although unduly reserved (for reasons which when revealed make the fault pardonable) she is a young woman of singular refinement and "true elegance," a phrase carrying great significance ("elegance of mind" involves a genuine sensibility to human values as well as the more superficial refinements of polished manner). She is, moreover, especially singled out for commendation by Mr. Knightley (whose judgment is recommended as invariably sound) and warmly liked (e.g., the very, very earnest shake of the hand) by Emma herself.

Now the critical question is whether the reader can be convinced that this Jane Fairfax would in fact play her essential part in the novel and marry Frank Churchill, a young man whose total quality is a good deal less than admirable. Many readers are not convinced. Are they right?

I think they are not right. It is true that Jane Fairfax is—we have been convinced—as good as she is clever and as clever as she is beautiful. But it is also true that Jane Fairfax is an unprovided woman with no prospects in life beyond those of earning her living as governess at Mrs. Smallridge's (and how well the nature of that establishment has been revealed to us through Mrs. Elton!) and passing her hard-earned holidays with Miss Bates. The quality of Jane's reaction to such a future has been clearly indicated:

> "I am not at all afraid [she says to Mrs. Elton] of being long unemployed. There are places in town, offices, where enquiry would soon produce something—Offices for the sale—not quite of human flesh—but of human intellect."
>
> "Oh! my dear, human flesh! You quite shock me; if you mean a fling at the slave-trade I assure you Mr. Suckling was always rather a friend to the abolition."
>
> "I did not mean, I was not thinking of the slave-trade" replied Jane, "governess-trade, I assure you, was all that I had in view; widely different certainly as to the guilt of those who carry it on; but as to the greater misery of the victims, I do not know where it lies. . . ." (II, xvii)

It is her horror of this alternative (notice the extraordinary force of the word "offices"; the sentence is broken in the sense of degradation) that those who are unconvinced by Jane's decision to marry Frank Churchill have, I think, overlooked. Perhaps all this makes Jane Fairfax less "good" than Emma thought her; but it does not make her less convincing to us. On the contrary a good deal of the moral passion of the book, as of her other novels, does undoubtedly arise from Jane Austen's understanding of and feeling about the problems of women in her society. It is this realistic, unromantic, and indeed, by orthodox standards, subversive concern with the position of women that gives the tang and force to her consideration of marriage. Jane Fairfax's marriage has not, indeed, been made in heaven, and it is unlikely that Frank Churchill will turn out to be an ideal husband; but is that not precisely Jane Austen's point?

More vulnerable is the marrying-off of Harriet Smith and Robert Martin. Here it is not the probability that is to be questioned but the manner. The treatment is altogether too glib and the result is to weaken the pattern of the novel. Since the experiences of Emma—her blunders and romanticisms—are the core of the book, and what most intimately illuminate the theme of marriage, it is essential to Jane Austen's plan that these experiences should be in no way muffled or sentimentalized. We must feel the whole force of them. The marriage of Harriet is presented in a way which does, to some extent, sentimentalize. Emma is allowed too easy a way out of her problem and the emotional force of the situation is thereby weakened. The objection to too conventional a sense of happy ending is not that it is happy (we do not question that) but that it is conventional and so lulls our feelings into accepting it too easily.

Sufficient has perhaps been said to suggest that what gives *Emma* its power to move us is the realism and depth of feeling behind Jane Austen's attitudes. She examines with a scrupulous yet passionate and critical precision the actual problems of her world. That this world is narrow cannot be denied. How far its narrowness matters is an important question.

Its *smallness* does not matter at all. There is no means of measuring importance by size. What is valuable in a work of art is the depth and truth of the experience it communicates, and such qualities cannot be identified with the breadth of the panorama. We may find out more about life in a railway carriage between Crewe and Manchester than in making a tour round the world. A conversation between two women in the butcher's queue may tell us more about a world war than a volume of despatches from the front. And when Emma says to Mr. Knightley: "Nobody, who has not been in the interior of a family, can say what the difficulties of any individual of that family may be," she is dropping a valuable hint about Jane Austen's method. The silliest of all criticisms of Jane Austen is the one which blames her for not writing about the battle of Waterloo and the French Revolution. She wrote about what she understood and no artist can do more.

But did she understand enough? The question is not a silly one, for it must be recognized that her world was not merely small but narrow. Her novels are sometimes referred to as miniatures, but the analogy is not apt. We do not get from *Emma* a condensed and refined sense of a larger entity. Neither is it a symbolic work suggesting references far beyond its surface meaning. The limitations of the Hartfield world which are indeed those of Surrey in about 1814 are likely therefore to be reflected in the total impact of the novel.

The limitation and the narrowness of the Hartfield world is the limitation of class society. And the one important criticism of Jane Austen (we will suspend judgment for the moment on its truth) is that her vision is limited by her unquestioning acceptance of class society. That she did not write about the French Revolution or the Industrial Revolution is as irrelevant as that she did not write about the Holy Roman Empire; they were not her subjects. But Hartfield is her subject and no sensitive contemporary reader can fail to sense here an inadequacy (again, we will suspend judgment on its validity). It is necessary to insist, at this point, that the question at issue is not Jane Austen's failure to suggest a *solution* to the problem of class divisions but her apparent failure to notice the *existence* of the problem.

The values and standards of the Hartfield world are based on the assumption that it is right and proper for a minority of the community to live at the expense of the majority. No amount of sophistry can get away from this fact and to discuss the moral concern of Jane Austen without facing it would be hypocrisy. It is perfectly true that, within the assumptions of aristocratic society, the values recommended in *Emma* are sensitive enough. Snobbery, smugness, condescension, lack of consideration, unkindness of any description, are held up to our disdain. But the fundamental condescension, the basic unkindness which permits the sensitive values of *Emma* to be applicable only to one person in ten or twenty, is this not left unscathed? Is there not here a complacency which renders the hundred little incomplacencies almost irrelevant?

Now this charge, that the value of *Emma* is seriously limited by the class basis of Jane Austen's standards, cannot be ignored or written off as a nonliterary issue. If the basic interest of the novel is indeed a moral interest, and if in the course of it we are called upon to re-examine and pass judgment on various aspects of human behaviour, then it can scarcely be considered irrelevant to face the question that the standards we are called upon to admire may be inseparably linked with a particular form of social organization.

That the question is altogether irrelevant will be held, of course, by the steadily decreasing army of aesthetes. Those who try to divorce the values of art from those of life and consequently morality will not admit that the delight we find in reading *Emma* has in fact a moral basis. It is a position, I think, peculiarly hard to defend in the case of a Jane Austen novel, because of the obvious preoccupation of the novelist with social morality. If *Emma* is *not* concerned with the social values involved in and involving personal relationships (and especially marriage) it is difficult to imagine what it *is* about.

That the question though relevant is trivial will be held by those readers who consider class society either good or inevitable. Clearly, to those who think aristocracy today a morally defensible form of society, and are prepared to accept (with whatever modifications and protestations of innocence) the inevitability of a cultural *élite* whose superior standards depend on a privileged social position based on the exploitation of their inferiors, clearly such readers will not feel that Jane Austen's acceptance of class society weakens or limits her moral perspicacity. The suspicion that the true elegance which Emma so values could not exist in Hartfield without the condemnation to servility and poverty of hundreds of unnamed (though not necessarily unpitied) human beings will not trouble their minds as they admire the civilized sensibility of Jane Austen's social standards. The position of such readers cannot of course be objected to on logical grounds so long as all its implications are accepted.

At the other extreme of critical attitudes will be found those readers whose sense of the limitations of Jane Austen's social consciousness makes it impossible for them to value the book at all. How can I feel sympathy, such a reader will say, for characters whom I see to be, for all their charm and politeness, parasites and exploiters? How can I feel that the problems of such a society have a relevance to me? Now if art were a matter of abstract morality it would be impossible to argue against this puritan attitude; but in truth it misses the most essential thing of all about *Emma,* that it is a warm and living work of art. To reject *Emma* outright is to reject the humanity in *Emma,* either to dismiss the delight and involvement that we feel as we read it as an unfortunate aberration, or else to render ourselves immune to its humanity by imposing upon it an attitude narrower than itself.

More sophisticated than this philistine attitude to the problem is that which will hold that *Emma* does indeed reflect the class basis and limitations of Jane Austen's attitudes, but that this really does not matter very much or seriously affect its value. This is a view, plausible at first sight, held by a surprisingly large number of readers who want to have their novel and yet eat it. Yes indeed, such a reader will say, the moral basis of Jane Austen's novels is, for us, warped by her acceptance of class society; her standards obviously can't apply in a democratic society where the Emmas and Knightleys would have to work for their living like anyone else. But, after all, we must remember when Jane Austen was writing; we must approach the novels with sympathy in their historical context. Jane Austen, a genteel bourgeoise of the turn of the eighteenth century, could scarcely be expected to analyse class society in modern terms. We must make a certain allowance, reading the book with a willing suspension of our own ideas and prejudices.

This represents a view of literature which, behind an apparently historical approach, debases and nullifies the effects of art. It invites us to read *Emma* not as a living, vital novel, relevant to our own lives and problems, but as a dead historical "document." A work of art which has to be read in such a way is not a work of art. The very concept of "making allowances" of this sort for an artist is both insulting and mechanical. It has something of the puritan's contempt for those who have not seen the light, but it lacks the puritan's moral courage, for it is accompanied by a determination not to be done out of what cannot be approved. The final result is generally to come to terms with the aesthetes. For if *Emma* is morally undesirable and yet Art, then Art can have little to do with morality and some new, necessarily idealist, criteria must be found.

It is important, I believe, to realize the weakness of this pseudo-historical view of *Emma*. If, in whatever century she happened to live, Jane Austen were indeed nothing but a genteel bourgeoise "reflecting" the views of her day, she would not be a great artist and she could not have written *Emma*. The truth is that in so far as *Emma* does reveal her as a conventional member of her class, blindly accepting its position and ideology, the value of *Emma* is indeed limited, not just relatively, but objectively and always. But the truth is also that this is not the principal or most important revelation of *Emma*.

The limitation must not be ignored or glossed over. There can be no doubt that there *is* an inadequacy here, an element of complacency that does to some extent limit the value of *Emma*. The nature of the inadequacy is fairly illustrated by this description of Emma's visit, with Harriet, to a sick cottager:

> They were now approaching the cottage, and all idle topics were super-seded. Emma was very compassionate; and the distresses of the poor were as sure of relief from her personal attention and kindness, her counsel and her patience, as from her purse. She understood their ways, could allow for their ignorance and their temptations, had no romantic expectations of extraordinary virtue from those, for whom education had done so little, entered into their troubles with ready sympathy, and always gave her assistance with as much intelligence as good-will. In the present instance, it was sickness and poverty together which she came to visit; and after remaining there as long as she could give comfort or advice, she quitted the cottage with such an impression of the scene as made her say to Harriet, as they walked away——
> "These are the sights, Harriet, to do one good. How trifling they make every thing else appear!—I feel now as if I could think of nothing but these poor creatures all the rest of the day; and yet who can say how soon it may all vanish from my mind?"
> "Very true," said Harriet. "Poor creatures! one can think of nothing else."
> "And really, I do not think the impression will soon be over," said Emma,

as she crossed the low hedge and tottering doorstep which ended the narrow, slippery path through the cottage garden, and brought them into the
lane again. "I do not think it will," stopping to look once more at all
the outward wretchedness of the place, and recall the still greater within.

"Oh! dear, no," said her companion. They walked on. The lane made a
slight bend; and when that bend was passed, Mr. Elton was immediately
in sight; and so near as to give Emma time only to say farther,

"Ah! Harriet, here comes a very sudden trial of our stability in good
thoughts. Well, (smiling), I hope it may be allowed that if compassion has
produced exertion and relief to the sufferers, it has done all that is truly
important. If we feel for the wretched, enough to do all we can for them,
the rest is empty sympathy, only distressing to ourselves."

Harriet could just answer. "Oh! dear, yes," before the gentleman joined
them. (I, x)

Now there can be no doubt about the quality of the feeling here.
Harriet's silly responses underline most potently the doubt that Emma
herself feels as to the adequacy of her own actions. There can be no
point in this passage (for it has no inevitable bearing on the plot) save
to give a sense of the darker side of the moon, the aspect of Hartfield
that will not be dealt with. And it does indeed to a great extent answer
the doubt in the reader's mind that an essential side of the Hartfield
world is being conveniently ignored. But the doubt is not entirely
answered. After all, the important question is not whether Emma recognizes the existence of the poor at Hartfield, but whether she recognizes
that her own position depends on their existence. "Comfort or advice"
moreover remain the positives in Emma's attitudes and one's doubts as to
their sufficiency are in fact, like Emma's, swept away by the arrival of
Mr. Elton and the plot. The essential moral issue is shelved; and it is, in
general, the supreme merit of Jane Austen, that essential moral issues are
not shelved.

But that the inadequacy is not crippling the passage just quoted will
also suggest. That final remark of Emma's is very significant. The paren-
thesized "smiling" and the idiocy of Harriet's comment have the effect of
throwing into doubt the whole aristocratic philosophy that Emma is
expounding and that doubt, though it does not balance the shelving of
the problem, does at least extenuate it. We are not wholly lulled.

Against the element of complacency other forces, too, are at work.
We should not look merely to the few specific references to the poor to
confirm our sense that the inadequacies of Jane Austen's social philosophy are overtopped by other, more positive vibrations. Among these
positive forces are, as we have seen, her highly critical concern over the
fate of women in her society, a concern which involves a reconsideration
of its basic values. Positive also are her materialism and her unpreten-
tiousness. If aristocracy is implicitly defended it is at least on rational

grounds; no bogus philosophical sanctions are called in to preserve the *status quo* from reasonable examination. And no claim is made, explicit or implicit, that we are being presented with a revelation of a fundamental truth. Hartfield is offered to us as Hartfield, not as Life.

And this is ultimately, I think, the strength of *Emma*: this rejection of Life in favour of living, the actual, concrete problems of behaviour and sensibility in an actual, concrete society. It is Jane Austen's sensitive vitality, her genuine concern (based on so large an honesty) for human feelings in a concrete situation, that captures our imagination. It is this concern that gives her such delicate and precise insight into the problems of personal relationships (how will a group of individuals living together best get on, best find happiness?). And the concern does not stop at what, among the ruling class at Hartfield, is pleasant and easily solved.

It gives us glimpses of something Mr. Woodhouse never dreamed of—the world outside the Hartfield world and yet inseparably bound up with it: the world Jane Fairfax saw in her vision of offices and into which Harriet in spite of (no, *because of*) Emma's patronage, was so nearly plunged: the world for which Jane Austen had no answer. It is this vital and unsentimental concern which defeats, to such a very large extent, the limitations. So that when we think back on *Emma* we do not think principally of the narrow inadequacies of Hartfield society but of the delight we have known in growing more intimately and wisely sensitive to the way men and women in a particular, given situation, work out their problems of living.

Mansfield Park

by Lionel Trilling

Sooner or later, when we speak of Jane Austen, we speak of her irony, and it is better to speak of it sooner rather than later because nothing can so far mislead us about her work as a wrong understanding of this one aspect of it. Most people either value irony too much or fear it too much. This is true of their response to irony in its first simple meaning, that of a device of rhetoric by which we say one thing and intend its opposite, or intend more, or less, than we say. It is equally true of their response to irony in its derived meaning, the loose generalized sense in which we speak of irony as a quality of someone's mind, Montaigne's for example. Both the excessive valuation and the excessive fear of irony lead us to misconceive the part it can play in the intellectual and moral life. To Jane Austen, irony does not mean, as it means to many, a moral detachment or the tone of superiority that goes with moral detachment. Upon irony so conceived she has made her own judgment in the figure of Mr. Bennet of *Pride and Prejudice,* whose irony of moral detachment is shown to be the cause of his becoming a moral nonentity.

Jane Austen's irony is only secondarily a matter of tone. Primarily it is a method of comprehension. It perceives the world through an awareness of its contradictions, paradoxes, and anomalies. It is by no means detached. It is partisan with generosity of spirit—it is on the side of "life," of "affirmation." But it is preoccupied not only with the charm of the expansive virtues but also with the cost at which they are to be gained and exercised. This cost is regarded as being at once ridiculously high and perfectly fair. What we may call Jane Austen's first or basic irony is the recognition of the fact that spirit is not free, that it is conditioned, that it is limited by circumstance. This, as everyone knows from childhood on, is indeed an anomaly. Her next and consequent irony, has reference to the fact that only by reason of this anomaly does spirit have virtue and meaning.

"*Mansfield Park.*" From *The Opposing Self* (New York: Viking Press, 1955) by Lionel Trilling. Copyright © 1955 by Lionel Trilling. Reprinted by permission of The Viking Press.

In irony, even in the large derived sense of the word, there is a kind of malice. The ironist has the intention of practicing upon the misplaced confidence of the literal mind, of disappointing comfortable expectation. Jane Austen's malice of irony is directed not only upon certain of the characters of her novels but also upon the reader himself. We are quick, too quick, to understand that *Northanger Abbey* invites us into a snug conspiracy to disabuse the little heroine of the errors of her corrupted fancy—Catherine Morland, having become addicted to novels of terror, has accepted their inadmissible premise, she believes that life is violent and unpredictable. And that is exactly what life is shown to be by the events of the story: it is we who must be disabused of our belief that life is sane and orderly. The shock of our surprise at the disappointment of our settled views is of course the more startling because we believe that we have settled our views in conformity with the author's own. Just when we have concluded in *Sense and Sensibility* that we ought to prefer Elinor Dashwood's sense to Marianne Dashwood's sensibility, Elinor herself yearns toward the anarchic passionateness of sensibility. In *Emma* the heroine is made to stand at bay to our adverse judgment through virtually the whole novel, but we are never permitted to close in for the kill—some unnamed quality in the girl, some trait of vivacity or will, erects itself into a moral principle, or at least a vital principle, and frustrates our moral blood-lust.

This interference with our moral and intellectual comfort constitutes, as I say, a malice on the part of the author. And when we respond to Jane Austen with pleasure, we are likely to do so in part because we recognize in her work an analogue with the malice of the experienced universe, with the irony of circumstance, which is always disclosing more than we bargained for.

But there is one novel of Jane Austen's, *Mansfield Park*, in which the characteristic irony seems not to be at work. Indeed, one might say of this novel that it undertakes to discredit irony and to affirm literalness, that it demonstrates that there are no two ways about anything. And *Mansfield Park* is for this reason held by many to be the novel that is least representative of Jane Austen's peculiar attractiveness. For those who admire her it is likely to make an occasion for embarrassment. By the same token, it is the novel which the depreciators of Jane Austen may cite most tellingly in justification of their antagonism.

About this antagonism a word must be said. Few writers have been the object of an admiration so fervent as that which is given to Jane Austen. At the same time, she has been the object of great dislike. Lord David Cecil has said that the people who do not like Jane Austen are the kind of people "who do not like sunshine and unselfishness," and Dr. Chapman, the distinguished editor of Jane Austen's novels and letters, although dissenting from Lord David's opinion, has speculated that perhaps "a certain lack of charity" plays a part in the dislike. But Mark Twain, to take but one example, manifestly did not lack charity or dislike sunshine and unselfishness, and Mark Twain said of Jane Austen that she inspired in him an "animal repugnance." The personal intensity of both parties to the dispute will serve to suggest how momentous, how elemental, is the issue that Jane Austen presents.

The *animality* of Mark Twain's repugnance is probably to be taken as the male's revulsion from a society in which women seem to be at the center of interest and power, as a man's panic fear at a fictional world in which the masculine principle, although represented as admirable and necessary, is prescribed and controlled by a female mind. Professor Garrod, whose essay, "Jane Austen, A Depreciation,"* is a *summa* of all the reasons for disliking Jane Austen, expresses a repugnance which is very nearly as feral as Mark Twain's; he implies that a direct sexual insult is being offered to men by a woman author who "describes everything in the youth of women which does not matter" in such a way as to appeal to "that age in men when they have begun to ask themselves whether anything matters." The sexual protest is not only masculine— Charlotte Brontë despised Jane Austen for representing men and women as nothing but ladies and gentlemen.

The sexual objection to Jane Austen is a very common one, even when it is not made explicit. It is not valid, yet it ought to be taken seriously into account. But then there is Emerson with his characteristic sexual indifference, his striking lack of animality, and Emerson's objection to Jane Austen is quick and entire, is instinctual. He says that she is "sterile" and goes on to call her "vulgar." Emerson held this opinion out of his passion of concern for the liberty of the self and the autonomy of spirit, and his holding it must make us see that the sexual reason for disliking Jane Austen must be subsumed under another reason which is larger, and, actually, even more elemental: the fear of imposed constraint. Dr. Chapman says something of this sort when he speaks of "political prejudice" and "impatient idealism" as perhaps having something to do with the dislike of Jane Austen. But these phrases, apart from the fact that they prejudge the case, do not suggest the biological force of the resistance which certain temperaments offer to the idea of society as a limiting condition of the individual spirit.

Such temperaments are not likely to take Jane Austen's irony as a melioration of her particular idea of society. On the contrary, they are likely to suppose that irony is but the engaging manner by which she masks society's crude coercive power. And they can point to *Mansfield Park* to show what the social coercion is in all its literal truth, before irony has beglamoured us about it and induced us to be comfortable with it—here it is in all its negation, in all the force of its repressiveness.

* See note 2 to Introduction.—*Ed.*

Perhaps no other work of genius has ever spoken, or seemed to speak, so insistently for cautiousness and constraint, even for dullness. No other great novel has so anxiously asserted the need to find security, to establish, in fixity and enclosure, a refuge from the dangers of openness and chance.

There is scarcely one of our modern pieties that it does not offend. Despite our natural tendency to permit costume and manners to separate her world from ours, most readers have no great difficulty in realizing that all the other novels of Jane Austen are, in essential ways, of our modern time. This is the opinion of the many students with whom I have read the novels; not only do the young men controvert by their enthusiasm the judgment of Professor Garrod that Jane Austen appeals only to men of middle age, but they easily and naturally assume her to have a great deal to say to them about the modern personality. But *Mansfield Park* is the exception, and it is bitterly resented. It scandalizes the modern assumptions about social relations, about virtue, about religion, sex, and art. Most troubling of all is its preference for rest over motion. To deal with the world by condemning it, by withdrawing from it and shutting it out, by making oneself and one's mode and principles of life the very center of existence and to live the round of one's days in the stasis and peace thus contrived—this, in an earlier age, was one of the recognized strategies of life, but to us it seems not merely impracticable but almost wicked.

Yet *Mansfield Park* is a great novel, its greatness being commensurate with its power to offend.

Mansfield Park was published in 1814, only one year after the publication of *Pride and Prejudice*, and no small part of its interest derives from the fact that it seems to controvert everything that its predecessor tells us about life. One of the striking things about *Pride and Prejudice* is that it achieves a quality of transcendence through comedy. The comic mode typically insists upon the fact of human limitation, even of human littleness, but *Pride and Prejudice* makes comedy reverse itself and yield the implication of a divine enlargement. The novel celebrates the traits of spiritedness, vivacity, celerity, and lightness, and associates them with happiness and virtue. Its social doctrine is a generous one, asserting the right of at least the *good* individual to define himself according to his own essence. It is animated by an impulse to forgiveness. One understands very easily why many readers are moved to explain their pleasure in the book by reference to Mozart, especially *The Marriage of Figaro.*

Almost the opposite can be said of *Mansfield Park.* Its impulse is not to forgive but to condemn. Its praise is not for social freedom but for social stasis. It takes full notice of spiritedness, vivacity, celerity, and lightness, but only to reject them as having nothing to do with virtue and happiness, as being, indeed, deterrents to the good life.

Nobody, I believe, has ever found it possible to like the heroine of *Mansfield Park*. Fanny Price is overtly virtuous and consciously virtuous. Our modern literary feeling is very strong against people who, when they mean to be virtuous, believe they know how to reach their goal and do reach it. We think that virtue is not interesting, even that it is not really virtue, unless it manifests itself as a product of "grace" operating through a strong inclination to sin. Our favorite saint is likely to be Augustine; he is sweetened for us by his early transgressions. We cannot understand how any age could have been interested in Patient Griselda. We admire Milton only if we believe with Blake that he was of the Devil's party, of which we are fellow travelers; the paradox of the *felix culpa* and the "fortunate fall" appeals to us for other than theological reasons and serves to validate all sins and all falls, which we take to be the signs of life.

It does not reconcile us to the virtue of Fanny Price that it is rewarded by more than itself. The shade of Pamela hovers over her career. We take failure to be the mark of true virtue and we do not like it that, by reason of her virtue, the terrified little stranger in Mansfield Park grows up to be virtually its mistress.

Even more alienating is the state of the heroine's health. Fanny is in a debilitated condition through the greater part of the novel. At a certain point the author retrieves this situation and sees to it that Fanny becomes taller, prettier, and more energetic. But the first impression remains of a heroine who cannot cut a basket of roses without fatigue and headache.

Fanny's debility becomes the more striking when we consider that no quality of the heroine of *Pride and Prejudice* is more appealing than her physical energy. We think of Elizabeth Bennet as in physical movement; her love of dancing confirms our belief that she moves gracefully. It is characteristic of her to smile; she likes to tease; she loves to talk. She is remarkably responsive to all attractive men. And to outward seeming, Mary Crawford of *Mansfield Park* is another version of Elizabeth Bennet, and Mary Crawford is the antithesis of Fanny Price. The boldness with which the antithesis is contrived is typical of the uncompromising honesty of *Mansfield Park*. Mary Crawford is conceived—is calculated—to win the charmed admiration of almost any reader. She is all pungency and wit. Her mind is as lively and competent as her body; she can bring not only a horse but a conversation to the gallop. She is downright, open, intelligent, impatient. Irony is her natural mode, and we are drawn to think of her voice as being as nearly the author's own as Elizabeth Bennet's is. Yet in the end we are asked to believe that she is not to be admired, that her lively mind compounds, by very reason of its liveliness, with the world, the flesh, and the devil.

This strange, this almost perverse, rejection of Mary Crawford's vitality in favor of Fanny's debility lies at the very heart of the novel's intention.

"The divine," said T. E. Hulme in *Speculations*, "is not life at its intensest. It contains in a way an almost anti-vital element." Perhaps it cannot quite be said that "the divine" is the object of Fanny's soul, yet she is a Christian heroine. Hulme expresses with an air of discovery what was once taken for granted in Christian feeling. Fanny is one of the poor in spirit. It is not a condition of the soul to which we are nowadays sympathetic. We are likely to suppose that it masks hostility—many modern readers respond to Fanny by suspecting her. This is perhaps not unjustified, but as we try to understand what Jane Austen meant by the creation of such a heroine, we must have in mind the tradition which affirmed the peculiar sanctity of the sick, the weak, and the dying. The tradition perhaps came to an end for literature with the death of Milly Theale, the heroine of Henry James's *The Wings of the Dove*, but Dickens exemplifies its continuing appeal in the nineteenth century, and it was especially strong in the eighteenth century. Clarissa's sickness and death confirm her Christian virtue, and in Fielding's *Amelia*, the novel which may be said to bear the same relation to *Tom Jones* that *Mansfield Park* bears to *Pride and Prejudice*, the sign of the heroine's Christian authority is her loss of health and beauty.

Fanny is a Christian heroine: it is therefore not inappropriate that the issue between her and Mary Crawford should be concentrated in the debate over whether or not Edmund Bertram shall become a clergyman. We are not, however, from our reading of the novel, inclined to say more than that the debate is "not inappropriate"—it startles us to discover that ordination was what Jane Austen said her novel was to be "about." In the letter in which she tells of having received the first copies of *Pride and Prejudice*, and while she is still in high spirits over her achievement, she says, "Now I will try and write something else, and it shall be a complete change of subject—ordination." A novelist, of course, presents a new subject to himself, or to his friends, in all sorts of ways that are inadequate to his real intention as it eventually will disclose itself—the most unsympathetic reader of *Mansfield Park* would scarcely describe it as being about ordination. Yet the question of ordination is of essential importance to the novel.

It is not really a religious question, but, rather, a cultural question, having to do with the meaning and effect of a *profession*. Two senses of that word are in point here, the open avowal of principles and beliefs as well as a man's commitment to a particular kind of life work. It is the latter sense that engages us first. The argument between Fanny and Mary is over what will happen to Edmund as a person, as a *man*, if he chooses to become a clergyman. To Mary, every clergyman is the Mr. Collins of *Pride and Prejudice;* she thinks of ordination as a surrender of manhood. But Fanny sees the Church as a career that claims a man's best manly energies; her expressed view of the churchman's function is that which was to develop through the century, exemplified in, say, Thomas Arnold, who found the Church to be an adequate field for what he called his talents for command.

The matter of a man's profession was of peculiar importance to Jane Austen. It weighs heavily against Mr. Bennet that, his estate being entailed, he has made no effort to secure his family against his death, and by reason of his otiosity he is impotent to protect his family's good name from the consequences of Lydia's sexual escapade. He is represented as being not only less a man but also as less a gentleman than his brother-in-law Gardiner, who is in trade in London. Jane Austen's feelings about men in relation to their profession reach their highest intensity in *Persuasion*, in the great comic scene in which Sir Walter Elliot is flattered by Mrs. Clay's telling him that every profession puts its mark upon a man's face, and that a true gentleman will avoid this vulgar injury to his complexion. And in the same novel much is made of the professional pride of the Navy and the good effect it has upon the personal character.

In nineteenth century England the ideal of professional commitment inherits a large part of the moral prestige of the ideal of the gentleman. Such figures as the engineer Daniel Doyce of *Little Dorrit* or Dr. Lydgate of *Middlemarch* represent the developing belief that a man's moral life is bound up with his loyalty to the discipline of his calling. The concern with the profession was an aspect of the ethical concept which was prepotent in the spiritual life of England in the nineteenth century, the concept of duty. The Church, in its dominant form and characteristic virtue, was here quite at one with the tendency of secular feelings; its preoccupation may be said to have been less with the achievement of salvation than with the performance of duty.

The word grates upon our moral ear. We do what we should do, but we shrink from giving it the name of duty. "Cooperation," "social-mindedness," the "sense of the group," "class solidarity"—these locutions do not mean what duty means. They have been invented precisely for the purpose of describing right conduct in such a way as *not* to imply what duty implies—a self whose impulses and desires are very strong, and a willingness to subordinate these impulses and desires to the claim of some external nonpersonal good. The new locutions are meant to suggest that right action is typically to be performed without any pain to the self.

The men of the nineteenth century did not imagine this possibility. They thought that morality was terribly hard to achieve, at the cost of renunciation and sacrifice. We of our time often wonder what could have made the difficulty. We wonder, for example, why a man like Matthew Arnold felt it necessary to remind himself almost daily of duty, why he believed that the impulses must be "bridled" and "chained down," why he insisted on the "strain and labour and suffering" of the moral life. We are as much puzzled as touched by the tone in which F. W. H. Myers tells of walking with George Eliot in the Fellows' Garden at Trinity "on an evening of rainy May," and she, speaking of God, Immortality, and Duty, said how inconceivable was the first, how unbelievable the second, "yet how peremptory and absolute the third." "Never, perhaps, have sterner accents affirmed the sovereignty of impersonal and unrecompensing Law. I listened, and night fell; her grave majestic countenance turned towards me like a sybil's in the gloom; it was as though she withdrew from my grasp, one by one, the two scrolls of promise, and left me the third scroll only, awful with inevitable fate." [1]

The diminution of faith in the promise of religion accounts for much but not for all the concern with duty in nineteenth century England. It was not a crisis of religion that made Wordsworth the laureate of duty. What Wordsworth asks in his great poem "Resolution and Independence" is how the self, in its highest manifestation, in the Poet, can preserve itself from its own nature, from the very sensibility and volatility that define it, from its own potentiality of what Wordsworth calls with superb explicitness "despondency and madness." Something has attenuated the faith in the self of four years before, of "Tintern Abbey," the certitude that "Nature never did betray / The heart that loved her": a new Paraclete is needed and he comes in the shape of the Old Leech Gatherer, a man rocklike in endurance, rocklike in insensibility, annealed by a simple, rigorous religion, preserved in life and in virtue by the "anti-vital element" and transfigured by that element.

That the self may destroy the self by the very energies that define its being, that the self may be preserved by the negation of its own energies —this, whether or not we agree, makes a paradox, makes an irony, that catches our imagination. Much of the nineteenth century preoccupation

[1] But if we are puzzled by the tone of this, we cannot say that it is a tone inappropriate to its subject. The idea of duty was central in the English culture of the nineteenth century, and in general when Englishmen of the period speak about duty *in propria persona* they speak movingly. This makes it all the stranger that when they express the idea through a literary form they scarcely ever do so in an elevated manner. They seem to have thought of duty as an ideal to be associated in literature chiefly with domestic life or with dullness. As a consequence, everyone was delighted with the jig in *Ruddigore:* "For duty, duty must be done,/ The rule applies to everyone./ Unpleasant though that duty be,/ To shirk the task were fiddledeedee." It was left to foreigners to deal with the idea as if it were of *tragic* import. Melville in *Billy Budd* and Vigny in his military stories exploited the moral possibilities of the British naval tradition of Nelson and Collingwood which even Wordsworth had been able to represent only abstractly and moralistically in his "character" of the Happy Warrior; and Conrad is the first English novelist to make the idea of duty large and interesting. It is hard to believe that the moral idea which Emily Dickinson celebrates in her brilliant poem on Thermopylae and associates with high intelligence is the same idea that Tennyson celebrates in "The Charge of the Light Brigade" and associates with stupidity.

with duty was not a love of law for its own sake, but rather a concern with the hygiene of the self. If we are aware of this, we are prepared to take seriously an incident in *Mansfield Park* that on its face is perfectly absurd.

The great fuss that is made over the amateur theatricals can seem to us a mere travesty on virtue. And the more so because it is never made clear why it is so very wrong for young people in a dull country house to put on a play. The mystery deepens, as does our sense that *Mansfield Park* represents an unusual state of the author's mind, when we know that amateur theatricals were a favorite amusement in Jane Austen's home. The play is Kotzebue's *Lovers' Vows* and it deals with illicit love and a bastard, but Jane Austen, as her letters and novels clearly show, was not a prude. Some of the scenes of the play permit Maria Bertram and Henry Crawford to make love in public, but this is not said to be decisively objectionable. What is decisive is a traditional, almost primitive, feeling about dramatic impersonation. We know of this, of course, from Plato, and it is one of the points on which almost everyone feels superior to Plato, but it may have more basis in actuality than we commonly allow. It is the fear that the impersonation of a bad or inferior character will have a harmful effect upon the impersonator, that, indeed, the impersonation of any other self will diminish the integrity of the real self.

A right understanding of the seemingly absurd episode of the play must dispel any doubt of the largeness of the cultural significance of *Mansfield Park*. The American philosopher George Mead has observed that the "assumption of roles" was one of the most important elements of Romanticism. Mead conceived of impersonation as a new mode of thought appropriate to that new sense of the self which was Romanticism's characteristic achievement. It was, he said further, the self's method of defining itself. Involved as we all are in this mode of thought and in this method of self-definition, we are not likely to respond sympathetically to Jane Austen when she puts it under attack as being dangerous to the integrity of the self as a moral agent. Yet the testimony of John Keats stands in her support—in one of his most notable letters Keats says of the poet that, as poet, he cannot be a moral agent; he has no "character," no "self," no "identity"; he is concerned not with moral judgment but with "gusto," subordinating his own being to that of the objects of his creative regard. Wordsworth implies something of a related sort when he contrasts the poet's volatility of mood with the bulking permanence of identity of the Old Leech Gatherer. And of course not only the poet but the reader may be said to be involved in the problems of identity and of (in the literal sense) integrity. Literature offers the experience of the diversification of the self, and Jane Austen puts the question of literature at the moral center of her novel.

The massive ado that is organized about the amateur theatricals and the dangers of impersonation thus has a direct bearing upon the matter of Edmund Bertram's profession. The election of a profession is of course in a way the assumption of a role, but it is a permanent impersonation which makes virtually impossible the choice of another. It is a commitment which fixes the nature of the self.

The ado about the play extends its significance still further. It points, as it were, to a great and curious triumph of Jane Austen's art. The triumph consists in this—that although on a first reading of *Mansfield Park* Mary Crawford's speeches are all delightful, they diminish in charm as we read the novel a second time. We begin to hear something disagreeable in their intonation: it is the peculiarly modern bad quality which Jane Austen was the first to represent—insincerity. This is a trait very different from the *hypocrisy* of the earlier novelists. Mary Crawford's intention is not to deceive the world but to comfort herself; she impersonates the woman she thinks she ought to be. And as we become inured to the charm of her performance we see through the moral impersonation and are troubled that it should have been thought necessary. In Mary Crawford we have the first brilliant example of a distinctively modern type, the person who cultivates the *style* of sensitivity, virtue, and intelligence.

Henry Crawford has more sincerity than his sister, and the adverse judgment which the novel makes on him is therefore arrived at with greater difficulty. He is conscious of his charm, of the winningness of his personal style, which has in it—as he knows—a large element of *natural* goodness and generosity. He is no less conscious of his lack of weight and solidity; his intense courtship of Fanny is, we may say, his effort to add the gravity of principle to his merely natural goodness. He becomes, however, the prey to his own charm, and in his cold flirtation with Maria Bertram he is trapped by his impersonation of passion—his role requires that he carry Maria off from a dull marriage to a life of boring concupiscence. It is his sister's refusal to attach any moral importance to this event that is the final proof of her deficiency in seriousness. Our modern impulse to resist the condemnation of sexuality and of sexual liberty cannot properly come into play here, as at first we think it should. For it is not sexuality that is being condemned, but precisely that form of asexuality that incurred D. H. Lawrence's greatest scorn—that is, sexuality as a game, or as a drama, sexuality as an expression of mere will or mere personality, as a sign of power, or prestige, or autonomy: as, in short, an impersonation and an insincerity.

A passage in one of her letters of 1814, written while *Mansfield Park* was in composition, enforces upon us how personally Jane Austen was involved in the question of principle as against personality, of character as against style. A young man has been paying court to her niece Fanny

Knight, and the girl is troubled by, exactly, the effect of his principled-
ness on his style. Her aunt's comment is especially interesting because it
contains an avowal of sympathy with Evangelicism, an opinion which is
the reverse of that which she had expressed in a letter of 1809 and had
represented in *Pride and Prejudice,* yet the religious opinion is but
incidental to the affirmation that is being made of the moral advantage
of the profession of principle, whatever may be its effect on the personal
style.

> Mr. J. P.——has advantages which do not often meet in one person. His
> only fault indeed seems Modesty. If he were less modest, he would be more
> agreeable, speak louder & look Impudenter;—and is it not a fine Character
> of which Modesty is the only defect?—I have no doubt that he will get
> more lively & more like yourselves as he is more with you;—he will catch
> your ways if he belongs to you. And as to there being any objection from
> his *Goodness,* from the danger of his becoming even Evangelical, I cannot
> admit *that.* I am by no means convinced that we ought not all to be
> Evangelicals, & am at least persuaded that they who are so from Reason
> and Feeling, must be happiest & safest. Do not be frightened from the con-
> nection by your Brothers having most wit. Wisdom is better than Wit, &
> in the long run will certainly have the laugh on her side; & don't be fright-
> ened by the idea of his acting more strictly up to the precepts of the New
> Testament than others.

The great charm, the charming greatness, of *Pride and Prejudice* is
that it permits us to conceive of morality as style. The relation of
Elizabeth Bennet to Darcy is real, is intense, but it expresses itself as a
conflict and reconciliation of styles: a formal rhetoric, traditional and
rigorous, must find a way to accommodate a female vivacity, which in
turn must recognize the principled demands of the strict male syntax.
The high moral import of the novel lies in the fact that the union of
styles is accomplished without injury to either lover.

Jane Austen knew that *Pride and Prejudice* was a unique success and
she triumphed in it. Yet as she listens to her mother reading aloud from
the printed book, she becomes conscious of her dissatisfaction with one
element of the work. It is the element that is likely to delight us most,
the purity and absoluteness of its particular style.

> The work [she writes in a letter to her sister Cassandra] is rather too light,
> and bright, and sparkling; it wants to be stretched out here and there with
> a long chapter of sense, if it could be had; if not, of solemn specious non-
> sense, about something unconnected with the story; an essay on writing, a
> critique on Walter Scott, or the history of Buonaparté, or anything that
> would form a contrast, and bring the reader with increased delight to the
> playfulness and epigrammatism of the general style.

Her overt concern, of course, is for the increase of the effect of the "general style" itself, which she believes would have been heightened by contrast. But she has in mind something beyond this technical improvement—her sense that the novel is a genre that must not try for the shining outward perfection of style; that it must maintain a degree of roughness of texture, a certain hard literalness; that, for the sake of its moral life, it must violate its own beauty by incorporating some of the irreducible prosy actuality of the world. It is as if she were saying of *Pride and Prejudice* what Henry James says of one of the characters of his story "Crapy Cornelia": "Her grace of ease was perfect, but it was all grace of ease, not a single shred of it grace of uncertainty or of difficulty." [2]

Mansfield Park, we may conceive, was the effort to encompass the grace of uncertainty and difficulty. The idea of morality as achieved style, as grace of ease, is not likely ever to be relinquished, not merely because some writers will always assert it anew, but also because morality itself will always insist on it—at a certain point in its development, morality seeks to express its independence of the grinding necessity by which it is engendered, and to claim for itself the autonomy and gratuitousness of art. Yet the idea is one that may easily deteriorate or be perverted. Style, which expresses the innermost truth of any creation or action, can also hide the truth; it is in this sense of the word that we speak of "mere style." *Mansfield Park* proposes to use the possibility of this deception. If we perceive this, we cannot say that the novel is without irony—we must say, indeed, that its irony is more profound than that of any of Jane Austen's other novels. It is an irony directed against irony itself.

In the investigation of the question of character as against personality, of principle as against style and grace of ease as against grace of difficulty, it is an important consideration that the Crawfords are of London. Their

---

[2] This may be the place to remark that although the direct line of descent from Jane Austen to Henry James has often been noted, and although there can be no doubt of the lineage, James had a strange misconception of the nature of the art of his ancestress. "Jane Austen, with her light felicity," he says in *The Lesson of Balzac,* "leaves us hardly more curious of her process, or of the experience that fed it, than the brown thrush who tells his story from the garden bough." He says of her reputation that it is higher than her intrinsic interest and attributes it to "the body of publishers, editors, illustrators, producers of the present twaddle of magazines, who have found their 'dear,' our dear, everybody's dear, Jane so infinitely to their material purpose." An acid response to the "dear Jane" myth is always commendable, but it seems to have led James into a strange obtuseness: "The key to Jane Austen's fortune with posterity has been in part the extraordinary grace of her facility, in part of her unconsciousness. . . ." This failure of perception (and syntax) is followed by a long, ambiguous, and unfortunate metaphor of Jane Austen musing over her "work-basket, her tapestry flowers, in the spare, cool drawing room of other days." Jane Austen was, it need scarcely be said at this date, as little unconscious as James himself either in her intentions or (as the remarks about the style of *Pride and Prejudice* show) in her "process."

manner is the London manner, their style is the *chic* of the metropolis. The city bears the brunt of our modern uneasiness about our life. We think of it as being the scene and the cause of the loss of the simple integrity of the spirit—in our dreams of our right true selves we live in the country. This common mode of criticism of our culture is likely to express not merely our dissatisfaction with our particular cultural situation but our dislike of culture itself, or of any culture that is not a folk culture, that is marked by the conflict of interests and the proliferation and conflict of ideas. Yet the revulsion from the metropolis cannot be regarded merely with skepticism; it plays too large and serious a part in our literature to be thought of as nothing but a sentimentality.

To the style of London Sir Thomas Bertram is the principled antagonist. The real reason for not giving the play, as everyone knows, is that Sir Thomas would not permit it were he at home; everyone knows that a sin is being committed against the absent father. And Sir Thomas, when he returns before his expected time, confirms their consciousness of sin. It is he who identifies the objection to the theatricals as being specifically that of impersonation. His own self is an integer and he instinctively resists the diversification of the self that is implied by the assumption of roles. It is he, in his entire identification with his status and tradition, who makes of Mansfield Park the citadel it is—it exists to front life and to repel life's mutabilities, like the Peele Castle of Wordsworth's "Elegiac Verses," of which it is said that it is "cased in the unfeeling armor of old time." In this phrase Wordsworth figures in a very precise way the Stoic doctrine of *apatheia,* the principled refusal to experience more emotion than is forced upon one, the rejection of sensibility as a danger to the integrity of the self.

Mansfield stands not only against London but also against what is implied by Portsmouth on Fanny's visit to her family there. Fanny's mother, Lady Bertram's sister, had made an unprosperous marriage, and the Bertrams' minimal effort to assist her with the burdens of a large family had been the occasion of Fanny's coming to live at Mansfield nine years before. Her return to take her place in a home not of actual poverty but of respectable sordidness makes one of the most engaging episodes of the novel, despite our impulse to feel that it ought to seem the most objectionable. We think we ought not be sympathetic with Fanny as, to her slow dismay, she understands that she cannot be happy with her own, her natural, family. She is made miserable by the lack of cleanliness and quiet, of civility and order. We jib at this, we remind ourselves that for the seemliness that does indeed sustain the soul, men too often sell their souls, that warmth and simplicity of feeling may go with indifference to disorder. But if we have the most elementary honesty, we feel with Fanny the genuine pain not merely of the half-clean and the scarcely tidy, of confusion and intrusion, but also of the vulgarity that thrives in these surroundings. It is beyond human ingenuity to define what we mean by vulgarity, but in Jane Austen's novels vulgarity has these elements: smallness of mind, insufficiency of awareness, assertive self-esteem, the wish to devalue, especially to devalue the human worth of other people. That Fanny's family should have forgotten her during her long absence was perhaps inevitable; it is a vulgarity that they have no curiosity about her and no desire to revive the connection, and this indifference is represented as being of a piece with the general indecorum of their lives. We do not blame Fanny when she remembers that in her foster father's house there are many rooms, that hers, although it was small and for years it had been cold, had always been clean and private, that now, although she had once been snubbed and slighted at Mansfield, she is the daughter of Sir Thomas's stern heart.

Of all the fathers of Jane Austen's novels, Sir Thomas is the only one to whom admiration is given. Fanny's real father, Lieutenant Price of the Marines, is shallow and vulgar. The fathers of the heroines of *Pride and Prejudice, Emma,* and *Persuasion,* all lack principle and fortitude; they are corrupted by their belief in their delicate vulnerability—they lack *apatheia.* Yet Sir Thomas is a father, and a father is as little safe from Jane Austen's judgment as he is from Shelley's. Jane Austen's masculine ideal is exemplified by husbands, by Darcy, Knightley, and Wentworth, in whom principle and duty consort with a ready and tender understanding. Sir Thomas's faults are dealt with explicitly—if he learns to cherish Fanny as the daughter of his heart, he betrays the daughters of his blood. Maria's sin and her sister Julia's bad disposition are blamed directly upon his lack of intelligence and sensibility. His principled submission to convention had issued in mere worldliness—he had not seen to it that "principle, active principle" should have its place in the rearing of his daughters, had not given then that "sense of duty which alone can suffice" to govern inclination and temper. He knew of no other way to counteract the low worldly flattery of their Aunt Norris than by the show of that sternness which had alienated them from him. He has allowed Mrs. Norris, the corrupter of his daughters and the persecutor of Fanny, to establish herself in the governance of his home; "she seemed part of himself."

So that Mansfield is governed by an authority all too fallible. Yet Fanny thinks of all that comes "within the view and patronage of Mansfield Park" as "dear to her heart and thoroughly perfect in her eyes." The judgment is not ironical. For the author as well as for the heroine, Mansfield Park is the good place—it is The Great Good Place. It is the house "where all's accustomed, ceremonious," of Yeats's "Prayer for His Daughter"—

> How but in custom and ceremony
> Are innocence and beauty born?

Yet Fanny's loving praise of Mansfield, which makes the novel's last word, does glance at ironies and encompasses ironies. Of these ironies the chief is that Lady Bertram is part of the perfection. All of Mansfield's life makes reference and obeisance to Sir Thomas's wife, who is gentle and without spite, but mindless and moveless, concerned with nothing but the indulgence of her mild, inexorable wants. Middle-aged, stupid, maternal persons are favorite butts for Jane Austen, but although Lady Bertram is teased, she is loved. Sir Thomas's authority must be qualified and tutored by the principled intelligence, the religious intelligence— Fanny's, in effect—but Lady Bertram is permitted to live unregenerate her life of cushioned ease.

I am never quite able to resist the notion that in her attitude to Lady Bertram Jane Austen is teasing herself, that she is turning her irony upon her own fantasy of ideal existence as it presented itself to her at this time. It is scarcely possible to observe how *Mansfield Park* differs from her work that had gone before and from her work that was to come after without supposing that the difference points to a crisis in the author's spiritual life. In that crisis fatigue plays a great part—we are drawn to believe that for the moment she wants to withdraw from the exigent energies of her actual self, that she claims in fancy the right to be rich and fat and smooth and dull like Lady Bertram, to sit on a cushion, to be a creature of habit and an object of ritual deference, not to be conscious, especially not to be conscious of herself. Lady Bertram is, we may imagine, her mocking representation of her wish to escape from the requirements of personality.

It was Jane Austen who first represented the specifically modern personality and the culture in which it had its being. Never before had the moral life been shown as she shows it to be, never before had it been conceived to be so complex and difficult and exhausting. Hegel speaks of the "secularization of spirituality" as a prime characteristic of the modern epoch, and Jane Austen is the first to tell us what this involves. She is the first novelist to represent society, the general culture, as playing a part in the moral life, generating the concepts of "sincerity" and "vulgarity" which no earlier time would have understood the meaning of, and which for us are so subtle that they defy definition, and so powerful that none can escape their sovereignty. She is the first to be aware of the Terror which rules our moral situation, the ubiquitous anonymous judgment to which we respond, the necessity we feel to demonstrate the purity of our secular spirituality, whose dark and dubious places are more numerous and obscure than those of religious spirituality, to put our lives and styles to the question, making sure that not only in deeds but in *décor* they exhibit the signs of our belonging to the number of the secular-spiritual elect.

She herself is an agent of the Terror—we learn from her what our lives should be and by what subtle and fierce criteria they will be judged, and how to pass upon the lives of our friends and fellows. Once we have comprehended her mode of judgment, the moral and spiritual lessons of contemporary literature are easy—the metaphysics of "sincerity" and "vulgarity" once mastered, the modern teachers, Lawrence and Joyce, Yeats and Eliot, Proust and Gide, have but little to add save in the way of contemporary and abstruse examples.

To what extremes the Terror can go she herself has made all too clear in the notorious passage in *Persuasion* in which she comments on Mrs. Musgrove's "large, fat sighings" over her dead scapegrace son. "Personal size and mental sorrow have certainly no necessary proportions," she says. "A large bulky figure has as good a right to be in deep affliction as the most graceful set of limbs in the world. But fair or not fair, there are unbecoming conjunctions, which reason will patronize in vain—which taste cannot tolerate, which ridicule will seize." We feel this to be unconscionable, and Henry James and E. M. Forster will find occasion to warn us that it is one of the signs of the death of the heart to regard a human being as an object of greater or less *vertu;* in fairness to Jane Austen we must remember that the passage occurs in the very novel which deals mercilessly with Sir Walter Elliot for making just this illegitimate application of taste to life. But although this aesthetic-spiritual snobbery is for Jane Austen a unique lapse, it is an extension, an extravagance of her characteristic mode of judgment, and it leads us to see what is implied by the "secularization of spirituality," which requires of us that we judge not merely the moral act itself but also, and even more searchingly, the quality of the agent. This is what Hegel has in mind when he is at such pains to make his distinction between character and personality and to show how the development of the idea of personality is one of the elements of the secularization of spirituality. Dewey followed Hegel in this when, in his *Ethics,* he said that moral choice is not really dictated by the principle or the maximum that is applicable to the situation but rather by the "kind of selfhood" one wishes to "assume." And Nietzsche's conception of the Third Morality, which takes cognizance of the *real*—that is, the unconscious—intention of the agent, is the terrible instrument of criticism of this new development of the moral life. We are likely to feel that this placing of the personality, of the quality of being, at the center of the moral life is a chief glory of spirit in its modern manifestation, and when we take pleasure in Jane Austen we are responding to her primacy and brilliance in the exercise of this new mode of judgment. Yet we at times become aware of the terrible strain it imposes upon us, of the exhausting effort which the concept of personality requires us to make and of the pain of exacerbated sensitivity to others, leading to the *disgust* which is endemic in our culture.

Jane Austen's primacy in representing this mutation in the life of the spirit constitutes a large part of her claim to greatness. But in her representation of the modern situation *Mansfield Park* has a special place. It imagines the self safe from the Terror of secularized spirituality. In the person of Lady Bertram it affirms, with all due irony, the bliss of being able to remain unconscious of the demands of personality (it is a bliss which is a kind of virtue, for one way of being solid, simple, and sincere is to be a vegetable). It shuts out the world and the judgment of the world. The sanctions upon which it relies are not those of culture, of quality of being, of personality, but precisely those which the new conception of the moral life minimizes, the sanctions of principle, and it discovers in principle the path to the wholeness of the self which is peace. When we have exhausted our anger at the offense which *Mansfield Park* offers to our conscious pieties, we find it possible to perceive how intimately it speaks to our secret inexpressible hopes.

What Became of Jane Austen?
[Mansfield Park]

by Kingsley Amis

There is something to be said for the view, held by rational critics as well as by mere going-through-the-motions appreciators, that *Mansfield Park* is the best of Jane Austen's works. Although there is some loss of high spirits, that invigorating coldness prevails, so that we can believe at times that we are reading an eighteenth century novel, and the dialogue reaches new heights of flexibility and awareness, so much so that there are some distinct anticipations of the modern novel. Further, we have in Mrs. Norris the most hauntingly horrible of the author's horrible characters, and in Sir Thomas Bertram the most fully and firmly drawn and— but for his final obduracy towards his elder daughter—most sympathetic of her patriarchs. And negatively, it might be added, there is less concern here with "the amorous effects of 'brass' " (in Mr. Auden's phrase), with the minutiae of social obligation, with distinctions between a Tweedledum labelled "well-bred" and a Tweedledee labelled "coarse"— with some of the things, in fact, which render parts of Jane Austen's other work distasteful.

Correspondingly, however, defects which are incidental elsewhere become radical in *Mansfield Park*. Not even *Pride and Prejudice*, which plainly foreshadows much of the Henry Crawford theme in the later book, exhibits as glaringly the author's inclination to take a long time over what is of minor importance and a short time over what is major. Nor does *Persuasion*, despite the sneering vulgarity with which the character of Mrs. Clay is treated, embody to any comparable degree the Austen habit of censoriousness where there ought to be indulgence and indulgence where there ought to be censure. These are patently moral "oughts," and it is by moral rather than aesthetic standards that *Mansfield Park*, especially, is defective. Although it never holds up the admirable as vicious, it continually and essentially holds up the vicious as

"What Became of Jane Austen? [Mansfield Park]" by Kingsley Amis. From *The Spectator*, No. 6745 (October 4, 1957), pp. 339-340. Copyright © 1957 by *The Spectator*. Reprinted by permission of the author and the editor of *The Spectator*.

admirable, an inversion rendered all the more insidious by being associated with such dash and skill, and all the more repugnant by the co-presence of a moralistic fervour which verges at times on the evangelical.

It must be said at once that the book succeeds brilliantly whenever it aims to hold up viciousness of character as vicious. Mrs. Norris is very fully visualised in domestic and social terms, but these are the lineaments of a moral repulsiveness, and it is a superb if unintentional stroke of moral irony whereby she alone shows charity towards the disgraced and excommunicated Maria. Sir Thomas, again, represents an essay, carried out with scrupulous justice, on the case of the humane and high-principled man whose defects of egotism and a kind of laziness (to be seen running riot in the character of his wife) betray him into inhumanity and are shown as instrumental in the disasters visited upon his daughters. More important still, the unworthiness of Henry and Mary Crawford is allowed to emerge with an effect of inevitability that is only heightened by the author's freedom, almost audacity, in stressing their sprightliness and even their considerable share of right feeling. This is an achievement which changes in ethical outlook have left undimmed and which testifies to a unique and enviable moral poise.

All these, however, are relative triumphs. The characters mentioned, especially the Crawfords, exist less in their own right than in order to show up by contrast the virtues of the central pair, not only in the status of persons but as embodiments of rival ideologies and ways of life. In both capacities the hero and heroine are deficient. The fact that as social beings they are inferior to the Crawfords, that Henry and Mary are good fun and the other two aren't, is a very large part of the author's theme and is perfectly acceptable, even though this particular disparity sometimes goes too far for comfort and further, one cannot help feeling, than can have been intended: to invite Mr. and Mrs. Edmund Bertram round for the evening would not be lightly undertaken. More basically than this, Edmund and Fanny are both morally detestable and the endorsement of their feelings and behaviour by the author—an endorsement only withdrawn on certain easily recognisable occasions—makes *Mansfield Park* an immoral book. Let us consider first the less heinous of the two offenders.

Edmund's kindness to Fanny entitles him to initial respect, and the bantering form it occasionally takes recalls his far livelier forerunner, Henry Tilney of *Northanger Abbey*. But it is not long before Edmund is shocked by Mary Crawford's complaint—in company, too—that her uncle's rather ill-judged alterations to a cottage of his resulted in the garden being messed up for some time. Soon afterwards he conducts, with the untiringly sycophantic Fanny, a post-mortem on this affront to his "sense of propriety." This readiness to be shocked, in itself shocking, is not in evidence when, a few chapters later, the pair of them launch into a canting pietistic tirade against Mary's brother-in-law in her presence. Nor does the vaunted sense of propriety exclude boorishness—in reply, for instance, to a perfectly amiable suggestion from Henry Crawford about possible improvements to the Parsonage. But it is his objections to the proposed private theatricals that finally establish Edmund as repulsive, and are thus worth setting out in some detail.

Any such amusement, he considers, is "open to some objections"—though without divulging these—and in this case "want of feeling" would be involved, because Sir Thomas is at sea and might get drowned round about now. (The reasonable argument, that Sir Thomas would object to his house being disordered—as in the event he does—is not stressed.) It further transpires that the play proposed, *Lovers' Vows,* is so vicious that merely to rehearse it "must do away all restraints." Such scruples, as Mrs. Q. D. Leavis notes in her Introduction to the latest reprint of the novel, are "well grounded in conventional notions of decorum." But we are right to expect from Edmund something more intelligent, more liberal, more manly than that, and a cursory reading will show that *Lovers' Vows* is in fact innocuous rubbish. This being so, his eventual reluctant consent to participate, which we are invited to see as the tragic overthrow of a noble mind worked on by Mary Crawford, becomes a squalid and ridiculous belly-flop, and his consequent humiliation is deserved in two senses, since it is earned—can we really be reading Jane Austen?—not by being too priggish, but by not being priggish enough.

If Edmund's notions and feelings are vitiated by a narrow and unreflecting pomposity, Fanny's are made odious by a self-regard utterly unredeemed by any humour—is this still Jane Austen?—or even lightness. She is mortified by being excluded—at her own obstinate insistence—from the theatricals. She pities herself and does others the kindness of hoping that they will never know how much she deserves their pity. She feels that Henry's addresses involve "treating her improperly and unworthily, and in such a way as she had not deserved." She indulges in righteous anger a good deal, especially when her own interests are threatened. She is disinclined to force herself to be civil to those—a numerous company—whose superior she thinks herself to be; such people she regards with unflinching censoriousness. She is ashamed of her own home in Portsmouth, where there is much "error" and she finds "everybody underbred," and how relieved she is when the "horrible evil" of Henry lunching there is averted. Significantly, the climax of her objections to her mother is that Mrs. Price was too busy to take much notice of Miss Price from Mansfield Park. And, in the closing stages, her "horror" at the wretched Maria's elopement is such as to exclude pity in any word or thought.

This indictment could be greatly extended, notably in the direction of the "moral concern" Fanny feels at Mary's power over Edmund. The tendency of all this can perhaps be fixed by pointing out that the character of Fanny lacks self-knowledge, generosity, and humility, the three "less common acquirements" which her girl cousins are, near the outset, stated to lack and which, by implication, are to be demonstrated as existing in her. Instead it is a monster of complacency and pride who, under a cloak of cringing self-abasement, dominates and gives meaning to the novel. What became of that Jane Austen (if she ever existed) who set out bravely to correct conventional notions of the desirable and virtuous? From being their critic (if she ever was) she became their slave. That is another way of saying that her judgment and her moral sense were corrupted. *Mansfield Park* is the witness of that corruption.

Persuasion

by Andrew H. Wright

I. *Anne Elliot*

"There are those," Louis Kronenberger reminds us, "who think Jane Austen tea-tablish, as there are those who think that Mozart tinkles." [1] "Those" have never read *Persuasion,* a sad love story with a happy ending. Here, more clearly and more sweetly than in any of the other novels, is exposed the conflict between two schemes of values: those of prudence, and those of love. Anne Elliot contains both and the result is a contradiction which causes nearly a decade of unhappiness to her; her reconciliation with Captain Wentworth stems not from the resolution of these opposites, but from a series of fortuitous circumstances which makes the match possible after all. Never, even at the end of the book, can she abandon her commitment to the prudential values, even when she is happily betrothed to Captain Wentworth. Yet she is a complete, a fully human, heroine. John Bailey writes: "There are few heroines in fiction whom we love so much, feel for so much, as we love and feel for Anne Elliot." [2]

Anne Elliot is twenty-seven years old when the book opens and "with an elegance of mind and sweetness of character, which must have placed her high with any people of real understanding, was nobody with either father or sister: her word had no weight; her convenience was always to give way;—she was only Anne." [3] At first we see her as the only sensible member of her family, advising a programme of retrenchment which will permit the Elliots to continue at Kellynch Hall, despite financial difficulties—but strenuously opposed by her father, who then takes his lawyer's advice to let Kellynch and move to Bath. It is only when the estate is leased, to an Admiral Croft and his wife, that we learn of Anne's

---

[1] In his introduction to the Harper's Modern Classics edition of *Pride and Prejudice,* New York, 1950, p. xi.

[2] *Introductions to Jane Austen,* London, 1931, p. 94.

[3] *Persuasion,* p. 5.

other dimension: for Mrs. Croft is the sister of a Frederick Wentworth, who:

> had come into Somersetshire, in the summer of 1806 [when Anne was nineteen]; and having no parent living, found a home for half a year, at Monkford. He was, at that time, a remarkably fine young man, with a great deal of intelligence, spirit and brilliancy; and Anne an extremely pretty girl, with gentleness, modesty, taste, and feeling.—Half the sum of attraction, on either side, might have been enough, for he had nothing to do, and she had hardly any body to love; but the encounter of such lavish recommendations could not fail. They were gradually acquainted, and when acquainted, rapidly and deeply in love. It would be difficult to say which had seen highest perfection in the other, or which had been the happiest; she, in receiving his declarations and proposals, or he in having them accepted.[4]

But Sir Walter and Lady Russell both disapproved the match: Commander Wentworth was young, not rich, and in "a most uncertain profession": the Navy. Though he was confident, though he was brilliant, Lady Russell "deprecated the connexion in every light"; and Anne was "persuaded to believe the engagement a wrong thing—indiscreet, improper, hardly capable of success, and not deserving it." [5] This was the beginning, though not the end, of Anne Elliot's difficulty. She has never been able to forget Frederick Wentworth—nor could her prudence dictate a marriage to Charles Musgrove when she was twenty-two—three years later. Now, at twenty-seven, she is no more able to forget her first attachment.

Luckily, she stays behind at Uppercross Cottage with her sister Mary Musgrove and family, when Sir Walter and Elizabeth (accompanied by the egregious Mrs. Clay) go to Bath. And Frederick Wentworth does come to Kellynch Hall to visit the Crofts: but, having felt himself misused by Anne eight years before, it is natural that his meeting with her should be awkward and cool. He bows, she curtseys: that is all; and then she hears from Mary that Captain Wentworth thinks her " 'altered beyond his knowledge.' "

> He had thought her wretchedly altered, and, in the first moment of appeal, had spoken as he felt. He had not forgiven Anne Elliot. She had used him ill; deserted and disappointed him; and worse, she had shown a feebleness of character in doing so, which his own decided, confident temper could not endure. She had given him up to oblige others. It had been the effect of over-persuasion. It had been weakness and timidity.[6]

---

[4] *Ibid.*, p. 26.　　　　[5] *Ibid.*, p. 27.　　　　[6] *Ibid.*, p. 61.

The remainder of the novel, however, concerns itself with the reconstitution of an alliance which over-persuasion has put asunder. No reader can be in doubt, however, as to the final outcome; but, as the essence of suspense is waiting for the expected, the succeeding chapters are read with mounting interest—for we wonder how the lovers will, at last, be reunited. There are many difficulties to be overcome, the first of which is Captain Wentworth's deliberate lack of interest in Anne; the second his evident desire to marry—and probably one of the Miss Musgroves; the third, the red herring in the person of William Walter Elliot, heir to Kellynch.

In the natural course of events, Anne and Captain Wentworth must see a good deal of each other; they meet frequently at Uppercross Great House, where he goes to see the Miss Musgroves, and she because it is the home of Mary's parents-in-law; they meet also at Uppercross Cottage, because Charles Musgrove and Wentworth often go shooting together. All, however, is excessively formal and distant. To Anne, "his cold politeness, his ceremonious grace, were worse than any thing." [7] And she is galled by his warmth and gaiety of attitude towards both the Musgrove girls, though she is unable to tell which of them he prefers. She is surprised, agitated, and pleased when one day he quietly and unexpectedly removes little Charles Musgrove from her back;[8] but this incident cannot make her reflect that his attitude toward her is softening. On the other hand, she soon gets more comprehensive evidence that he cannot forgive her defection.

This comes when she overhears Captain Wentworth and Louisa Musgrove talking behind a hedgerow:

> "Your sister [he says] is an amiable creature; but *yours* is the character of decision and firmness, I see. If you value her conduct or happiness, infuse as much of your own spirit into her, as you can. But this, no doubt, you have been always doing. It is the worst evil of too yielding and indecisive character, that no influence over it can be depended on.—You are never sure of a good impression being durable. Every body may sway it; let those who would be happy be firm." [9]

Anne feels that this conversation should be taken as a rebuke to herself. It now also seems clear that Louisa is the girl of his choice, a hunch that gains weight as a reconciliation between Henrietta Musgrove and Charles Hayter takes place soon thereafter. To cap it all, she is present at a conversation between Admiral and Mrs. Croft during which the

---

[7] *Ibid.,* p. 72.

[8] "Don't you see," writes Maria Edgeworth, "Captain Wentworth, or rather don't you in her place feel him, taking the boisterous child off her back as she kneels by the sick boy on the sofa?" A. J. C. Hare, ed., *The Life and Letters of Maria Edgeworth,* Boston, 1895, I, 260 (to Mrs. Ruxton, 21 February 1818).

[9] *Persuasion,* p. 88.

former states with some assurance that Frederick will certainly marry one of the Musgrove girls.

So all seems settled; at least it seems certain that Captain Wentworth has determined to forget Anne Elliot, and is succeeding in doing so. Then comes the journey to Lyme, where she meets Captain Wentworth's friends, the Harvilles, and the recently bereaved Captain Benwick, whose grief, ironically, she helps to alleviate.

> When the evening was over, Anne could not but be amused at the idea of her coming to Lyme, to preach patience and resignation to a young man whom she had never seen before; nor could she help fearing, on more serious reflection, that, like many other great moralists and preachers, she had been eloquent on a point in which her own conduct would ill bear examination.[10]

This, however, is not the climax of this visit—only a commentary on Anne's state of mind. The climax comes on the final walk which the party takes before leaving the watering place.

> There was too much wind to make the high part of the new Cobb pleasant for the ladies, and they agreed to get down the steps to the lower, and all were contented to pass quietly and carefully down the steep flight, excepting Louisa; she must be jumped down them by Captain Wentworth. In all their walks, he had had to jump her from the stiles; the sensation was delightful to her. The hardness of the pavement for her feet, made him less willing upon the present occasion; he did it, however; she was safely down, and instantly, to shew her enjoyment, ran up the steps to be jumped down again. He advised her against it, thought the jar too great; but no, he reasoned and talked in vain; she smiled and said, "I am determined I will": he put out his hands; she was too precipitate by half a second, she fell on the pavement on the lower Cobb, and was taken up lifeless! [11]

Everyone is too upset to think—everyone but Anne. Mary's reaction is, " 'She is dead! She is dead?' " Henrietta faints, and Captain Wentworth calls for help, while Captain Benwick and Charles Musgrove stand by ineffectually. But Anne takes over: with calmness and decision, she orders Benwick and her brother-in-law to give some assistance to Wentworth; she suggests that a surgeon be fetched; and that Louisa be carried to the inn.

So ends the first volume of the novel, though Anne is not soon to learn what a profound impression her behaviour at the accident has made upon Captain Wentworth. Several days later, she is gratified to learn (from the Crofts) that he has inquired particularly after her; but any possible resurgence of hope is quashed when she learns that he is going to Shropshire to visit his brother.

[10] *Ibid.*, p. 101.   [11] *Ibid.*, p. 109.

Besides, she and Lady Russell go to Bath to join Sir Walter, Elizabeth, and Mrs. Clay. Here there is a new interest: William Walter Elliot, for many years estranged from the rest of the family because of his marriage to a girl other than Elizabeth (which particularly enraged Sir Walter), is in Bath, a recent widower, and fully attentive to his relations. Anne has a moment of suspicion at his wishing to effect a reconciliation after so many years; but when she sees him, she is much pleased.

> He was quite as good-looking as he had appeared at Lyme [where she had caught a glimpse of him], his countenance improved by speaking, and his manners were so exactly what they ought to be, so polished, so easy, so particularly agreeable, that she could compare them in excellence to only one person's manners. They were not the same, but they were, perhaps, equally good.[12]

And this pleasure continues, even increases as she hears from Lady Russell that she has been the subject of close inquiry, and fulsome praise, by the heir to Kellynch. She enjoys toying with the idea of marrying him, and likes to think of being the future Lady Elliot of Kellynch Hall: but, after a month, she feels some hesitation:

> Mr. Elliot was too generally agreeable. Various as were the tempers in her father's house, he pleased them all. He endured too well,—stood too well with everybody.[13]

It is wise for the reader to pause and reflect here that Anne, who as yet knows nothing but good about Mr. Elliot, rejects the possibility of marrying him, despite the prudential values inherent in such an attachment: her rejection is based on the commitment to another and opposing standard.

Meanwhile, Captain Wentworth arrives in Bath and encounters her with William Walter Elliot. Her former fiancé "was obviously more struck and confused by the sight of her, than she had ever observed before; he looked quite red." [14] She too is affected, and in her own mind all the more disdains Mr. Elliot, especially when Captain Wentworth begins not only to show some signs of resurgent affection, but to manifest a jealousy of the other man.

> Jealousy of Mr. Elliot! It was the only intelligible motive. Captain Wentworth jealous of her affection! Could she have believed it a week ago—three hours ago! For a moment the gratification was exquisite. But alas! There were very different thoughts to succeed. How was such jealousy to be quieted? How was the truth to reach him? How, in all the peculiar dis-

[12] *Ibid.*, p. 143.   [13] *Ibid.*, p. 161.   [14] *Ibid.*, p. 175.

advantages of their respective situations, would he ever learn her real sentiments? It was misery to think of Mr. Elliot's attentions.—Their evil was
incalculable.[15]

Then Anne learns from Mrs. Smith, a former school friend and now
a widow in unhappy circumstances, that William Walter Elliot is de-
ceitful, hypocritical, dishonest. So Anne is—as far as the book's terms are
concerned—now free to reject him both because the attachment would
be without love and because it would be imprudent. Now the book can
move quickly on to its happy *dénouement*, although there is to be fuller
clarification of the issues on the way.

In a discussion with Captain Harville (which is overheard by Wentworth), Anne discloses her own strong commitment to a certain aspect of
the system of values implied by the word *love*. She says (apropos of the
characteristics of women as against those of men):

> "Oh!" cried Anne eagerly, "I hope I do justice to all that is felt by
> you, and by those who resemble you. God forbid that I should undervalue
> the warm and faithful feelings of any of my fellow-creatures. I should deserve
> utter contempt if I dared to suppose that true attachment and constancy
> were known only by woman. No, I believe you capable of every thing
> great and good in your married lives. I believe you equal to every im-
> portant exertion, and to every domestic forbearance, so long as—if I may
> be allowed the expression, so long as you have an object. I mean, while the
> woman you love lives, and lives for you. All the privilege I claim for my
> own sex (it is not a very enviable one, you need not covet it) is that of
> loving longest, when existence or when hope is gone." [16]

This warm and enthusiastic statement spurs Captain Wentworth at
last to tender Anne a proposal of marriage; it takes but little time to
effect a joyous reconciliation not only to each other—but to the rest of
the family. One reason why Captain Wentworth is now acceptable is that
he has fulfilled every promise which his optimistic temperament declared
nine years before. Anne's judgment is now maturer and firmer than it
was when she was a girl of nineteen; she could now more reasoningly disagree with Lady Russell. Nevertheless, she cannot regret her decision to
take Lady Russell's advice.

> "I have been thinking over the past, and trying impartially to judge of
> the right and wrong, I mean with regard to myself; and I must believe that
> I was right, much as I suffered from it, that I was perfectly right in being
> guided by the friend whom you will love better than you do now. To me,
> she was in the place of a parent. Do not mistake me, however. I am not

[15] *Ibid.*, pp. 190, 191.   [16] *Ibid.*, p. 235.

saying that she did not err in her advice. It was, perhaps, one of those cases in which advice is good or bad only as the event decides; and for myself, I certainly never should, in any circumstance of tolerable similarity, give such advice. But I mean, that I was right in submitting to her, and that if I had done otherwise, I should have suffered more in continuing the engagement than I did even in giving it up, because I should have suffered in my conscience. I have now, as far as such a sentiment is allowable in human nature, nothing to reproach myself with; and if I mistake not, a strong sense of duty is no bad part of a woman's portion." [17]

It is plain, then, that the ironic dilemma (which is the problem posed by the novel) is never resolved. Although, owing to many happily fortuitous circumstances, Anne Elliot and Frederick Wentworth are reunited at the end—there still exists potentially in every relationship between a man and a woman the conflict between love and prudence.

II. *Frederick Wentworth and William Walter Elliot*

Frederick Wentworth's real rival in *Persuasion* is not William Walter Elliot but over-conventionality. The heroine never forgets her first love, neither does she abandon hope; the sanguine naval officer is, like Christopher Newman in *The American,* "a good man wronged,"—and, as with James's hero, the wrongdoers are not so much competitors for the heroine's hand, but adherents to a set of standards which he cannot give subservient allegiance to. Young Mr. Elliot, like Lord Deepmere, is a red herring.

When we first meet Frederick Wentworth, he is a young and promising commander, "a remarkably fine young man, with a great deal of intelligence, spirit and brilliancy. . . ." [18] He is subtly uncomplicated—simple and straightforward, but clever.

Captain Wentworth had no fortune. He had been lucky in his profession, but spending freely, what had come freely, had realized nothing. But, he was confident that he should soon be rich;—full of life and ardour, he knew that he should soon have a ship, and soon be on a station that would lead to every thing he wanted. He had always been lucky; he knew he should be so still.—Such confidence, powerful in its own warmth, and bewitching in the wit which often expressed it, must have been enough for Anne; but Lady Russell saw it very differently.— His sanguine temper, and fearlessness of mind, operated very differently on her. She saw in it but an aggravation of the evil. It only added a dangerous character to himself. He was brilliant, he was headstrong.—Lady Russell had little taste

for wit; and of anything approaching to imprudence a horror. She deprecated the connexion in every light.[19]

So Anne, having been persuaded not only by Lady Russell but also by
Sir Walter, turns him down, and he leaves the neighbourhood, a disappointed man—to return almost eight years later with the very natural
determination not to reopen the affair. He is cool to Anne. But now,
having fulfilled all his early promise, he wishes to marry. As he says to
his sister, only half-playfully:

> "Yes, here I am, Sophia, quite ready to make a foolish match. Any body
> between fifteen and thirty may have me for asking. A little beauty, and a
> few smiles, and a few compliments to the navy, and I am a lost man.
> Should not this be enough for a sailor, who has had no society among
> women to make him nice?" [20]

He is jocose with the Miss Musgroves, whose high spirits and flattery delight him; extraordinarily kind to Mrs. Musgrove, whose retrospective
grief over poor Richard evokes astringent criticism from Jane Austen; but
deliberately unresponsive to Anne Elliot.

Yet he cannot ignore her altogether, for in the nature of things they
are thrown together a great deal, on account of the family connections.
He is thus able to perform the small but moving act of kindness, in
removing young Charles Musgrove from Anne's back. It is, however, at
Lyme, that he is forced to return all of his attention and affection to his
first love—when Louisa behaves so stupidly, and Anne so coolly. At Bath,
very much later, we learn what he has been thinking in this period:

> . . . he had meant to forget her, and believed it to be done. He had imagined
> himself indifferent, when he had only been angry; and he had been unjust
> to her merits, because he had been a sufferer from them . . . but he was
> obliged to acknowledge that only at Uppercross had he learnt to do her
> justice, and only at Lyme had he begun to understand himself.[21]

But the reunion is gloriously happy—and as he tells Anne, " 'I must endeavour to subdue my mind to my fortune. I must learn to brook being
happier than I deserve.' " [22]

William Walter Elliot appears first under a cloud. As heir to Kellynch,
he was expected to marry Elizabeth; instead, to the mortification of Sir
Walter and his eldest daughter, young Mr. Elliot married "a rich
woman of inferior birth." But, more than that, he has spoken ill of the
Elliots of Kellynch Hall, and it is a severe commentary on Sir Walter,
Elizabeth, and Lady Russell that he should be welcomed so readily back

[19] *Ibid.*, p. 27.   [20] *Ibid.*, p. 62.   [21] *Ibid.*, pp. 241, 242.   [22] *Ibid.*, p. 247.

into their good graces when, as a personable widower, he shows up at
Bath. Only Anne has some doubts:

> . . . she had the sensation of there being something more than immedi-
> ately appeared, in Mr. Elliot's wishing, after an interval of so many years,
> to be well received by them.[23]

Yet he is courteous, attractive—altogether very pleasing. Anne, in fact,
soon finds him "too generally agreeable" to every one; she begins to
suspect his motives, though she cannot understand what they can be. But
from Mrs. Smith she finds out the truth about her personable young
cousin—that he is in fact a heartless wretch; not a mere hypocrite but a
false friend: heartless, indifferent, selfish. He has come to Bath to keep
Sir Walter from marrying Mrs. Clay, and thus from the possibility of
producing a male heir to Kellynch. Young Mr. Elliot succeeds in that
endeavour—by enticing Mrs. Clay to London, out of harm's way.

Generally speaking—and to summarize this chapter in a sentence—
Jane Austen's characters are instruments of a profound vision: she laughs
at man, but only because she takes him seriously; examines humanity
closely, but the more she perceives the less she understands—or perhaps
one had better say, the more she understands, the more is she perplexed
by the contradictions which she finds. She has what Vivas calls "a conception of the total personality." Man, he says:

> the actual actor of the moral drama, as we have come to know him through
> the efforts of poets and sages, is a complex, burdened, pitiful, and wonder-
> ful creature. He may be the paragon of animals, of noble reason and in-
> finite faculty; in action he may be like an angel and in apprehension like
> a god; but he is also a petulant thinking reed and a hopeless mess. He is in
> love with life but also hates it deeply and subtly. He is capable of crime and
> sin but also has a tyrannical and whimsical conscience that tortures him
> for trivial misdemeanors as brutally as it punishes him for unpardonable sins.
> Narcissistic, he hates himself; full of insufferable vanity, he seeks to humili-
> ate himself; the victim of systematic self-deception, he is capable of unspar-
> ing self-knowledge. But, above all, in what he wants he is hopelessly con-
> fused, vague, self-deceived, inconsistent, and divided. Nothing, I suspect,
> would give him a worse sense of misery and of guilt than letting him have
> all that he wants. In any case it would take an Augustine, a Freud, a Dosto-
> evski, a Kierkegaard, and a Shakespeare, aided by a Boas and a Machiavelli,
> pooling their several talents and techniques, to split open the secret heart
> of this contemptible lump of living clay and extract its wonderful essence.[24]

And Jane Austen makes no inconsiderable contribution in this quest.

---

[23] *Ibid.*, p. 140.
[24] Eliseo Vivas, *The Moral Life and the Ethical Life,* Chicago, 1950, p. 60.

Jane Austen and the Peerage

by Donald J. Greene

In a note appended to his novel *The Fountain* (New York, 1932), Charles Morgan explains why he names certain of his characters as he does. "A novelist," he says, "may suggest ancient nobility in England by an invented name, but the great aristocracy of Holland is so narrowly restricted and so well known that any fictitious title would give a false, and probably ridiculous, impression. I have therefore been bound to choose, in van Leyden, the name of a noble family extinct before my own sojourn in Holland. It has the right ring." Certainly few novelists treating of "ancient nobility in England" have allowed themselves to be hampered by any such scruples as Morgan's; and a complete peerage and baronetage of British fiction, running from magnates as illustrious as the Pallisers, Dukes of Omnium, and the Tanville-Tankertons, Dukes of Dorset, down to such small fry as Sir Pitt Crawley and Sir Alastair Digby-Vane-Trumpington, Barts., would be an imposing monument to the exuberance of the story-writer's fertility in the invention of "aristocratic" names and titles. It has not perhaps been sufficiently remarked that Jane Austen's practice in this matter stands in rather striking contrast to that of most of her fellow novelists; that when she creates families with any pretensions to gentle birth, she almost always endows them with names belonging to actual British families, sometimes with an extinct title of nobility, sometimes with a living one.

One may concede that in doing so Jane Austen was setting herself, consciously or unconsciously, an ideal of verisimilitude comparable to Morgan's. But when one looks closely into the names that she chooses, one runs into certain interesting "coincidences" that seem to throw light not only on Jane Austen's technique as a novelist but also on her milieu and her social attitudes. . . .

One great family connection of northern England seems in particular to have caught Jane Austen's fancy. The major character in her novels who possesses the highest social standing is probably Fitzwilliam Darcy, Esquire, of Pemberley Hall, Derbyshire: "one of the greatest personages

"Jane Austen and the Peerage" by Donald J. Greene. From *PMLA*, LXVIII (December 1953), pp. 1017-1031. Reprinted by permission of the author and the editors of *PMLA*. Slightly abridged by the author for this edition.

in the land," Mr. Collins describes him. Mr. Collins may be reasonably suspected of exaggeration; yet Darcy's combination of money, manners, influence, ancestry, and arrogance is somehow so awe-inspiring that his plain esquireship tends to eclipse the knighthoods, baronetcies, and even minor peerages that crop up elsewhere in the novels. In his edition of the *Novels* R. W. Chapman has noted incidentally that Darcy's name combines those of two great Yorkshire families—the D'Arcys, Earls of Holdernesse, whose title became extinct in 1778, and the Fitzwilliams, Earls Fitzwilliam. Chapman is here speculating whether Fanny Burney's *Cecilia*, with its use of the phrase "pride and prejudice," could have helped to inspire Jane Austen's novel. He mentions Miss Burney's "Duke of Derwent" and suggests that the title could have directed Miss Austen's attention to the northern nobility (II, 408).

But the matter seems to be more complex than this. Robert D'Arcy, fourth and last Earl of Holdernesse (1718-1778), and William Fitzwilliam, fourth Earl Fitzwilliam (1748-1833), were both great men in Whig political circles, holding high ministerial office from time to time. They had a colleague and relation, even more prominent in affairs of state, whose family names are also of interest to readers of Jane Austen. In 1782 (when Jane Austen was seven) the Marquessate of Rockingham became extinct, on the sudden death of Charles Watson Wentworth, of Wentworth Woodhouse in Yorkshire, Marquess of Rockingham, Prime Minister of Great Britain, and political head of the Whig aristocracy. The Wentworth and Woodhouse families were united in the thirteenth century, when one Robert Wentworth married a great heiress, Emma Wodehous. The senior line of the Wentworth Woodhouse family achieved a baronetcy under James I. A sister of the first baronet married the heir of the D'Arcys, and the eldest son of the first baronet was the great Thomas Wentworth, Earl of Strafford, Charles I's ill-fated minister. Strafford's only son left no issue, and his estate descended to the children of his sister Anne Wentworth, who had married Lord Rockingham, head of the Watson family. It was a later Anne Wentworth who, in 1744, married the third Earl Fitzwilliam; and on the death of her brother the Prime Minister, who was childless, the fortunes of the Watsons, Wentworths, and Woodhouses all devolved on the Fitzwilliams.[1]

The reader of Jane Austen is intrigued to find in this one pedigree the title-role of one of her fragmentary novels (*The Watsons*);[2] the name of her most vividly drawn male character, the hero of *Pride and Prejudice;* the name of the imperious heroine of *Emma;* and what is to be the married name (Anne Wentworth) of the heroine of *Persuasion.* The

---

[1] The genealogical data in this article come mainly from Arthur Collins, *The Peerage of England* (London, 1756), and W. and R. A. Austen-Leigh, *Jane Austen, Her Life and Letters* (London, 1913), hereafter cited in my text as *LL*.

[2] The title of the novel was, of course, supplied by a later editor.

Brontës' juvenile obsession with the family names and titles of the Duke of Wellington comes to the mind;[3] and one may speculate that, as the Brontë sisters were attracted to the Wellesley family by the history of the great Duke's feats and their own Tory upbringing, so young Jane Austen's fierce, half-comical devotion to the House of Stuart may have directed her towards the figure of Strafford, always a romantic one in royalist eyes, and so to the ramifications of his family tree.

Also, in considering Jane Austen's practice in this matter of nomenclature, we must bear in mind her own social status. It was, after all, a cut or two above that of Fanny Burney, the daughter of a professional musician of obscure ancestry. Jane Austen was related, if distantly, to many of the nobility. She was the great-great-granddaughter of James Brydges, eighth Lord Chandos, and great-grandniece of the magnificent first Duke of Chandos. It seems likely that the curious name Cassandra, so dear to Jane as that of her beloved older sister, came into the family from the Brydges connection, and that Jane's mother, Cassandra Leigh, and her first cousin, another Cassandra Leigh (Mrs. Cooke), were named after their great-aunt, Cassandra, Duchess of Chandos,[4] a sister of Thomas Willoughby, first Lord Middleton (names familiar to readers of *Sense and Sensibility*). The Leighs of Adlestrop, Mrs. Austen's family, were a (senior) collateral branch of the Leighs, Lords Leigh of Stoneleigh—the "loyal Leighs," who had been ennobled as a reward for their services on the royalist side in the Civil War. Two of Jane Austen's brothers married Loyds, cousins of the Earl of Craven. There are many more distant relationships with other noble families; indeed, remote connections can be traced, through the Leighs and Cravens, between Jane Austen and the Fitzwilliams and Wentworths themselves.

Jane Austen cannot have been unaware of these relationships. "It is pleasant to be among people who know one's connections and care about them," she writes Cassandra in 1808, while visiting her somewhat grand relatives in Kent, the Knights and Knatchbulls.[5] Two incidents about this time must have particularly emphasized for her the aristocratic connections of her family. In 1806, with the extinction of the Leighs of Stoneleigh, the Stoneleigh Abbey estate devolved on the Leighs of Adlestrop; and the unusual terms of the last Lord Leigh's will caused a great deal of searching of pedigrees before it could be decided which member of the Leigh family was heir to Stoneleigh. Jane and her mother visited Stoneleigh Abbey to take part in the negotiations of the time (LL, pp.

[3] C.f., e.g., Lawrence Hanson, *The Four Brontës* (London, 1949), pp. 16ff.
[4] She was the second wife (dying 1735) of the first Duke. Those who are interested in the Christian names of Jane Austen's women characters might notice that his third Duchess' names were Lydia Catherine. The Duchess Cassandra was a remarkable woman in her own right: see C. H. Collins Baker and M. I. Baker, *The Life and Circumstances of James Brydges, First Duke of Chandos* (Oxford, 1949).
[5] *Letters*, ed. R. W. Chapman (Oxford, 1932), I, p. 207.

194-197). The other incident concerns the Brydges connection. The Chandos peerage became extinct in 1789, and for many years, Sir Samuel Egerton Brydges, voluminous and almost forgotten novelist, poet, essayist, bibliographer, antiquary, and genealogist, fought an epic battle to establish the claim to it, first of his elder brother and later of himself. The case, with its minute and lengthy investigation of the Brydges pedigree, was adversely decided by the House of Lords in 1803.[6] Egerton Brydges and Jane Austen were acquaintances; they became connected by marriage through the Lefroys of Ashe; and Brydges' sister, Mrs. George Lefroy, was one of Jane Austen's nearest neighbors and most intimate friends. Jane could not have remained unaware of this prolonged litigation, which was the central event of Egerton Brydges' life, or of her own Brydges ancestry, even if Egerton's proved spurious.

Matters being so, it is unlikely that Jane Austen required the aid of Fanny Burney to direct her attention to the existence of Fitzwilliams and D'Arcys, or Willoughbys and Middletons. More probably she would be a little contemptuous of the somewhat amateurish nomenclature employed by her fellow novelists when dealing with the gentry, and would seek "the right ring" and "avoid a false and probably ridiculous impression" by using the genuine article, with which she had every reason to be familiar.

It is a fascinating pastime for the reader of Jane Austen to thumb through Collins' *The Peerage of England* and note the occurrence of the familiar names: Bertrams and Musgraves[7] appear in the Fitzwilliam pedigree; an ancestor of the Earls Ferrers marries Eleanor, daughter of Sir Hugh Willoughby of Middleton (Viscount Higham of Higham-Ferrers is also one of Lord Rockingham's titles); we meet the Dashwoods, Lords LeDespencer, and the Eliots (spelt various ways), afterwards Earls of St. Germans; turning over the page after reading the account of the Bennets, Earls of Tankerville, we come upon a mention of the extinct barony of Bingley. In the early juvenile works, names of great families are even more frequent and more obvious. The central characters of *Evelyn* are Gowers (Marquesses of Stafford and Dukes of Sutherland). In *Catharine, or the Bower* we meet Stanleys (Earls of Derby) and Wynnes (Lord Portsmouth, the great man of the Steventon neighborhood, whose heir the Rev. George Austen tutored, was a cousin of the Welsh magnate, Sir Watkin Williams Wynne) and the humble Petersons, who, in spite of young Jane's characterization of them as being of "mean" ("no" erased) family, are promoted in revision to Percivals (Earls of Egmont). The villains of the piece are "Mr. Dudley, who was the Younger Son of a very

---

[6] *DNB*, s.v. "Brydges," and Egerton Brydges, *Autobiography* (London, 1834), *passim*.
[7] The family in *Persuasion* are, of course, Musgroves, but there are Musgraves in *The Watsons*.

noble Family, of a Family more famed for their pride than their opulence
. . . ," his wife, "an ill-educated, untaught woman of ancient family,"
who "was proud of that family almost without knowing why, and like
him too was haughty and quarrelsome, without considering for what,"
and their gauche daughter.[8] Is Mrs. Dudley a trial run for Lady Catherine
de Bourgh? The Leighs had reason to regret their connection with the
Dudleys; young Jane Austen, who was an avid reader (and writer) of
history, may well have heard of her collateral ancestress, Alice Leigh, *suo
jure* Duchess Dudley, the deserted wife of a rapscallion son of Queen
Elizabeth's Robert Dudley, Earl of Leicester (*DNB*, s.v. "Dudley"). Many
other similar names could be recorded from the writings both of Jane
Austen's youth and of her maturity.

Was there a copy of Collins' *Peerage* in the Steventon rectory library?
I have come across no specific reference to it—the *Baronetage* used by
Sir Walter Elliot, Chapman says, would have been Debrett's (*Persuasion,*
v, 295), though a Collins' *Baronetage* was also in existence at the time.
But one would suppose that a copy of the *Peerage* would have been
indispensable to the tutor of the future Earl of Portsmouth and to the
Austen ladies with their frequent visits to outlying ramifications of the
Leigh clan and to the gentry of east Kent. There were editions in 1756,
1768, and 1779; finally the "standard" edition appeared in 1808, thoroughly revised and reworked by, as it happened, Sir Edgerton Brydges,
Jane Austen's acquaintance and would-be relation.

Arthur Collins (1682?-1760), the original compiler of the *Peerage*, must
have been a curious person. No one ever loved a lord more. His biog-
rapher in *DNB* tells us, "In prosecuting his unrequited, or very tardily
requited, labours, on which he expended not only a lifetime but all that
he possessed, his motive was . . . 'an innate desire to preserve the
memory of famous men'; and his general disinterestedness must be set off
against what may often seem adulation of rank and birth."

It may seem so indeed. His dedications of the several volumes of the
Peerage are masterpieces even of an age of fulsome dedication. He continually apologizes for intruding his dedications on their recipients, and
thanks them for letting him approach them at all. To the Earl of North-
umberland he writes, "I am greatly obliged for the Honour of being
constantly received by You, with great Candour and Affability, an amiable Part in the Character of every one; but particularly conspicuous in
your Lordship . . .";[9] of the Countess of Oxford, "Her Ladyship justly
observed, *That Merit appears not only Estimable, but Attractive.* . . .
I am now to mention, that her Ladyship shewed a Generous and Affable

---

[8] Jane Austen, *Volume the Third,* ed. R. W. Chapman (Oxford, 1951), p. 37; *Works,*
ed. R. W. Chapman (Oxford, 1954), VI, p. 195.

[9] Vol. IV (1756), Dedication. The material quoted in this paragraph is absent from
the 1779 edition; I have not seen that of 1768.

Deportment to all Honoured with Access to Her" [10] (shades of Lady Catherine!); and to Robert D'Arcy, Earl of Holdernesse, "I am sensible how much this Address is breaking and interrupting your most important Thoughts and Business, which the Honour and Interest of our most gracious SOVEREIGN, and the Nation, can but ill dispense with, at the present critical Juncture. And fearing to offend you, by expatiating on the Affability, Candor, and Humanity, which has gained you universal Applause among all Ranks of the People; therefore shall conclude this epistle. . . ." [11] This is a Collins addressing a D'Arcy, and surely it has the authentic ring. Are the names a mere coincidence?

As for that strange individual, Egerton Brydges, some extracts from the Table of Contents of one of the chapters of his *Autobiography* will suffice: "Author's fondness for the old aristocracy natural—Old aristocracy respected by the people—National debt and taxation have nearly destroyed it. . . . Extraordinary passages from 'Cobbett's Register' in favour of the old nobility, and against the modern monied interest, and exclaiming against the bad passions of *parvenus*—A great fund of good sense, sagacity, and truth in these passages. . . . Ancient family of Mainwaring of Pever—Their high quality proved by their intermarriage with a co-heir of the earls palatine of Chester. . . . Present possessors of the estate and name adopted by Sir Henry and only related to him by his mother." (I, xxiii)

Jane Austen dearly loved Brydges' sister, her neighbor Mrs. Lefroy Brydges, who was thirteen years older than Jane Austen and survived her by two decades, spent some time at Ashe when she was a child, and two of the scanty contemporary memorials of her come from his *Autobiography* (II, 41). How well acquainted Jane Austen was with her friend's brother and what she thought of him can be inferred from a short but pregnant passage in one of her letters. In 1798 she has been reading his newly published novel *Arthur Fitzalbini,* which is a hodgepodge of the same sort of "sensibility" and snobbery that make up so much of the *Autobiography.* With characteristic acerbity she remarks, "My father is disappointed—*I* am not, for I expected nothing better. Never did any book carry more internal evidence of its author. Every sentiment is completely Egerton's" (*Letters,* I, 32). Brydges seems to have reciprocated: though much given to tedious comment on contemporary writers he has known, his one reference to Jane Austen's authorship seems to be the dry comment that, when he knew her in 1803, "I did not know that she was addicted to literary composition" (II, 41).

I have suggested that Jane Austen was well aware of her own social status, and that she was not diffident about making use of her familiarity

[10] Vol. V (1756), Addenda, Mm3,1ᵛ.
[11] Vol. III (1756), Dedication.

with the appellations of the nobility and gentry in order to secure greater realism in her novels. It may be objected that those on whom she bestows such names are by no means always of a station adequate to them. That is true, even of the Rockingham names. "The Watsons" are a poor family, and Captain Wentworth specifically disclaims—or rather Sir Walter Elliot disclaims for him—any relationship to the noble clan: "Mr. Wentworth was nobody . . . quite unconnected; nothing to do with the Strafford family." Yet Sir Walter's next sentence, complexly ironical, makes the reader speculate whether Jane Austen is not anticipating the objection and laughing both at the objector and at himself—as well, of course, as at poor Sir Walter—"One wonders how the names of many of our nobility become so common."

But the Fitzwilliams of *Pride and Prejudice* are a different matter. There is no doubt about *their* claim to aristocracy. Before their marriages Lady Catherine de Bourgh and Lady Anne Darcy were Lady Catherine Fitzwilliam and Lady Anne Fitzwilliam; they are the daughters of an earl—their nephew, Colonel Fitzwilliam, is a younger son of the present earl, their brother. Now when *Pride and Prejudice* was written there was one, and only one, earl in the British realm whose family name was Fitzwilliam—the Whig magnifico, nephew of Rockingham and heir to his wealth and influence, one of the leaders of the "coalition Whigs" whose political position was so important to Great Britain in the dangerous years of the French Revolution. It was Fitzwilliam's short and confused tenure of the Lord Lieutenancy of Ireland in 1795 that caused so much embarrassment to Pitt's administration and perhaps paved the way for the Irish rebellion of 1798 and the abortive French invasion of Ireland of the same year. He was the "Noble Lord" to whom Burke's great "Letter" of 1796 was addressed. He was, in all seriousness, "one of the greatest personages in the land." Lord Fitzwilliam had a number of sisters . . . surely Jane Austen here is sailing far closer to the wind than any modern novelist, even when protected by the conventional disclaimer at the beginning of the novel, could possibly dream of doing.

One seeks some sort of explanation for Jane Austen's astounding choice of the name Fitzwilliam for the earldom from which flows the "pride" of the Darcys and De Bourghs. Was she unaware of the existence of so famous a family as the real Fitzwilliams? Those who still think of Jane Austen as a naïve and gentle spinster, ignorant of the world outside the walls of a country rectory, may vote for this solution. But no one can possibly think so who has read the scanty records of her life and thought and knows that she was well aware of what was going on in the world around her. The original version of *Pride and Prejudice*, we are told, was composed in 1796. It is inconceivable that so assiduous a historian as Jane Austen, the reader of Henry and Bigland, could have forgotten the rancorous and strenuous debate that Fitzwilliam's perhaps calculated maladroitness in Ireland the previous year had set off, or that the news of Burke's last great polemic on the war with France should not have penetrated to the rectory at Steventon. Jane Austen's brothers were fighting in that war, and Fitzwilliam's actions could—and in Ireland perhaps did—seriously affect its course and outcome.

What else then? Did she expect that such magnificent personages would never trouble themselves about a mere woman novelist? Possibly so; and perhaps the ironic disclaimer about the Wentworth name in *Persuasion* is evidence that she had learned caution since her first published novels. Yet that still does not explain the choice of the particular name Fitzwilliam. Is it possible—I suppose that no one before has ventured to suggest that Jane Austen is being consciously political in her novels—that the quiet Tory daughter of a quiet Tory parson deliberately wants her readers to find in the arrogant possessors of the great Whig names of Fitzwilliam and D'Arcy a satire on an aspect of Whiggism most obnoxious to Pittite Tories?

It was, we know, part of Pitt's policy to reduce the power of the Whig aristocracy by swamping the House of Lords with new peerages conferred on men who had risen to prominence in business and the professions. Egerton Brydges more than once relieves his feelings by a tirade on the subject: "The deterioration and proximate annihilation of them ['the higher classes of landed gentry'] is a grievous loss to the state and the people. It was much accelerated by the character of Pitt's government, by his financial measures, and his ill-selected profusion of honours; by his palpable preference of mercantile wealth, and by his inborn hatred of the old aristocracy. . . . Look at the greater part of the men who have been advanced from nothing in the last fifty years—they are a miserable set. . . . It is true that there ought to be two or three lawyers in the Upper House, but not twenty or thirty" (I, 196; II, 49-50).

There is a great deal of this sort of thing in Brydges. It reminds one irresistibly of Sir Walter Elliot: "I have two strong grounds of objection to it [the navy]. First, as being the means of bringing persons of obscure birth into undue distinction and raising men to honours which their fathers and grandfathers never dreamt of. . . . A man is in greater danger in the navy of being insulted by the rise of one whose father his father might have disdained to speak to." As we know, the navy was, in fact, the means of bringing at least two persons of relatively "obscure birth," Jane Austen's brothers Charles and Francis, into distinction— they both eventually became admirals and Francis a knight. It is easy to believe that in all this Jane Austen is on the side of Pitt rather than the side of Sir Walter Elliot and Sir Egerton Brydges, on the side of the rising middle class as against the hereditary aristocracy.

Can this suggestion be reconciled with the earlier one that Jane Austen was well aware of her own connections with the hereditary aristocracy and by no means inclined to despise them? I am not sure that Jane Austen herself was ever able to reconcile the two attitudes; but their simultaneous existence can perhaps be explained. It may be a source of legitimate pride and pleasure to be able to trace one's descent from an ancient and honorable lineage; but it cannot have been so pleasant to be snubbed by those closer to the charmed center of the aristocratic circle[12] Jane Austen must have been subjected to a wealth of condescension before the picture of Lady Catherine de Bourgh, in all its virulence, took final shape. Lady Catherine's married, as well as her maiden, name is not without significance. Arthur Collins informs us that the noble name of Brydges was "anciently written Brugge, Burg, Bruges, etc.," and Egerton Brydges is at some pains to assure us that "my male stock is baronial from the Conquest; ascending . . . to Johannes de Burgo (Monoculus), founder also of the House of De Burgh." [13] Brydges cannot have failed to inform his sister and his putative cousin, Jane Austen, of this momentous fact about their family tree.

Slight as this sort of evidence is, it seems to point to one conclusion: that much of the social criticism in Jane Austen's novels (and there is really a great deal of social criticism in them) is not that of a cool, detached, impersonal observer, but comes from one who is herself deeply and personally involved with the social phenomena which she describes and passes judgment on. A case might be made out for saying that the unifying thesis of Jane Austen's novels is the rise of the middle class, a process of which the middle class itself became acutely conscious when Pitt, in effect, overthrew the entrenched political power of the Whig aristocracy in 1784. In *Pride and Prejudice* it is the middle-class Bennets and Gardiners who compel the noble Fitzwilliams and Darcys to take them seriously; in *Persuasion* it is Wentworths against Elliots; in *Northanger Abbey*, Morlands against Tilneys; in *Sense and Sensibility*, Dashwoods against Ferrarses.

"Middle class" is our term, of course, not Jane Austen's. Jane Austen is at pains to emphasize, if in no other way than by her use of such names as Bennet and Wentworth and Dashwood for her "middle-class" protagonists, that their possessors are of as good a "class" as those who treat them superciliously: "He is a gentleman; I am a gentleman's daughter" is Elizabeth Bennet's magnificent retort to the divinities that hedge about Fitzwilliam Darcy. The barriers of caste with which the Fitzwil-

---

[12] See a strange letter, purporting to be from Fanny Knight, Lady Knatchbull (Jane Austen's favorite niece), in her old age, quoted in G. B. Stern's *Benefits Forgot* (New York, 1949), pp. 242-243, and Sylvia Townsend Warner, *Jane Austen*, Bibliographical Supplements to British Book News (London, 1951), p. 19. The extract quoted begins, "Yes my love it is very true that Aunt Jane from various circumstances was not so *refined* as she ought to have been from her *talent*," and goes on to discuss in detail Jane and Cassandra's deficiencies "as to good Society and its ways."

[13] *Autobiography*, II, p. 422.

liams and Darcys have surrounded themselves are artificial and invalid; of their own making and comparatively recent making at that. This is good eighteenth century Tory doctrine, and would have been subscribed to by any country squire, glancing contemptuously and perhaps a little enviously at the first Duke of Newcastle or the first Duke of Chandos.

This is to reduce the problem to its lowest terms, of course. It is not as simple as all that, and Jane Austen is well aware that it isn't. When Elizabeth informs Lady Catherine that she is a gentleman's daughter, she is telling a splendid half-truth: she knows that she is not a gentlewoman's daughter and that nothing will redeem her mother's and her sisters' vulgarity. When all is said and done, Fitzwilliam Darcy remains the "greatest personage" in the novel; it is because he so magnificently lives up to the ideal of his rank that things end happily for Elizabeth. When Emma Woodhouse tries to put her egalitarian theories into practice with Harriet Smith, they simply don't work—and even then Emma feels it necessary to postulate an aristocratic natural father for Harriet. Possibly it is in *Mansfield Park* that Jane Austen comes as close as she ever does to a thoroughgoing presentation of a theory of Tory democracy, when Fanny and William Price, from an incurably lower-middle-class home, "make good" and the high-bred Maria Bertram is disgraced. But the future of the other Prices is far less hopeful.

In spite of their obvious antipathy to each other, Jane Austen and Egerton Brydges had certain things in common. They were both born on the fringes of aristocracy; they both had a respect—perhaps partly romantic in nature: it was the age of Walter Scott—for the good things they felt aristocracy might stand for, and they were proud of their connection with it. At the same time, they both had clever and sensitive minds, easily detecting and resenting condescension; they both had a talent for writing, an occupation not wholly respectable among the country gentry; they were acutely conscious of their intellectual superiority to many of those who patronized them. It is wryly amusing to find Egerton Brydges at one time panegyrizing "the higher classes of landed gentry" as "the most manly, and best-educated, and most useful rank of society" in England, and at another characterizing the landed genry of east Kent, the home of the Knights and Knatchbulls, as a "mean, bigoted, and ignorant clanship." "I never could bear the talk of country squires," he says; "and as they suspected this, my society was a wet sheet upon them. . . . I could not talk of sheep and bullocks; examine a horse's mouth, or discuss his points. I could not tell what wind would give a good scenting day; nor what course the fox would take, when he broke cover" (I, 46, 85-86).

The emotional tensions resulting from such ambivalence can be gauged by the almost hysterical tone that permeates both Brydges' early *Fitzalbini* (obviously an autobiographical fantasy) and his late *Autobiography*. At one moment he is extravagantly rhapsodizing on the natural aristocracy of talent and the necessity for despising man-created distinctions of rank; at the next he is presenting an interminable list of the noble families of the time of the Norman Conquest to whom he is related (thirty years after the House of Lords has judicially pronounced that he is related to none of them). Such neurosis could only disgust Jane Austen; and perhaps the virulence of her comment on *Fitzalbini*, corrosive even for Jane Austen, is an indication that she was only too familiar with the sources of Brydges' emotionality.

The resultant of such tensions in Jane Austen was not hysteria, but irony. It is important not to mistake the nature of that irony. Critics have seen it as "irony of defense," as the mechanism of a refusal to make moral judgments about the world or to become emotionally involved with it: "To events, literary and actual, she allowed herself no public response except the socially conventional or the ironic: for neither of these endangered her reserve, both put off self-commitment and feeling. . . ." [14] This seems to me a fundamentally mistaken line of approach to any supremely great artist like Jane Austen. I do not think great art is ever compatible with a deficiency of a *desire* to commit oneself, with the deliberate abdication, "putting off," of the capacity to feel. *Control,* perhaps, of the expression of powerful feeling by the artistic perception, the sensitivity to form; but not suppression or attenuation of the feeling itself. Possibly much ironic expression, both in literature and in day-to-day living, stems rather from the converse of the kind of sensibility postulated—from a tendency to feel *too* deeply, to feel as it were on both sides of a question. It is a question of psychology, of course: is the person who avoids definite commitment and indulges in irony emotionally shallower than the person who commits himself whole-heartedly to a cause and expresses himself in positive assertions? Hamlet, I suppose, is the classic type of the former; King Harry the Fifth of the latter.

So much has been said in the past about Jane Austen's "limitations" that it is important not to misinterpret her restraint, if restraint it is. Certainly one cannot say that Jane Austen avoids making moral judgments: she makes them, often and vigorously, in both her letters and her novels; and if strong expression of like and dislike is any criterion of a capacity for feeling, again Jane Austen shows no evidence of emotional sterility, or even emotional "reserve." Quoting such diverse marginal comments on her copy of Goldsmith's *History* as "Every ancient custom ought to be Sacred, unless it is prejudicial to Happiness" and "How much are the poor to be pitied, and the Rich to be Blamed!", an earlier writer remarks, in words that are still relevant: "It must be left to those critics who have described Jane Austen's disposition as 'calm,' 'unemotional,' 'unsentimental,' 'passionless,' to reconcile such epithets with these

---

[14] Marvin Mudrick, *Jane Austen: Irony as Defense and Discovery* (Princeton, 1952), p. 1.

eager outpourings, which are given here for the benefit of all who may care to form some truer conceptions of the real Jane than the tame and colourless personality, devoid of all enthusiasm and ardour, which has at times been set before the public as hers." [15] As a child of her times, the contemporary of William Pitt and Walter Scott and Edmund Burke, the disciple of Dr. Johnson and Cowper, she found it possible to be enthusiastic both for the notion of *noblesse oblige* and for the notion of *la carrière ouverte aux talents*. If she sometimes found the two sympathies hard to reconcile, she was neither the first nor the last "Tory democrat" to do so.

[15] Mary Augusta Austen-Leigh, *Personal Aspects of Jane Austen* (London, 1920), pp. 28-29.

Regulated Hatred: An Aspect of
the Work of Jane Austen

by D. W. Harding

I

The impression of Jane Austen which has filtered through to the reading public, down from the first-hand critics, through histories of literature, university courses, literary journalism, and polite allusion, deters many who might be her best readers from bothering with her at all. How can this popular impression be described? In my experience the first idea to be absorbed from the atmosphere surrounding her work was that she offered exceptionally favourable openings to the exponents of urbanity. Gentlemen of an older generation than mine spoke of their intention of re-reading her on their deathbeds; Eric Linklater's cultured Prime Minister in *The Impregnable Women* passes from surreptitious to abandoned reading of her novels as a national crisis deepens. With this there also came the impression that she provided a refuge for the sensitive when the contemporary world grew too much for them. So Beatrice Kean Seymour writes (*Jane Austen*): "In a society which has enthroned the machine-gun and carried it aloft even into the quiet heavens, there will always be men and women—Escapist or not, as you please—who will turn to her novels with an unending sense of relief and thankfulness."

I was given to understand that her scope was of course extremely restricted, but that within her limits she succeeded admirably in expressing the gentler virtues of a civilised social order. She could do this because she lived at a time when, as a sensitive person of culture, she could still feel that she had a place in society and could address the reading public as sympathetic equals; she might introduce unpleasant people into her stories but she could confidently expose them to a public opinion that condemned them. Chiefly, so I gathered, she was a delicate satirist, reveal-

"Regulated Hatred: An Aspect of the Work of Jane Austen" by D. W. Harding. Reprinted from *Scrutiny*, VIII (1940) pp. 346-62, by permission of the author and the editors of *Scrutiny*.

ing with inimitable lightness of touch the comic foibles and amiable weaknesses of the people whom she lived amongst and liked.

All this was enough to make me quite certain I didn't want to read her. And it is, I believe, a seriously misleading impression. Fragments of the truth have been incorporated in it but they are fitted into a pattern whose total effect is false. And yet the wide currency of this false impression is an indication of Jane Austen's success in an essential part of her complex intention as a writer: her books are, as she meant them to be, read and enjoyed by precisely the sort of people whom she disliked; she is a literary classic of the society which attitudes like hers, held widely enough, would undermine.

In order to enjoy her books without disturbance those who retain the conventional notion of her work must always have had slightly to misread what she wrote at a number of scattered points, points where she took good care (not wittingly perhaps) that the misreading should be the easiest thing in the world. Unexpected astringencies occur which the comfortable reader probably overlooks, or else passes by as slight imperfections, trifling errors of tone brought about by a faulty choice of words. Look at the passage in *Northanger Abbey* where Henry Tilney offers a solemn reprimand of Catherine's fantastic suspicions about his father:

"Dear Miss Morland, consider the dreadful nature of these suspicions you have entertained. What have you been judging from? Remember the country and the age in which we live. Remember that we are English, that we are Christians. Consult your own understanding, your own sense of the probable, your own observation of what is passing around you. Does our education prepare us for such atrocities? Do our laws connive at them? Could they be perpetrated without being known, in a country like this, where social and literary intercourse is on such a footing, and where roads and newspapers lay everything open?"

Had the passage really been as I quote it nothing would have been out of tone. But I omitted a clause. The last sentence actually runs: "Could they be perpetrated without being known, in a country like this, where social and literary intercourse is on such a footing, where every man is surrounded by a neighbourhood of voluntary spies, and where roads and newspapers lay everything open?" "Where every man is surrounded by a neighbourhood of voluntary spies"—with its touch of paranoia that surprising remark is badly out of tune both with "Henry's astonishing generosity and nobleness of conduct" and with the accepted idea of Jane Austen.

Yet it comes quite understandably from someone of Jane Austen's sensitive intelligence, living in her world of news and gossip interchanged amongst and around a large family. She writes to Cassandra (September 14th, 1804), "My mother is at this moment reading a letter from my aunt. Yours to Miss Irvine of which she had had the perusal (which by the bye in your place I should not like) has thrown them into a quandary about Charles and his prospects. The case is that my mother had previously told my aunt, without restriction, that . . . whereas you had replied to Miss Irvine's inquiries on the subject with less explicitness and more caution. Never mind, let them puzzle on together." And when Fanny Knight (her niece) writes confidentially about her love affair, Jane Austen describes ruses she adopted to avoid having to read the letter to the family, and later implores Fanny to "write *something* that may do to be read or told" (November 30th, 1814).

Why is it that, holding the view she did of people's spying, Jane Austen should slip it in amongst Henry Tilney's eulogies of the age? By doing so she achieves two ends, ends which she may not have consciously aimed at. In such a speech from such a character the remark is unexpected and unbelievable, with the result that it is quite unlikely to be taken in at all by many readers; it slips through their minds without creating a disturbance. It gets said, but with the minimum risk of setting people's backs up. The second end achieved by giving the remark such a context is that of off-setting it at once by more appreciative views of society and so refraining from indulging an exaggerated bitterness. The eulogy of the age is not nullified by the bitter clause, but neither can it wipe out the impression the clause makes on those who attend to it.

One cannot say that here the two attitudes modify one another. The technique is too weak. Jane Austen can bring both attitudes into the picture but she has not at this point made one picture of them. In *Persuasion* she does something of the same kind more delicately. Miss Elliot's chagrin at having failed to marry her cousin is being described in the terms of ordinary satire which invites the reading public to feel superior to Miss Elliot:

> There was not a baronet from A to Z whom her feelings could have so willingly acknowledged as an equal. Yet so miserably had he conducted himself, that though she was at this present time (the summer of 1814) wearing black ribbons for his wife, she could not admit him to be worth thinking of again. The disgrace of his first marriage might, perhaps, as there was no reason to suppose it perpetuated by offspring, have been got over, had he not done worse;

—and then at this point the satire suddenly directs itself against the public instead of Miss Elliot—

> but he had, as by the accustomary intervention of kind friends they had been informed, spoken most disrespectfully of them all. . . .

In *Emma* the same thing is done still more effectively. Again Jane Austen seems to be on perfectly good terms with the public she is addressing and to have no reserve in offering the funniness and virtues of Mr. Woodhouse and Miss Bates to be judged by the accepted standards of the public. She invites her readers to be just their natural patronising selves. But this public that Jane Austen seems on such good terms with has some curious things said about it, not criticisms, but small notes of fact that are usually not made. They almost certainly go unnoticed by many readers, for they involve only the faintest change of tone from something much more usual and acceptable.

When she says that Miss Bates "enjoyed a most uncommon degree of popularity for a woman neither young, handsome, rich, nor married," this is fairly conventional satire that any reading public would cheerfully admit in its satirist and chuckle over. But the next sentence must have to be mentally re-written by the greater number of Jane Austen's readers. For them it probably runs, "Miss Bates stood in the very worst predicament in the world for having much of the public favour; and she had no intellectual superiority to make atonement to herself, or compel an outward respect from those who might despise her." This, I suggest, is how most readers, lulled and disarmed by the amiable context, will soften what in fact reads, ". . . and she had no intellectual superiority to make atonement to herself, or frighten those who might hate her into outward respect." Jane Austen was herself at this time "neither young, handsome, rich, nor married," and the passage perhaps hints at the functions which her unquestioned intellectual superiority may have had for her.

This eruption of fear and hatred into the relationships of everyday social life is something that the urbane admirer of Jane Austen finds distasteful; it is not the satire of one who writes securely for the entertainment of her civilised acquaintances. And it has the effect, for the attentive reader, of changing the flavour of the more ordinary satire amongst which it is embedded.

Emma is especially interesting from this point of view. What is sometimes called its greater "mellowness" largely consists in saying quietly and undisguisedly things which in the earlier books were put more loudly but in the innocuous form of caricature. Take conversation for instance. Its importance and its high (though by no means supreme) social value are of course implicit in Jane Austen's writings. But one should beware of supposing that a mind like hers therefore found the ordinary social intercourse of the period congenial and satisfying. In *Pride and Prejudice* she offers an entertaining caricature of card-table conversation at Lady Catherine de Bourgh's house.

> Their table was superlatively stupid. Scarcely a syllable was uttered that did not relate to the game, except when Mrs. Jenkinson expressed her

fears of Miss de Bourgh's being too hot or too cold, or having too much or
too little light. A great deal more passed at the other table. Lady Catherine
was generally speaking—stating the mistakes of the three others, or relating
some anecdote of herself. Mr. Collins was employed in agreeing to everything her ladyship said, thanking her for every fish he won, and apologising
if he thought he won too many. Sir William did not say much. He was
storing his memory with anecdotes and noble names.

This invites the carefree enjoyment of all her readers. They can all
feel superior to Lady Catherine and Mr. Collins. But in *Emma* the style
changes: the talk at the Coles' dinner party, a pleasant dinner party
which the heroine enjoyed, is described as ". . . the usual rate of conversation; a few clever things said, a few downright silly, but by much
the larger proportion neither the one nor the other—nothing worse than
everyday remarks, dull repetitions, old news, and heavy jokes." "Nothing
worse"!—that phrase is typical. It is not mere sarcasm by any means. Jane
Austen genuinely valued the achievements of the civilisation she lived
within and never lost sight of the fact that there might be something
vastly worse than the conversation she referred to. "Nothing worse" is a
positive tribute to the decency, the superficial friendliness, the absence
of the grosser forms of insolence and self-display at the dinner party. At
least Mrs. Elton wasn't there. And yet the effect of the comment, if her
readers took it seriously would be that of a disintegrating attack upon
the sort of social intercourse they have established for themselves. It is not
the comment of one who would have helped to make her society what
it was, or ours what it is.

To speak of this aspect of her work as "satire" is perhaps misleading.
She has none of the underlying didactic intention ordinarily attributed
to the satirist. Her object is not missionary; it is the more desperate one
of merely finding some mode of existence for her critical attitudes. To
her the first necessity was to keep on reasonably good terms with the
associates of her everyday life; she had a deep need of their affection and
a genuine respect for the ordered, decent civilisation that they upheld.
And yet she was sensitive to their crudenesses and complacencies and
knew that her real existence depended on resisting many of the values
they implied. The novels gave her a way out of this dilemma. This, rather
than the ambition of entertaining a posterity of urbane gentlemen, was
her motive force in writing.

As a novelist, therefore, part of her aim was to find the means for
unobtrusive spiritual survival, without open conflict with the friendly
people around her whose standards in simpler things she could accept
and whose affection she greatly needed. She found, of course, that one of
the most useful peculiarities of her society was its willingness to remain
blind to the implications of a caricature. She found people eager to laugh
at faults they tolerated in themselves and their friends, so long as the

faults were exaggerated and the laughter "good-natured"—so long, that is, as the assault on society could be regarded as a mock assault and not genuinely disruptive. Satire such as this is obviously a means not of admonition but of self-preservation.

Hence one of Jane Austen's most successful methods is to offer her readers every excuse for regarding as rather exaggerated figures of fun people whom she herself detests and fears. Mrs. Bennet, according to the Austen tradition, is one of "our" richly comic characters about whom we can feel superior, condescending, perhaps a trifle sympathetic, and above all heartily amused and free from care. Everything conspires to make this the natural interpretation once you are willing to overlook Jane Austen's bald and brief statement of her own attitude to her: "She was a woman of mean understanding, little information, and uncertain temper." How many women amongst Jane Austen's acquaintance and amongst her most complacent readers to the present day that phrase must describe! How gladly they enjoy the funny side of the situations Mrs. Bennet's unpleasant nature creates, and how easy it is made for them to forget or never observe that Jane Austen, none the less for seeing how funny she is, goes on detesting her. The thesis that the ruling standards of our social group leave a perfectly comfortable niche for detestable people and give them sufficient sanction to persist, would, if it were argued seriously, arouse the most violent opposition, the most determined apologetics for things as they are, and the most reproachful pleas for a sense of proportion.

Caricature served Jane Austen's purpose perfectly. Under her treatment one can never say where caricature leaves off and the claim to serious portraiture begins. Mr. Collins is only given a trifle more comic exaggeration than Lady Catherine de Bourgh, and by her standards is a possible human being. Lady Catherine in turn seems acceptable as a portrait if the criterion of verisimilitude is her nephew Mr. Darcy. And he, finally, although to some extent a caricature, is near enough natural portraiture to stand beside Elizabeth Bennet, who, like all the heroines, is presented as an undistorted portrait. The simplest comic effects are gained by bringing the caricatures into direct contact with the real people, as in Mr. Collins' visit to the Bennets and his proposal to Elizabeth. But at the same time one knows that, though from some points of view caricature, in other directions he does, by easy stages, fit into the real world. He is real enough to Mrs. Bennet; and she is real enough to Elizabeth to create a situation of real misery for her when she refuses. Consequently the proposal scene is not only comic fantasy, but it is also, for Elizabeth, a taste of the fantastic nightmare in which economic and social institutions have such power over the values of personal relationships that the comic monster is nearly able to get her.

The implications of her caricatures as criticism of real people in real

society is brought out in the way they dovetail into their social setting.
The decent, stodgy Charlotte puts up cheerfully with Mr. Collins as a
husband; and Elizabeth can never quite become reconciled to the idea
that her friend is the wife of her comic monster. And that, of course, is
precisely the sort of idea that Jane Austen herself could never grow
reconciled to. The people she hated were tolerated, accepted, comfortably
ensconced in the only human society she knew; they were, for her, society's embarrassing unconscious comment on itself. A recent writer on
Jane Austen, Elizabeth Jenkins, puts forward the polite and more comfortable interpretation in supposing Charlotte's marriage to be explained
solely by the impossibility of young women's earning their own living at
that period. But Charlotte's complaisance goes deeper than that: it is
shown as a considered indifference to personal relationships when they
conflict with cruder advantages in the wider social world:

> She had always felt that Charlotte's opinion of matrimony was not ex-
> actly like her own, but she could not have supposed it possible that, when
> called into action, she would have sacrificed every better feeling to worldly
> advantage.

We know too, at the biographical level, that Jane Austen herself, in a
precisely similar situation to Charlotte's, spent a night of psychological
crisis in deciding to revoke her acceptance of an "advantageous" proposal
made the previous evening. And her letters to Fanny Knight show how
deep her convictions went at this point.

It is important to notice that Elizabeth makes no break with her
friend on account of the marriage. This was the sort of friend—"a friend
disgracing herself and sunk in her esteem"—that went to make up the
available social world which one could neither escape materially nor be
independent of psychologically. The impossibility of being cut off from
objectionable people is suggested more subtly in *Emma,* where Mrs.
Elton is the high light of the pervasive neglect of spiritual values in social
life. One can hardly doubt that Jane Austen's own dealings with society
are reflected in the passage where Mr. Weston makes the error of inviting
Mrs. Elton to join the picnic party which he and Emma have planned:

> . . . Emma could not but feel some surprise, and a little displeasure, on
> hearing from Mr. Weston that he had been proposing to Mrs. Elton, as her
> brother and sister had failed her, that the two parties should unite, and
> go together, and that as Mrs. Elton had very readily acceded to it, so it was
> to be, if she had no objection. Now, as her objection was nothing but her
> very great dislike of Mrs. Elton, of which Mr. Weston must already be
> perfectly aware, it was not worth bringing forward: it could not be done
> without a reproof to him, which would be giving pain to his wife; and she
> found herself, therefore, obliged to consent to an arrangement which she

would have done a great deal to avoid; an arrangement which would, probably, expose her even to the degradation of being said to be of Mrs. Elton's party! Every feeling was offended; and the forbearance of her outward submission left a heavy arrear due of secret severity in her reflections, on the unmanageable good-will of Mr. Weston's temper.

"I am glad you approve of what I have done," said he, very comfortably. "But I thought you would. Such schemes as these are nothing without numbers. One cannot have too large a party. A large party secures its own amusement. And she is a good-natured woman after all. One could not leave her out."

Emma denied none of it aloud, and agreed to none of it in private.

This well illustrates Jane Austen's typical dilemma: of being intensely critical of people to whom she also has strong emotional attachments.

II

The social group having such ambivalence for her, it is not surprising if her conflict should find some outlets not fully within her conscious control. To draw attention to these, however, is not to suggest that they lessen the value of her conscious intention and its achievements.

The chief instance is the fascination she found in the Cinderella theme, the Cinderella theme with the fairy godmother omitted. For in Jane Austen's treatment the natural order of things manages to reassert the heroine's proper pre-eminence without the intervention of any human or quasi-human helper. In this respect she allies the Cinderella theme to another fairy-tale theme which is often introduced—that of the princes brought up by unworthy parents but never losing the delicate sensibilities which are an inborn part of her. This latter theme appears most explicitly in *Mansfield Park*, the unfinished story of *The Watsons*, and, with some softening, in *Pride and Prejudice*. The contrast between Fanny Price's true nature and her squalid home at Portsmouth is the clearest statement of the idea, but in the first four of the finished novels the heroine's final position is, even in the worldly sense, always above her reasonable social expectations by conventional standards, but corresponding to her natural worth.

To leave it at this, however, would be highly misleading. It is the development which occurs in her treatment of the Cinderella theme that most rewards attention. In *Northanger Abbey, Sense and Sensibility,* and *Pride and Prejudice* it is handled simply; the heroine is in some degree isolated from those around her by being more sensitive or of finer moral insight or sounder judgment, and her marriage to the handsome prince at the end is in the nature of a reward for being different from the rest and a consolation for the distresses entailed by being different. This is true even of *Northanger Abbey* in spite of the grotesque error of judgment that Catherine Morland is guilty of and has to renounce. For here Jane Austen was interested not so much in the defect in her heroine's judgment as in the absurdly wide currency of the "gothick" tradition that entrapped her. Catherine throws off her delusion almost as something external to herself. And this is so glaring that Jane Austen seems to have been uncomfortable about it: in describing it she resorts to a rather factitious semi-detachment from her heroine.

> Her mind made up on these several points, and her resolution formed, of always judging and acting in future with the greatest good sense, she had nothing to do but to forgive herself and be happier than ever; and the lenient hand of time did much for her by insensible gradations in the course of another day.

In *Sense and Sensibility* and *Pride and Prejudice* the heroines are still nearer perfection and even the handsome princes have faults to overcome before all is well. Immediately after her final reconciliation with Mr. Darcy, Elizabeth Bennet is tempted to laugh at his over-confident direction of his friend Bingley's love affair, ". . . but she checked herself. She remembered that he had yet to learn to be laughed at, and it was rather too early to begin."

To put the point in general terms, the heroine of these early novels is herself the criterion of sound judgment and good feeling. She may claim that her values are sanctioned by good breeding and a religious civilisation, but in fact none of the people she meets represents those values so effectively as she does herself. She is never in submissive alliance with the representatives of virtue and good feeling in her social world— there is only a selective alliance with certain aspects of their characters. The social world may have material power over her, enough to make her unhappy, but it hasn't the power that comes from having created or moulded her, and it can claim no credit for her being what she is. In this sense the heroine is independent of those about her and isolated from them. She has only to be herself.

The successful handling of this kind of theme and this heroine brought Jane Austen to the point where a development became psychologically possible. The hint of irrationality underlying the earlier themes could be brought nearer the light. She could begin to admit that even a heroine must owe a great deal of her character and values to the social world in which she had been moulded, and, that being so, could hardly be quite so solitary in her excellence as the earlier heroines are. The emphasis hitherto had been almost entirely on the difference between the heroine and the people about her. But this was to slight the reality of her bond with the ordinary "good" people; there was more to be said for the fundamentals of virtue and seemliness than she had been implying. And so, after the appearance of *Pride and Prejudice*, she wrote to Cassandra, "Now I will try and write of something else, and it shall be a complete change of subject—ordination . . ." (January 29th, 1813).

This sets the tone of *Mansfield Park*, the new novel. Here her emphasis is on the deep importance of the conventional virtues, of civilised seemliness, decorum, and sound religious feeling. These become the worthy objects of the heroine's loyalties; and they so nearly comprise the whole range of her values that Fanny Price is the least interesting of all the heroines. For the first time, Jane Austen sets the heroine in submissive alliance with the conventionally virtuous people of the story, Sir Thomas and Edmund. Mistaken though these pillars of society may in some respects be, the heroine's proper place is at their side; their standards are worthy of a sensitive person's support and complete allegiance.

It is a novel in which Jane Austen pays tribute to the virtuous fundamentals of her upbringing, ranging herself with those whom she considers right on the simpler and more obvious moral issues, and withdrawing her attention—relatively at least—from the finer details of living in which they may disturb her. She allies herself with virtues that are easy to appreciate and reasonably often met with. The result, as one would expect, is a distinct tendency to priggishness. And, of course, the book was greatly liked. "Mr. H[aden] is reading *Mansfield Park* for the first time and prefers it to *P. and P.*" (November 26th, 1815). "Mr. Cook [himself a clergyman] says 'it is the most sensible novel he ever read,' and the manner in which I treat the clergy delights them very much" (June 14th, 1814). Compared with *Mansfield Park*, Jane Austen is afraid that *Emma* will appear "inferior in good sense" (December 11th, 1815). It was after reading *Mansfield Park*, moreover, that the pompously self-satisfied Librarian to the Prince Regent offered her, almost avowedly, his own life story as the basis for a novel about an English clergyman. He must have been one of the first of the admirer-victims who have continued to enjoy her work to this day. And her tactful and respectful reply ("The comic part of the character I might be equal to, but not the good, the enthusiastic, the literary") illustrates admirably her capacity for keeping on good terms with people without too great treachery to herself.

The priggishness of *Mansfield Park* is the inevitable result of the curiously abortive attempt at humility that the novel represents. Although it involves the recognition that heroines are not spontaneously generated but owe much of their personality to the established standards of their society, the perfection of the heroine is still not doubted. And so the effort towards humility becomes in effect the exclamation, "Why, some of the very good people are nearly as good as I am and really do deserve my loyalty!"

There is no external evidence that Jane Austen was other than highly satisfied with *Mansfield Park*, which is, after all, in many ways interesting and successful. But its *reductio ad absurdum* of the Cinderella theme and the foundling princess theme could hardly have been without effect. This, I think, is already visible in the last chapter, which, with its suggestion of a fairy-tale winding up of the various threads of the story, is ironically perfunctory. For instance:

> I purposely abstain from dates on this occasion, that every one may be at liberty to fix their own, aware that the cure of unconquerable passions, and the transfer of unchanging attachments, must vary much as to time in different people. I only entreat everybody to believe that exactly at the time when it was quite natural that it should be so, and not a week earlier, Edmund did cease to care about Miss Crawford, and became as anxious to marry Fanny as Fanny herself could desire.

And Sir Thomas's "high sense of having realised a great acquisition in the promise of Fanny for a daughter, formed just such a contrast with his early opinion on the subject when the poor little girl's coming had first been agitated, as time is for ever producing between the plans and decisions of mortals, for their own instruction and their neighbours' entertainment."

Whether or not Jane Austen realised what she had been doing, at all events the production of *Mansfield Park* enabled her to go on next to the extraordinary achievement of *Emma*, in which a much more complete humility is combined with the earlier unblinking attention to people as they are. The underlying argument has a different trend. She continues to see that the heroine has derived from the people and conditions around her, but she now keeps clearly in mind the objectionable features of those people; and she faces the far bolder conclusion that even a heroine is likely to have assimilated many of the more unpleasant possibilities of the human being in society. And it is not that society has spoilt an originally perfect girl who now has to recover her pristine good sense, as it was with Catherine Morland, but that the heroine has not yet achieved anything like perfection and is actually going to learn a number of serious lessons from some of the people she lives with.

Consider in the first place the treatment here of the two favourite themes of the earlier novels. The Cinderella theme is now relegated to the sub-heroine, Jane Fairfax. Its working out involves the discomfiture of the heroine, who in this respect is put into the position of one of the ugly sisters. Moreover the Cinderella procedure is shown in the light of a social anomaly, rather a nuisance and requiring the excuse of unusual circumstances.

The associated theme of the child brought up in humble circumstances whose inborn nature fits her for better things is frankly parodied and deflated in the story of Harriet Smith, the illegitimate child whom Emma tries to turn into a snob. In the end, with the insignificant girl cheerfully married to a deserving farmer, "Harriet's parentage became known. She proved to be the daughter of a tradesman, rich enough to afford her the comfortable maintenance which had ever been hers, and decent enough to have always wished for concealment. Such was the blood of gentility which Emma had formerly been so ready to vouch for!"

Thus the structure of the narrative expresses a complete change in Jane Austen's outlook on the heroine in relation to others. And the story no longer progresses towards her vindication or consolation; it consists in her gradual, humbling self-enlightenment. Emma's personality includes some of the tendencies and qualities that Jane Austen most disliked—self-complacency, for instance, malicious enjoyment in prying into embarrassing private affairs, snobbery, and a weakness for meddling in other people's lives. But now, instead of being attributed in exaggerated form to a character distanced into caricature, they occur in the subtle form given them by someone who in many ways has admirably fine standards.

We cannot say that in *Emma* Jane Austen abandons the Cinderella story. She so deliberately inverts it that we ought to regard *Emma* as a bold variant of the theme and a further exploration of its underlying significance for her. In *Peruasion* she goes back to the Cinderella situation in its most direct and simple form, but develops a vitally important aspect of it that she had previously avoided. This is the significance for Cinderella of her idealised dead mother.

Most children are likely to have some conflict of attitude towards their mother, finding her in some respects an ideal object of love and in others an obstacle to their wishes and a bitter disappointment. For a child such as Jane Austen who actually was in many ways more sensitive and able than her mother, one can understand that this conflict may persist in some form for a very long time. Now one of the obvious appeals of the Cinderella story, as of all stories of wicked step-mothers, is that it resolves the ambivalence of the mother by the simple plan of splitting her in two: the ideal mother is dead and can be adored without risk of disturbance; the living mother is completely detestable and can be hated wholeheartedly without self-reproach.[1]

In her early novels Jane Austen consistently avoided dealing with a mother who could be a genuinely intimate friend of her daughter. Lady Susan, of the unfinished novel, is her daughter's enemy. In *Northanger Abbey* the mother is busy with the household and the younger children. In *Sense and Sensibility* she herself has to be guided and kept in hand by her daughter's sounder judgment. In *Pride and Prejudice* she is Mrs.

[1] This is, needless to say, only a very small part of the unconscious significance which such stories may have for a reader. Most obviously it neglects the relationships of the stepmother and the heroine to the father.

Bennet. In *Mansfield Park* she is a slattern whom the heroine only visits once in the course of the novel. In *Emma* the mother is dead and Miss Taylor, her substitute, always remains to some extent the promoted governess. This avoidance may seem strange, but it can be understood as the precaution of a mind which, although in the Cinderella situation, is still too sensitive and honest to offer as a complete portrait the half-truth of the idealised dead mother.

But in *Persuasion* she does approach the problem which is latent here. She puts her heroine in the Cinderella setting, and so heightens her need for affection. And then in Lady Russell she provides a godmother, not fairy but human, with whom Anne Elliot can have much the relationship of a daughter with a greatly loved, but humanly possible, mother. Jane Austen then goes on to face the implications of such a relationship—and there runs through the whole story a lament for seven years' loss of happiness owing to Anne's having yielded to her godmother's persuasion.

The novel opens with her being completely convinced of the wrongness of the advice she received, and yet strongly attached to Lady Russell still and unable to blame her. Her attitude is, and throughout the book remains, curiously unresolved. "She did not blame Lady Russell, she did not blame herself, for having been guided by her; but she felt that were any young person in similar circumstances to apply to her for counsel, they would never receive any of such certain immediate wretchedness, such uncertain future good." But for all that the rest of the book shows Anne repeatedly resisting fresh advice from her godmother and being completely vindicated in the upshot.

This might mean that Anne was a repetition of the earlier heroines, detached by her good sense and sound principles from the inferior standards of those about her. That would be true of her relations with her father and eldest sister. But she had no such easy detachment from her godmother. Lady Russell was near enough to the ideal mother to secure Anne's affection, to make her long for the comfort of yielding to her judgment. This satisfaction—the secure submission to a parent who seems completely adequate—was denied Anne by her superior judgment. She was strong enough to retain the insight that separated her from Lady Russell—they never mentioned the episode in the years that followed and neither knew what the other felt about it—but she never came to feel her partial detachment from her as anything but a loss. Nor could she ever regret having yielded to Lady Russell's advice, even though she regretted that the advice had been so mistaken. At the end of the story, reverting to the old dilemma, she tells the lover whom she has now regained:

"I have been thinking over the past, and trying to judge of the right and wrong—I mean with regard to myself; and I must believe that I was right, much as I suffered from it—that I was perfectly right in being guided by the friend whom you will love better than you do now. To me, she was in the place of a parent. Do not mistake me, however. I am not saying that she did not err in her service. It was, perhaps, one of those cases in which advice is good or bad only as the event decides and for myself, I certainly never should, in any circumstances of tolerable similarity, give such advice. But I mean that I was right in submitting to her, and that if I had done otherwise, I should have suffered more in continuing the engagement than I did even in giving it up, because I should have suffered in my conscience."

It is in *Persuasion* that Jane Austen fingers what is probably the tenderest spot for those who identify themselves with Cinderella: she brings the idealised mother back to life and admits that she is no nearer to perfection than the mothers of acute and sensitive children generally are.

This attempt to suggest a slightly different emphasis in the reading of Jane Austen is not offered as a balanced appraisal of her work. It is deliberately lop-sided, neglecting the many points at which the established view seems adequate. I have tried to underline one or two features of her work that claim the sort of readers who sometimes miss her—those who would turn to her not for relief and escape but as a formidable ally against things and people which were to her, and still are, hateful.

Chronology of Important Dates

1775	Jane Austen born December 16 at Steventon in Hampshire, where father, George Austen, is minister. Seventh of eight children.
1793-1795	Writes various farces, parodies, and short tales (now collected in the *Minor Works*) and an early version of *Sense and Sensibility* called *Elinor and Marianne*.
1796	Began a novel called *First Impressions*, the basis of *Pride and Prejudice*.
1797	George Austen writes to a publisher, Cadell, offering the novel for publication.
1801	George Austen retires; family moves to Bath.
1803	A novel in three volumes entitled *Susan* (an early form of *Northanger Abbey*) bought by a London publisher, but not published.
1805	Death of George Austen; mother, Jane, and one sister, Cassandra, move to Southhampton in the following year.
1809	Moved to Chawton Cottage in Hampshire, a house owned by her brother, Edward.
1811	*Sense and Sensibility* published at her own expense and, like all her other works, anonymously.
1813	*Pride and Prejudice* published.
1814	*Mansfield Park* published.
1816	*Emma* published. Health failing.
1817	Unfinished novel, *Sanditon*, begun. Dies at Winchester July 18.
1818	*Northanger Abbey* and *Persuasion* published posthumously.

Notes on the Editor and Authors

IAN WATT (b. 1917), the editor of this volume, was Professor of English at the University of California in Berkeley, and now teaches at the University of East Anglia, Norwich. He is the author of *The Rise of the Novel* and numerous articles.

KINGSLEY AMIS (b. 1922), British novelist, poet, and university teacher, is the author of *Lucky Jim* and *Take a Girl Like You*. He is a Fellow of Peterhouse College, Cambridge.

REUBEN A. BROWER (b. 1908), Professor of English at Harvard University, is the author of *Alexander Pope: The Poetry of Allusion*.

DONALD J. GREENE (b. 1916), Professor of English at the University of New Mexico, is the author of *The Politics of Samuel Johnson* and many other studies, mainly in eighteenth century literature.

D. W. HARDING (b. 1906), Professor of Psychology at Bedford College, is the author of *Social Psychology and Individual Values*, and was editor of and frequent contributor to *Scrutiny*.

ARNOLD KETTLE (b. 1916), Senior Lecturer in English Literature at Leeds University, is the author of *An Introduction to the English Novel* (two volumes).

C. S. LEWIS (b. 1892), Professor of Medieval and Renaissance English at Cambridge University, is the author of *The Allegory of Love, English Literature in the Sixteenth Century, The Screwtape Letters,* and many other books and articles.

ALAN D. MCKILLOP (b. 1892), Emeritus Professor of English at the Rice Institute, is the author of *Samuel Richardson, Printer and Novelist,* and *The Early Masters of English Fiction*.

MARVIN MUDRICK (b. 1921), Professor of English at the University of California in Santa Barbara, is the author of *Jane Austen: Irony as Defense and Discovery*.

MARK SCHORER (b. 1908) is Chairman of the Department of English at the University of California in Berkeley. Besides novels and short stories, he has written *William Blake: The Politics of Vision, Sinclair Lewis: A Biography,* and is editor of the volume on Sinclair Lewis in this series.

LIONEL TRILLING (b. 1905) is Professor of English at Columbia University and author of many critical works including *Matthew Arnold, E. M. Forster,* and *The Liberal Imagination*.

Edmund Wilson (b. 1895), man of letters, is the author of *Axel's Castle, To the Finland Station,* and many other historical, critical, political, and fictional writings.

Virginia Woolf (1882-1941), novelist and critic, is the author of *To the Lighthouse, Mrs. Dalloway,* and *The Common Reader.*

Andrew H. Wright (b. 1923) is Professor of English at Ohio State University and author of *Joyce Cary: A Preface to His Novels.*

Selected Bibliography

Works by Jane Austen

NOVELS

Emma. London: John Murray, 1816. Three volumes, 12°.

Mansfield Park. London: T. Egerton, Military Library, Whitehall, 1814. Three volumes, 12°.

Northanger Abbey, and Persuasion. London: John Murray, Albermarle Street, 1818. With a biographical notice of the author. Four volumes, 12°.

Pride and Prejudice. London: T. Egerton, Military Library, Whitehall, 1813. Three volumes, 12°.

Sense and Sensibility. London: T. Egerton, Whitehall, 1811. Three volumes, 12°.

The Novels of Jane Austen. The Text based on Collation of the Early Editions by R. W. Chapman. Oxford, 1923. Five volumes, 8°. Large-paper limited edition. Illustrated. Third edition, 1933; some further corrections in 1952.

OTHER WRITINGS

Jane Austen's Letters to Her Sister Cassandra and Others. Collected and edited by R. W. Chapman. Oxford, 1932. Second edition, 1952.

Minor Works. Edited by R. W. Chapman. Oxford, 1954. Collection of all juvenilia and unfinished works; volume six of Chapman's edition of the novels.

Works on Jane Austen

BIOGRAPHY

Austen-Leigh, James Edward. *A Memoir of Jane Austen.* London, 1870. Ed. R. W. Chapman. Oxford, 1926.

Austen-Leigh, William and Richard A. *Jane Austen: Her Life and Letters, a Family Record.* London, 1913.

Chapman, R. W. *Jane Austen: Facts and Problems.* Oxford, 1948.

Jenkins, Elizabeth. *Jane Austen, a Biography.* London, 1930.

CRITICISM

In addition to the studies mentioned in the Introduction or reprinted here, the following are of particular interest:

BOOKS

Lascelles, Mary. *Jane Austen and Her Art*. London, 1939.

ARTICLES

Cecil, Lord David. *Jane Austen*. Cambridge, 1935.

Farrer, Reginald. "Jane Austen," *Quarterly Review*, CCXXVIII (1917), 1-30.

Gorer, Geoffrey. "The Myth in Jane Austen," *American Imago*, II (1941), 197-204.

Leavis, Q. D. "Introduction," *Mansfield Park*. MacDonald Illustrated Classics, London, 1957. Also an essay on *Sense and Sensibility* in the same series (1958), and three articles in *Scrutiny*, for which see Chapman's *Bibliography*, listed below.

Schorer, Mark. "Fiction and the 'Analogical Matrix'," *Critiques and Essays on Modern Fiction*, ed. John W. Aldridge. New York, 1952.

————. "Introduction," *Pride and Prejudice*, Riverside Edition, Boston, 1956.

Trilling, Lionel. "Introduction," *Emma*. Riverside Edition, Boston, 1957.

Van Ghent, Dorothy. "On *Pride and Prejudice*," *The English Novel: Form and Function*. New York, 1953.

BIBLIOGRAPHIES

Chapman, R. W. *Jane Austen: A Critical Bibliography*. Oxford, 1953; second edition, 1955.

Keynes, Geoffrey. *Jane Austen: A Bibliography*. London, 1929.

STUDIES OF JANE AUSTEN CRITICISM

Duffy, Joseph M., Jr. "Jane Austen and the Nineteenth Century Critics of Fiction, 1812-1913." Dissertation, University of Chicago, 1954.

Hogan, Charles Beecher, "Jane Austen and Her Early Public," *Review of English Studies*, N.S. I (1950), 39-54.

Link, Frederick Martin. "The Reputation of Jane Austen in the Twentieth Century . . . ," Dissertation, Boston University, 1958.

American Authors in the Twentieth Century Views Series

European Authors in the Twentieth Century Views Series